FIRST WOMAN PRESIDENT OF INDIA
PRATIBHA PATIL

FIRST WOMAN PRESIDENT OF INDIA PRATIBHA PATIL

Edited by

PROF. RAMESH CHANDRA

MRS. NEELA GOKHALE

KALPAZ PUBLICATIONS
DELHI-110052

First Woman President of India Pratibha Patil

Rs. 540

ISBN: 9788178356396

Published in 2008 in India by
Kalpaz Publications
C-30, Satyawati Nagar,
Delhi-110052
E-mail: kalpaz@hotmail.com
Phone : 9212729499

Lasser Type Setting by: Rudra Computer Graphics, Delhi
Printed at : Singhal Print Media, Delhi

Contents

Preface

Entering into her sixtieth year of independence, India can say that she has taken certain huge steps on an epic journey from the time when Prime Minister Jawaharlal Nehru flew the tricolor atop Red Fort on the 15 th of August, 1947. And what better way to mark her entry into the sixtieth year of freedom and sovereignty, by electing a woman as the 13th President of the country?

Pratibha Patil may perhaps be one of the most controversial candidates to be ever elected into the offices of the President of the country, but one thing that can never be taken away from her, is the fact that she alone will have the distinction of becoming the first woman President of the country.

Some questions will remain - as to whether Pratibha Patil was the best choice that the country ever had for the role of the President, and even to the point where questions may arise over her integrity only by the virtue of the fact that she was elected into office by the ruling Indian National Congress alliance, who unmistakably had the majority in case of numbers in parliament.

The first part of the dilemma can be easily comprehended, because the fact of the matter remains that Patil was assuming the offices just vacated by an enigmatic personality, Dr APJ Abdul Kalam. The country would never have been able to accept any other person in his place, namely because of his demure personality and electric sharp intellect and therefore to pinpoint Patil as the only perpetrator would be extremely unethical and amoral. This contradiction has got unified in her case only because of the fact that she remained as the only candidate who would certainly have taken over from him and therefore conclusions in this regard seem to be completely biased.

As to the other concern that the people of the country have – as to the fact of Pratibha Patil being a mere rubber stamp president, who was propped up by the ruling alliance to satisfy their own ends and means, that too, after having twelve presidents to precede her, seems rather unjustified and wrong. She is not the first president of the country to be elected by a ruling party – it should be categorically remembered that the first President of the country, Dr Rajendra Prasad was also supported by the Congress Party under the leadership of Pt Jawaharlal Nehru. (And consequently, it should also be remembered, that Dr Prasad was the only Indian President who had served the complete two terms that were prescribed for the First Citizen of the country.)

The point that needs to be appreciated is that the quality of people who have had in the recent past as presidents have not been in the same league as the people who held this eminent position. There are examples which do not support the above statement. Dr Kalam has been voted as the best President we have had so far, a people's President. At the same time it needs to be reckoned that Dr Zail Singh, Dr S D Sharma, M N Venkataraman were great names, respected as some of the achievers in their field but they were not in the same league as Dr Radhakrishnan or Dr Zakir Hussain. The last two had been awarded the Bharat Ratna for their eminence even before they became the President. The first President, Dr Rajendra Prasad was a Gandhian to the core. He went back to his ashram in Patna after demitting office, that too after two terms. He led an austere life, away from public glare. Babu Rajendra Prasad's differences with Pt Jawaharlal Nehru, is public knowledge, despite the fact both of them were colleagues in the Congress Party and a part of Bapu's team.

The concept of the rubber stamp came in perhaps only in Indira Gandhi's time and perhaps somewhere, after Giani Zail Singh's decision to back the government to carry out *Operation Blue Star*, that rubber stamp once again disappeared as the country prepared to see through the omnipotent red-tapism and corruption that was perhaps sweeping through the country. And therefore, to already reach a verdict regarding Pratibha Patil in this context is but a false assumption.

She defeated towering figures in her journey to become the 13th President of the country and the first woman president at that, in the form of immediate past Vice-President, Bhairon Singh Shekhawat, and also defeated a motion to bring back Dr Kalam for a second term; she assumed offices under numerous allegations regarding her character and also to a certain extent her criminal record; she has been made to go through what mythology describes as the *agni-parikhsha* and perhaps the fact that she finally scaled the wall to assume to topmost office of the country are proof enough of the fact that she has the spirit and the power to go the distance. To judge her, we have another five years to go ... and only then can the country perhaps pull her up into her virtual judiciary and award her freedom or a sentence.

Introduction

Pratibha Devisingh Patil was born in the house of Narayan Rao in Nadgaon, Maharashtra on December 19, 1934. She studied at R.R. School at Jalgaon. She completed her M.A. from M.J. College, Jalgaon, and obtained a Law Degree from the Government Law College, Mumbai. During her college days, she excelled in table tennis, winning shields in inter-college tournaments. In 1962, Pratibha Patil was voted "College Queen" of Mooljee Jaitha (MJ) College in Jalgaon. The same year, she won an assembly election from Edlabad constituency on the Indian National Congress ticket. She married Devisingh Ransingh Shekhawat on July 7, 1965. As she was active in Maharashtra politics she preferred to keep her maiden surname. The couple has a son and a daughter.

From 1962 to 1985, Pratibha Patil was a member of the Maharashtra Legislative Assembly in which she represented Edlabad constituency of Jalgaon District. She held various posts during this time.

During 1967-72, she was Deputy Minister, Public Health, Prohibition, Tourism, Housing and Parliamentary Affairs. During 1972-74, she was Cabinet Minister, Social Welfare. During 1974-75, she was Cabinet Minister, Public Health and Social Welfare. During 1975-76, she was Cabinet Minister, Prohibition, Rehabilitation and Cultural Affairs.

During 1977-78, she was Cabinet Minister, Education.

From July 1979 to February 1980, she was Leader of Opposition in Maharashtra Legislative Assembly. From 1982 to 1985, she was Cabinet Minister, Urban Development and Housing.

She held the post of deputy chairperson of the Rajya Sabha during 1986 – 1988. She represented Amravati in the Lok Sabha during 1991 - 1996.

On November 8, 2004, she became the 16th Governor of Rajasthan and was the first woman governor of the state.

Pratibha Patil is active in various social work. She has contributed greatly in various fields, specially education. Together with her husband, she set up an educational institute, Vidya Bharati Shikshan Prasarak Mandal, which runs a chain of schools and colleges in Jalgaon and Mumbai. She has also set up Shram Sadhana Trust that runs hostels for working women in New Delhi and Mumbai, an engineering college for rural youths in Jalgaon. She also founded and was the chairperson of a cooperative sugar factory known as Sant Muktabai Sahakari Sakhar Karkhana and a cooperative bank named after herself as Pratibha Mahila Sahakari Bank. She was also involved in setting up an Industrial Training School for the visually challenged in Jalgaon and running a school for poor children of Vimukta Jamatis and Nomadic Tribes.

POLITICAL LIFE[H]

Pratibha Patil joined politics in 1962 at the age of 27. Under the guidance of senior Congress leader Yashwantrao Chavan, she became a deputy minister for education after re-election in 1967. In her next terms (1972-78) she was a full cabinet minister for the state. In successive congress governments, she handled the portfolios of tourism, social welfare and housing under several chief ministers, Vasantdada Patil, Babasaheb Bhosle, S. B. Chavan and Sharad Pawar. She was continually re-elected to the assembly, either from Jalgaon or the nearby Edlabad constituencies, until 1985, when she was elected to the Rajya Sabha as a Congress candidate. She has never lost an election that she has contested.

In 1977, the Congress party split up after Indira Gandhi's defeat following the Indian Emergency (1975–1977). Many senior leaders of state Congress(I), including Pratibha's mentor Chavan and his protege Sharad Pawar, as well as much of the rank and file joined the Congress (Urs) party floated by Devraj Urs. However, Pratibha preferred to remain with Indira Gandhi, though it verged on inviting political ridicule. This act of loyalty to the Gandhi family would be remembered later by Rajiv Gandhi and subsequently, Sonia Gandhi.She protested the arrest of Indira Gandhi in December 1977 and spent 10 days in prision. In 1978, when the Congress (Urs) came to power in Maharashtra, she became Leader of the Opposition in the state assembly.

In 1980, the Congress (I) swept back into power, and her name was considered a front-runner for the Chief Minister's post. However, the post went to Sanjay Gandhi's confidant A. R. Antulay, who was soon forced to resign on corruption charges. Subsequently, she became a minister again in the Vasantdada Patil ministry. Following differences between Patil and then Maharashtra Pradesh Congress Committee (MPCC) chief Prabha Rau, Rajiv Gandhi appointed her as MPCC chief (1988-90).

In 1985, she was elected to the Rajya Sabha, and served as its deputy chairperson from November 1986 to November 1988. Her term expired in April 1990. The following year, in the elections when Rajiv Gandhi was assassinated she won 10th Lok Sabha from elections the Amravati constituency, her husband's city, where he had once been mayor, thus first time entering in lower house of national parliament.

She has also served as Director of National Federation of Urban Co-operative Banks & Credit Societies and the Member of Governing Council, National Co-operative, Union of India.

As Governor of Rajasthan[sh]

In November 2004, eight years after her term in the 10th Lok Sabha, Pratibha Patil was recalled to become the first woman Governor of Rajasthan. She was the second politician from Maharashtra in this post, the first being Vasantdada Patil. With Pratibha Patil as Governor, Rajasthan had women in three significant positions of power in the state, including Chief Minister Vasundhara Raje and Assembly Speaker Sumitra Singh.In April 2006, the Rajasthan Legislative Assembly passed the Rajasthan Freedom of Religion Bill 2006. The objective of the bill was to control "unlawful conversion from one religion to another by allurement or by fraudulent means or forcibly." However, some Christian organizations opposed the bill alleging that the bill was an outcome of the rightist policies of Sangh Parivar. However, Pratibha Patil returned the bill unsigned, stating certain clauses in the Bill infringed on "the fundamental rights such as freedom of speech and expression, freedom of conscience and freedom to profess, practice and propagate religion." The Government of Rajasthan re-sent the bill to her in May 2006 noting that similar anti-conversion laws enacted by Congress governments in Madhya Pradesh and Orissa over 40 years ago were upheld by the Supreme Court of India and that the head of the Constituent Assembly, Dr B R Ambedkar, while drafting Article 25 of the Constitution had said that it would be best to leave it to the state legislatures to make laws to regulate conversions.

After sitting on the bill for over a year she sent it to the President of India just a day before she resigned as governor of Rajasthan. A similar bill named Himachal Pradesh Freedom of Religion Act 2006 passed later was promptly signed by the state governor. Pratibha Patil resigned as the Governor of Rajasthan on June 21, 2007, due to her presidential candidacy.

Nomination for Presidential Election 2007

On 14th June, UPA, the ruling alliance of political parties in India headed by Congress (I), and the Indian left parties nominated her as their candidate for the Presidential Election. She emerged as a compromise candidate after the Left parties would not agree to the nomination of present Home Minister Shivraj Patil. At that point, Sonia Gandhi proposed Pratibha Patil's name. Her loyalty to Nehru-Gandhi family was widely perceived to be a major factor in her nomination as UPA-Left Presidential candidate.

This makes her the first woman President of India. UPA Chairperson Sonia Gandhi described her nomination as a "historic occasion" in India's 60th year of independence.

She filed her nomination on 23 January which has been found to be valid after scrutiny. She faced Bhairon Singh Shekhawat a NDA supported candidate in a straight contest. She extensively campaigned in the South India, starting from Kerala, Andhra Pradesh and in Jammu & Kashmir. She won the Presidential election on 19th July, 2007.

1

Pratibha Patil: An Obvious Exemplary

Having attempted to focus our eyes on what is essential and basic in Pratibha Patil, we must widen our view to take in her surroundings and environment.

Pratibha Patil was born on December 19, 1934 in Nandgao, Maharashtra. Her father, Narayan Rao, was the member of a Maratha Sub-Caste known as Kunbis or Kunbi Marathas.

Kunbis, a group scattered in clans across the state of Maharashtra, has an elongated and complicated history that dates back even to biblical times. Gifted with a cultural history, mythologies and folk-lore, Kunbis have lifted themselves into progressive land-owning class from a comparatively lower stratum of peasant and agriculture community. This upwardly mobile progressive cluster has constantly developed themselves according to the norms of changing time; but, surprising enough, Indian Constitution has labeled them as "OBC".

Narayan Rao, father of Pratibha Patil, was born in the city of Jalgaon. In the north-west region of the state of Maharashtra, in the middle of the steppe, the mountains or the impenetrable rivers, you sometimes come across small unattractive banana trees, with one or – at the most – four million inhabitants, and many colleges. Jalgaon is really like the big towns in the vicinity of Maharashtra. Narayan Rao, educated largely in Indian Literature and classics, was a man of the last century. Happy with his lineage, he was gifted with that inexpressible graciousness of personality, self-confidence, friendliness, sociability and extravagance which was not very familiar to the youth of that time.

Simple and religious in mind, he lived an old, solid and consecrated life by the years. His appearance excited curiosity. A tall, dignified stature, a habit of shrugging his shoulders, eyes which were always jovial, a large curved nose, uneven lips which congested uneasily but comfortably, and a large hairless spot extending all over his head—a look by means of which he not only managed to make the repute of himself, but to be so and to please every one without exception, people of all classes and conditions, and particularly those whom he preferred to please.

He understood how to get the upper hand in all his business. He was among those who could solve life's riddles almost always, eventually to bear rich and sweet fruits. Without ever having been a member of the very uppermost society, he had always had interaction with individuals belonging to that sphere, and of such a sort that he was always respected. He understood that great assess of pride and self-confidence which, without offending others, raised him in the judgment of the humanity.

A fixed opinion on things generally, and unalterable principles, formulated themselves in his mind as Rao grew older — but solely on practical grounds. Still another legacy was a broad secular outlook. He and his wife were immensely proud of their daughter; though his wife was more expressive in her probe of affection.

Unlike Narayan Rao, Pratibha's mother, as one might expect of a woman coming from a very conventional family, was extremely pious. She had little formal education, and never fully approved of her husband's habits, though she adjusted to them in time. According to people, who knew her well, she was a polite and subtle person, a delicate woman, distressed with physical weakness; she was a modest, gentle Hindu wife whose life was surrounded with husband and children. Yet, she did influence them all, though indirectly.

In her marriage, she occupied a submissive vital role in the home. Of fair complexion, she was a small frame with small beautifully shaped hands and feet. She had a devoted husband, and children upon whom she could dote to her heart's content. Most of her life was absorbed in her children and home.

Childhood Days

Then, Pratibha Patil's ancestral factor, itself, coincides with some interesting but contradictory points:

(1) By birth she belongs to Kunbis, and therefore a descendant of Indo-Aryan race
(2) By her time, this lower peasant caste has been developed into a landowning class
(3) Though the caste lifted themselves in a higher economic position, they remained marginalized 'socially'
(4) Later Indian Constitution listed Kunbis as OBC

But in considering Pratibha Patil's relation to these forces and to her family background in general we must first note that the fact that she was born as sub-caste, seems to have had no influence over her whatever. She was born a sub-caste subject, but her family appeared to have given her all the necessities without any hesitation or reluctance. Hence Pratibha, the object of their complete devotion and love, showed excellent promise for the future.

Life at home was not unpleasant. She was blissfully happy at home. An environment of refuge permeated. Every material comfort was available. Nothing was spared in Narayan Rao's endeavor to make accessible each console to his daughter. All of Narayan Rao's children acknowledged his predominant control within the family. Pratibha's attitude to her father was ambivalent. She admired her father enormously, saw him as the image of power, valor and intelligence, but feared him also.

The gap between father and daughter in those early days left lasting impressions on Pratibha Patil. The daughter inclined to aesthetics, stood in awe of her father's personality. There was no encouragement to make decisions, for her father provided the symbol and substance of security.

Because of Narayan Rao's preoccupation with work, and her mother's protective love, she was drawn to her in the early years. Her mother was a devout Hindu, and she raised her kids as "good" Hindu, that is, the kind who goes to Temples, say their prayers. At any rate, she grew up with a healthy sense of right and wrong.

The young Pratibha's leisure hours were whiled away in various games but she was especially fond of table tennis and enjoyed swimming.

She developed a taste for serious reading and an endearment to poetry. She also acquired an ardent interest in science. Pratibha began to read, with admiration, the Hindu classics, such as the Bhagavad-Gita and the Upanishads.

Thus, for all practical purposes, the young Pratibha lived in comfortable surroundings throughout the formative period of her life. In her early education, the young Pratibha was subjected to good influences. All who knew her agree that she was a brilliant and vivacious figure, with a remarkable strength of character and rock-like will.

Education

Pratibha started her education at early age in R.R. School at Jalgaon. Pratibha, for the first two years, was its youngest pupil.

Pratibha played in the R.R. School's junior table tennis team before captaining the Intermediate team. R.R. School was very strong at table tennis. Its Intermediate team was holder of zonal level trophy in table tennis. One of Pratibha's friends who played with her at both school level and university level remembered Pratibha as a player with finesse and who was totally committed, and giving everything a go. She continued to play brilliantly, and she was such a livewire that the rest of the team was inspired by her performance.

Pratibha experimented unsuccessfully at school with other sports such as chess as she lacked the patience and lost concentration quickly. But she was a physical fitness preak and that could be seen by the number of games she played regularly. From about the age of ten, Pratibha enjoyed playing games especially basketball, badminton and table tennis.

R.R. School had a strict and very formal schedule with a limited choice of academic subjects. The syllabi consisted of Hindi, Marathi, Social Studies, Mathematics and Science. Pratibha's academic record at R.R. School over the entire years was very distinguished. She appears to have relied on her lively intelligence and good memory rather than the labour of concentrated and relentless study. Apart from Marathi, in which she was usually near to if not at the top of the class, she was rarely in the top third in any subject, and this was reflected in the principal's overall comment each term, usually a 'satisfactory'. Pratibha loathed the discipline and tedium of learning English language but did well in it.

In a testimonial written for Pratibha on leaving school, the principal gave a reasonably positive assessment of Pratibha's achievements and potential: 'Her results are highly creditable to her, for to her natural ability she has added a strong degree of thoroughness and determination. The combination of innate talents and the faculty to concentrate should take her far in future'.

After completing her schooling, Pratibha joined Mooljee Jaitha (MJ) College in Jalgaon. Established in 1945 Mooljee Jaitha College was the premier academic institution and the oldest College of the North Maharashtra region. It provided education in various under-graduate and post-graduate courses in the faculties of Arts, Commerce and Science. It prepared students from diverse backgrounds for productive careers by providing them with a student-centered, practically focused quality-learning experience.

College life was a lot different than high school. Pratibha decided to walk to college walking. The first thing she noticed was the workload. It was heavier and more intense than she ever experienced before. The major challenges of college work were the large volume of reading, the short deadlines, and continuous writing which brought her the desired MA Degree.

Legal Education

The next episode in Pratibha's education was her training in the law, which began when she took admission in Government Law College, Mumbai. This law institute has played an endless role in the judicial, political, social life and historical background of India.

When she took it up, she was far from excited by its allurements. She proved to have a strong natural affinity for the subject, and necessity forced her to plough through its maze of rules and laws. Some vital lessons for her career as a public person resulted. She learned that liberty and compliance with prescribed rules of behavior are not opposites that must somehow be balanced, as they had seemed earlier, but are complementary and inseparable. She learned to temper her human skepticism with principles of natural law, and thus to reconcile political theory with practical experience and to reconcile both with her deepest rooted feelings.

Most importantly, she learned an elementary fact about the law which, applied on a larger scale, would constitute a new idea in the art of politics. Blackstone had defined the law as "a rule of civil conduct prescribed by the supreme power in a state, commanding what is right and prohibiting what is wrong"; Pratibha perceived that this characteristic of the law could be consciously applied not merely to bringing government under law through a constitution but to the grand goal of transforming society. She saw that one could best combine freedom and energy in people, and infuse them with industry and love of country, by establishing the ways that things be done rather than trying to order what needed to be done.

A problem arose in the beginning. In law schools in those days; young women were not commanly seen. There were very few women in her college but this did not deter her and she determinedly went ahead with her studies.

For all the speed with which she prepared himself for the bar, Pratibha took her time about commencing her practice. Once she got under way, she was immediately successful. Connections helped. Her services had won her considerable renown and facilitated the making of contacts with eminent people. Her political activities had established her reputation for ability and integrity and led to firm personal relations with influential people.

NOTES

Jalgaon

Jalgaon District is located in the north-west region of the state of Maharashtra. It is bounded by Satpuda mountain ranges in the north, Ajanta mountain ranges in the south. The principal natural feature is the Tapti River which flows westward from headwaters in eastern Maharashtra to empty into the Arabian Sea. The rich volcanic soil is well suited for cotton production.

Jalgaon has got pretty diverse climate. It is exceptionally hot and dry during summer with temperature reaching as high as 45 degrees Celsius. Jalgaon receives about 700 mm rainfall during monsoons, which is followed by pleasant temperature in winter.

It is abounded by many religious places and cultural establishments. The major tourist attractions are Pal hill station at Raver, Patnadevi temple at the confluence of Tapi and Purna rivers and hot water springs at Unapdev in Chopda Taluka.

The World famous Heritage site Ajanta Caves is near to Jalgaon (50 kms) making it as one of major International Tourist hub. The District has excellent rail and road connectivity and is a central destination to reach out to major places in India.

Languages spoken are Marathi, Ahirani, Hindi, and English. It hosts a population of about 4 million in an area of about 11,700 sq km.

Jalgaon Market is mainly known for Gold, Pulses, Wholesale Tea, Agriculture, and Grains Trading. Banana and cotton are its main crops. Jalgaon is largest banana growing district in India.

Jalgaon is also growing up as a premier educational place with many colleges in the field of engineering and computer science. Modern Jalgaon is now boasts of vast industrial area, educational institutes and good hospitals. The city is well developed with good roads, shopping centres, residential areas, with good infrastructure in communication and transport.

Kunbis

Kunbis of Maharashtra only are known as Marathas as they form the farming section of Marathas. They are also known as Patils, Patels or Patidars. Chatrapati Shahu Maharaj coined the word Maratha for the peasant section, so as to stand united against the priestly domination that existed for around 1,900 years. Kunbis from Maharashtra have a 12 and 1/2 (also known as Saade Bara) clan system. The 12 clans predominantly consists of Indo-Aryan race and 1/2 part consists of other clans.

The Kunbi are mainly scattered across the state of Maharashtra, especially in the region of Nagpur and Konkan. They are also found in Western Litoral, from Sindh, Kutch, Gujarath, Saurashtra/Kathiawar, Tuluva-Haiva, Kerala, etc.

Some scholars believe the name Kunbi is derived from the Sanskrit word *krishi* which means cultivation. Some authors attempt to trace the origin of the Kunbi to the Gods Rama and Indra, the established symbols of the Kshatriya (second highest level in the Hindu caste hierarchy) and thereby attempt to claim a higher caste origin.

The Kunbi genealogists and historians maintain that the Kunbi are divided into more than 1500 sub-castes. But the more rational view is that of the Kunbi having twelve main divisions. Colloquially, some Kunbi are distinguished by the regions from which they hail; such as those from Sindh are known as Sindhi Kunbi, those from Kutch, the Kutchi Kunbi, and those from Madhya Pradesh as the Manwa Kunbi.

The Kunbi are non-vegetarian and their staple food includes wheat, rice and legumes such as gram, arhar and moong. They eat seasonal vegetables, fruit, roots and tubers, as well as milk and milk products. Alcoholic drinks are socially prohibited but some Kunbi are addicted to them.

The Kunbi are mainly a peasant community and agriculture is their traditional occupation, but today Kunbis have risen into prominence and occupy high position in politics, bureaucracy and society. Successive waves of land reform legislation all over India since the 1950s abolished the prevalent *zamindari* (landlord) system. This turned the cultivating caste of Kunbi, who largely used to be tenant farmers, into a landowning caste. The Kunbi also domesticate cows and buffalo. Some of them are sharecroppers, while a few impoverished ones work as agricultural labourers. Among the Kunbi there are also businessmen, government servants at various levels, engineers, doctors and defence personnel. In Delhi they are mainly engaged as industrial workers, daily-wage labourers or are self-employed; running shops or dairies.

The Kunbi are listed in the Other Backward Classes (OBC) list in the Indian Constitution. This provides them with benefits such as quotas in government jobs and development schemes, reserved seats in medical and engineering colleges, etc.

Culture:

Many Hindu-Kunbis perform the Upanayana, Samskara as per their family traditions. In the past Kunbis have larger houses - some were called Wada, some were Garhi (fortressed complex) and some also had Kila (a fort). Most of the historical evidences are as on date managed and maintained by National (India) and State (Maharashtra) level government departments, although there are many families who maintain their own set of documents or evidences as a mark of family assets. Large scale Kunbi farmers generally maintain large herds of dairy cattle and a number of horses.

Marriages among the Kunbi usually occur only within their sub-community, but outside their clan. But the trend is now veering towards extending the marital restrictions by considering the entire Kunbi community as a group. Marriages are arranged by negotiation among the elders of the concerned families. Child marriages, which are still quite common in the rural areas, are increasingly being discontinued in favour of adult marriages. In case of child marriage the *gaona* (bride's departure to the husband's house) takes place after she reaches puberty. Monogamy is the norm and dowry is paid in cash and kind. Glass bangles, *sindur* (a reddish-brown mark on the forehead), and nose-rings are the prescribed symbols of marriage and are usually strictly observed. Divorce is socially permitted and may be sought on grounds such as adultery, impotence and maladjustment and compensation may be given to the aggrieved party. Generally, the caste *panchayat's* (council) decision is binding on both parties. Widow and widower remarriage is also allowed.

The Kunbi have an oral tradition of folklore and folktales passed down over the generations. Women sing folk songs on auspicious occasions like marriage, childbirth, etc. The musical accompaniments are usually the *dholak*, a cylindrical or slightly barrel-shaped double-headed drum, and the *manjira*, a pair of small cymbals.

The All India Kunbi Mahasabha (Great Council), their national level caste organization, looks after the welfare and development of the community. Since India's independence this umbrella organisation of the Kunbi has tended to become a political pressure group. The political elite among the Kunbi have also grown in number and status and there have been, and are, Kunbi ministers at Central and State levels. The Mahasabha has various regional and local councils as its components and they exercise social control over the areas under their jurisdiction. Instances of adultery, rape, elopement, disrespect for traditional norms, contempt towards the caste council and matrimonial disputes are handled by them. Defaulters are punished by levying cash fines or excommunication.

The Kunbi profess Hinduism and worship Ram and Vishnu (the preserver in the Hindu trinity) as their family deities. The goddesses Kali (the fierce black goddess of destruction) and Durga (a form of Kali, she rides a tiger, and is destroyer of evil and protector of the faithful), and the god Hanuman, alias Bajrangbali, are their regional deities. They celebrate prominent Hindu festivals like Diwali (festival of lights), Holi (festival of colours), Shivaratri (Shiva's Night-celebrating Shiva's marriage with goddess Parvati), Dussehra (celebrating the victory of Rama over the demon king Ravana), etc.

The Kunbi engage Brahmin (highest Hindu caste) priests to perform their sacred, life-cycle rites and rituals which are generally similar to those of other Hindus. Shaving a portion of the scalp (*mundan*) is a ritual performed in childhood while adolescent boys go through the rite of wearing the sacred thread (*janeu*). The dead are cremated. The ashes are immersed in a river, preferably the sacred Ganges River.

The Kunbi are a classic example of a lower peasant caste trying to raise its status by mythologically deriving its origin from a higher warrior caste. This may have helped them gain a sense of increased self-respect, or imagined superiority. But the stark fact remains that they are still blindly groping through the maze of Hindu social hierarchy and are lost in the dark, idolatrous world of various demons and demigods, pagan rites and rituals.

Kunbi Clans

Tirole, Deshmukhs and Jadav (administration, business, farming and now politically dominant) Ahire, Bawne, Vanjari and Dhanoje (money lenders, business and farming), Lonare, Zade, Beldar, Ghatole, Killedar and Dhakane, Mana, Karadi and Khedule Khaire and Jungli (tribals involved in farming). In the Konkan region, many Kunbis are Christian, who was converted to Christianity by Portugese. Many Kunbi groups in the Konkan and Goa region have their own churches. The famous cricketer Vijay Hazare was a Goan Christian.

Common Surnames

Adik, Aware, Bachale, Bhalerao, Brahmankar, Bele,Bhagavath Bhope, Belkar, Bhoir, Bodhale, Chowdhary, Choudhari, Chavan, Dhone, Dange, Dongre, Dore, Desai, Dhawle, Dhanwate, Deshmukh, Deoskar, Deorkar, Dhamankar, Dhande, Dubey, Dhamakar, Dhadse,

Gaonkar, Geete, Gurve, Gaithonde, Gore, Gode, Gaikwad, Gedam, Gawande, Gurve, Gaidhane, Gharat, Jadhav, Junarkar, Jichkar, Khandar, Kadam, Kedar, Kale, Kor, Lunge, Lalke, Lambat, Lode, Misal, Mathankar, More, Mahajan, Manik, Mate, Mane, Mahale, Nagle, Nagale, Navalkar, Naik, Nayak, Nigam, Nikunj, Pabley, Parimal, Patil, Pawar, Pandey, Premkhede, Pashte, Rode, Raut, Rane, Rasal, Raul, Shinde, Sable, Sawant, Salve, Shinde, Shelar, Taiwade, Thakur, Thakre, Taley, Tambe, Thape, Tope, Thombre, Uparker, Wankhade, Wankhede, Watonde, Wagh, Waghmare

FAMOUS KUNBI PERSONALITIES[MH]

SAINTS[H]

Saint Tukaram[SH]

Saint Tukaram was born in Dehu village eighteen miles away from Pune, Tukaram (c. 1598-1649 A.D.) is the most popular saint of Maharashtra. His parents were poor agriculturists of Maratha community but of pious and charitable nature. Their family deity was Vithoba of Pandarpur. Married at the age of fifteen, Tukaram lost his wife and son who died of starvation in a famine. His second wife Jeejabai was a capable but worldly woman who could not understand or appreciate her husband's *spiritual* aspirations, and took to nagging. They had two children.

As a petty farmer and trader, Tukaram was innocent of worldly ways, and was cheated and humiliated in dealings. His life is a favorite topic for Keertankars (reciters and story tellers in praise of God) as it is full of dramatic incidents of misadventures of an unworldly man. He spent much of his spare time in contemplation and studying works of Jnaneswar, Namdev and Eknath, other famous saints of his native land. One guru, Raghava Chaitanya provided spiritual guidance in dream. After a period of contemplation in isolation and *sadhana* of severe kind, poetry dawned on him. His *abhangs* reveal the great inner struggle he had to undergo. But they also provide insight into stages of God-realization through the medium of Bhakti or devotion. The separation of the soul from the God gives intense pain to the devotee. This is known as Viraha to Hindu *mystics* and "Dark night of the soul" to Christian mystics.

Singing and chanting of God's glory was a surest path of god-realization to Tukaram. Perhaps attainment of inner purity and complete self-surrender enabled him to visualize God's presence and his *abhangs* attest that he felt god's presence every where and in everything.

Caste and class do not come in the way of God-realization, he declared. There are many stories and miracles attached to

Tukaram. One narrates of jealous Brahmins who admonished him, a non-Brahmin, for writing *prayer* songs based on Vedas and *puranas* and forced him to throw the palm-leaf books on which he had composed *abhangs*. Since it was the local Dharmadhikari who told him to destroy his compositions, Tukaram immersed all the books with great anguish in the river. He then sat meditating on a rock on the bank of Indrayani River.

After twelve days, Lord Panduranga is said to appeared to him and told that the songs will come back to him. Early next morning, copies of songs came floating to *the rock* on which Tukaram was lost in contemplation. Chatrapati Shivaji came to know about this famous saint and his immense popularity of his *abhangs* which were recited by people of all castes and communities. He sent expensive presents through the entourage. But such worldly possessions had no meaning to the saint and he sent them back, much to the chagrin of his nagging wife. Later Shivaji himself came and sought his blessings from this great soul. Tukaram sensed his end was nearing. He asked his wife whether she could accompany him on the last journey. "How can I leave behind the children, family, cattle and calves and come with you?" she retorted. Devotees believe that Tukaram went to Indrayani river and entered forward in deep waters. His rug, cymbals and Tanpura came floating. But the body was missing. They believe that he went bodily to heaven.

Siddharameshwar Maharaj[sh]

Shri Samartha Siddharameshwar Maharaj is one of the greatest unknown saints of the age. He was born in the month of August 1888 A.D. in a small village called "Pathri" in the district Sholapur of India.

On the sixth day of his birth, his grandmother had a dream in which great Saint Siddheshwar appeared before her and told her that the boy who is born, is his incarnation and asked her to name him Siddheshwar. He also said that one day the boy will become a great Saint. And hence his name was kept Siddharamappa. Later on he was known as "Siddharameshwar Maharaj."

Even in his childhood he was very much sharp, active and had the capacity to imbibe things very quickly. He did not study much at the school level but he was very intelligent, clever and smart in all his behaviour. He was always very straight forward and spoke with a thoughtful idea. He retorted his answers to every question with full meaning. At the age of 16, even though he was premature to work, he took up a job of an accountant in a Marwadi firm at Bijapur. He did his work with earnestness and settled down in Bijapur. Here he met his Master Shri Bhausaheb Maharaj, who has built a monastery in the small village called Inchgiri in Karnataka State of India which started in the year 1885.

Shri Bhausaheb Maharaj, understanding the mental capacity and lifestyle of the people then, started teaching "Meditation" to his disciples at this monastery. The main aim or goal of teaching meditation was to attain Final Reality. The meditation method he used was known as Pipilika Marg or the ant's way, a slow process of attaining Final Reality.

Shri Siddharameshwar Maharaj, after passing away of his Master Bhausaheb Maharaj in the year 1914, was meditating on the teachings of his Master. In 1918, he renounced the world and joined his four brother disciples to popularize his Master's teachings. In the year 1920, when he was on tour popularizing his Master's teachings, he got the idea that one should go beyond meditation because meditation is an initial stage to attain Final Reality. Brother disciples disagreed with Shri Siddharameshwar Maharaj, saying that their Master Shri Bhausaheb Maharaj has not told them so. He agreed with them, but reiterated, "Okay! Can one not go beyond that?"

He decided to set out on that arduous path on his own, left his brother disciples, and returned to his home in Bijapur. He started his meditation in Bijapur on the raised platform like a minaret sitting over an old gun and he meditated for nine months without a break. Since his Master had taught him only meditation, there was no alternative for him to find out the way to attain the Final Reality, that is, Enlightenment, without meditation. He made the ceaseless efforts to achieve this Final Reality. He said "I will attain the Final Reality even at the cost of my life."

His efforts were finally rewarded as total and Full Realization blessed him. He then explained that one can achieve the Final Reality via Vihangam Marg (the birds' way), that is, by realizing through thought processes that Ignorance has come by hearing it over and over for generations. Only by practising and hearing otherwise, the truth, from the teachings of the Master(s) and thinking over it, just like the bird flies from one tree to another, one can attain Final Reality very fast. This is the shortest way to achieve the Final Reality.

In conjunction he taught that the path to Final Reality is reached by slipping easily through the gate of Laya, which is a clear sign of one's progress — the danger being in mistaking it for the final goal of spiritual practice — thus being deceived. Ignorance and thoughts are hand maidens. If the thoughts are absorbed in reality, one can go on to ultimate reality. He then started preaching his disciples to attain Final Reality via Vihangam Marg (the bird's way). First he gave the Knowledge of Final Reality to his disciples and then asked them to renounce and then told them to renounce even the act of renunciation. Finally he gave the knowledge of Vignana — the Thoughtless Reality.

He preached in a very simple, lucid and sane language, by giving examples from daily life. He was of the opinion that Parmarth — understanding of Final Reality should be taught in a very simple language without using high sounding or bombastic words, to make the people understand the Ultimate Reality. This he did from year 1925 to 1936. The Maharaj passed away on 9th November, 1936, in Bombay, giving full understanding of the Final Reality to his disciples, especially so to two of the most accomplished followers Sri Nisargadatta Maharaj and Sri Ranjit Maharaj.

Siddharameshwar Maharaj's book "Master Key to Final Realization" explains only one of the ways to attain Final Reality. That is, the knowledge that you are apart from the four bodies and that there remains the Ego of knowledge which should be dissolved in Final Reality that is called "Laya" (Absorbtion).

Shri Siddharameshwar Maharaj preached step by step in a very simple language how to attain Final Reality during the years 1925 to 1936. These teachings of his have been published in Marathi as "Amrut Laya."

Siddharameshwar Maharaj's efforts were finally rewarded with full and total Realization. He then explained that one can achieve the Final Reality via Vihangam Marg (the birds' way), that is, by realizing through thought processes that Ignorance has come by hearing it over and over for generations. Only by practising and hearing otherwise, the truth from the teachings of the Master(s) and thinking over it, just like the bird flies from one tree to another, one can attain Final Reality very fast.

Nisargadatta Maharaj[sh]

Sri Nisargadatta Maharaj also known as Maruti was born on April 17, 1897 was a master of spirituality, considered to have attained the supreme state of moksha and to be a jivan-mukta. Nisargadatta is widely considered to be one of the 20th century's most direct followers of the school of Advaita Vedanta or nondualism, successful in his direct explanation of non-dualism to both easterners and westerners. Maharaj was world-renowned and admired for his direct and informal teachings, a selection of which are in his most famous and widely-translated book *I Am That*. Nisargadatta continued to receive and teach visitors in his home until his death in 1981 at the age of 84.

Nisargadatta's father, Shivrampant, worked as a domestic servant in Mumbai and later as a petty farmer in Kandalgaon, a small village in the back-woods of Ratnagiri district of Maharashtra. He had a Hindu background and upbringing. At 18 Maruti's father died, prompting him and his brother to leave their family behind to find work in Mumbai. Maruti found work as a small-time clerk but quickly opened a small-goods store, mainly selling bidis – leaf-rolled cigarettes. In 1924 he married Sumatibai and they had three daughters and a son.

At the age of 34, Maruti was introduced to his future guru, Sri Siddharameshwar Maharaj, the head of the Inchegeri branch of the Navnath Sampradaya by his friend Yashwantrao Baagkar. Maharaj His guru told him to concentrate on the feeling "I Am" and to remain in that state.

Sri Siddharameshwar died not long after their meeting, and three years later in 1936 Maruti reached self-awareness, adopted the new name of Nisargadatta and inherited membership into the Navnath Sampradaya sect. He then took off to the Himalayas to further his understanding but eventually returned to his family in Mumbai. It was there that he spent the rest of his life, working as a bidi vendor and giving teachings in his home. He was a smoker and died of throat cancer on September 8, 1981

His genius is in making abstract ideas clear to everyone. He explained that the purpose of advanced spirituality is to simply know who you are. Through his many talks given in his humble flat in the slums of Bombay, he showed a direct way in which one could become aware of one's original nature. Many of these talks were recorded, and these recordings form the basis of *I Am That* and his other books. His words are free from cultural and religious trappings, and the knowledge he expounds is stripped bare of all that is unnecessary.

Nisargadatta's teachings are grounded in the Advaita Vedanta interpretation of the Hindu idea Tat Tvam Asi, literally "That Thou Art", meaning You are one with Divinity. According to Nisargadatta, our true nature is perpetually free peaceful awareness, in Hinduism referred to as Brahman. Awareness is the source of, but different from, the personal, individual consciousness, which is related to the body. The mind and memory are responsible for association with a particular body; awareness exists prior to both mind and memory. It is only the idea that we are the body that keeps us from living what he calls our "original essence", the True Self, in Hinduism referred to as Atman.

He describes this essence as pure, free, and unaffected by anything that occurs. He likens it to a silent witness that watches through the body's senses, yet is not moved, either to happiness or sadness, based on what it sees.

For Nisargadatta, the Self is not one super-entity which knows independently, regardless of things; there is no such super-entity, no Creator with infinite intellect. God does not exist independently from creation. What does exist is the "total acting" (or functioning) of the Ultimate or Absolute Reality along the infinite varying forms in manifestation. This Absolute Reality is identical to The Self.

Nisargadatta also predicates the radical idea that there is no such thing as a "doer". According to him and other teachers of Vedanta, since our true nature or identity is not the mind, is not the body, but the witness of the mind and body, we, as pure awareness, do nothing. The mind and body act of their own accord, and we are the witness of them, though the mind often thinks it acts.

Rashtra Saint Tukdoji Maharaj[SH]

Rashtrasant Tukdoji was born in a remote village, viz. Yawali in Amravati district of Maharashtra on 30th April 1909 in the poverty-ridden family. He completed his primary education at Yawali and Warkhed. In early life, he came in contact with many noble saints. Samartha Adkoji Maharaj showered love on him and graced him with yogic power. Later on Tukdoji underwent yogic practices in the deep jungles of Ramtek, Ramdighi, Gondoda and Salburdi hills. Out of great reverence people called him 'Devababa'. His devotional songs at the rhythm of his khajedi attracted thousands of people of the area.

In 1935 Tukdoji had organised a Maharudra Yojna on the hills of salburdi where more than three lakhs of people came to participate. After this Yojna, his fame spread far and wide came to be respected throughout Madhya Pradesh. In 1936 he was invited by Mahatma Gandhi to his Sewagram Ashram where stayed a month. Thereafter Tukdoji started mass awakening through cultural and spiritual programmes and plunged ahead long into the national freedom struggled in 1942. Ashti-Chimur freedom-struggle was the result of the clarion call of Rashtrasant Tukdoji. He was arrested at Chandrapur and imprisoned in Nagpur and Raipur jails for 100 days i.e. from 28th August to 2nd December 1942.

Tukdoji after his release from the jail, initiated social reform movements and struggled hard against blind faith, untouchabilty, superstition, cow-slaughter and other social evils, He established his Gurukunj Ashram at Mozari village about 120 Km from Nagpur, where constructive programmes were implemented with active participation of his followers.

His congregational prayer could captivate the minds of the masses irrespective of caste, creed of religion. He established the all India Shree Gurudeva Sava Mandal to propagate the Collective Dinner, Congregational Prayer, Ramdhun, Village health and sanitation, Child care and women's uplift, village arts and crafts, physical culture. Ayurveda including wresting matches and physical parades, yoga and other programmes of integrated rural development.

After the dawn of independence, Tukdoji concentrated his full attention to rural reconstruction works and organised many kinds of camps for constructive workers. His activities were impressive and of great national interest. Dr. Rajendrea Prasad, Prasident of India showered love on him respectfully bestowed the honor 'Rashtrasant' in one of the great gatherings at Gurukunj Ashram. Thereafter people widely called him 'Rashtrasant' with great respect.

Rashtrasant Tukdoji celebrated the death anniversary of Mahatma Gandhi with rural oriented constructive programmes in hundreds of villages, establishing ideal village, at Gurukunj. Amagaon and Wadi Bajar. Many national leaders visited those ideal villages and upheld his idea. of rural development, by appreciating the work of Rashtrasant Tukdoji.

On the basis of his experience and insight the Rashtrasant composed 'Gramgeeta' wherein he exposed the present realities and gave a new concept of development for rural India. In 1955 he was invited to Japan for World Religions' Parliament and World Peace Conference. Both the Conferences were inaugurated with the tone of Khanjedi of Rashtrasant Tukdoji with great appreciation from thousands in the audience present in the Conference Hall.

In 1956 Rastrasant Tukdoji oraganised Bharat Sadhu Samaj with the active participations of many heads of sects, creeds and religious institutions. It was the first Organization of all the ascetic orders of India with Tukdoji Maharaj as the first president. During 1956 to 1960. He was invited to many conferences to address or to preside. A few of them can be mentioned as Bharat sevak Samaj Sammelan, Harijan Conference, Sarva Seva Sangh Sammelan, Sarvodaya Sammelan, Vidarbha Literacy Sammelan, All India Vedanta Conference, Ayurveda Sammelan and numerous others. He was one of founder Vice President of Vishwa Hindu Parishad. He was on many fronts for national cause, at the hour Bengal famine (1945), at the time of China war (1962), and aggression of Pakistan (1965), of Koyana earth quake devastation (1962) Rashtrasant went with his mission to help the affected and organised the constructive relief works.

His Literary contribution is also immense and of high order. He has composed both in Hindi and Marathi three thousand Bhajans, two thousand Abhangas, five thousand ovis and contributed more than six hundred articles on religious, social and national aspects and on formal and informal education. Rashtrasant a self illuminating star and a dynamic leader of divert actions. He was well known for many arts and a skills. In the spiritual field, he was a great yogi, and in cultural field, he was a treat orator and musician. His personality was unparallel and unique. His personality had many facets and. His teachings are everlasting and useful for the generations to come. In his last days, he was suffering from cancer. All possible efforts were made to cure the fatal disease, but Rashtrasant left his mortal body on 11th October 1968 at 4.58 p.m. in the Gurukunj Ashram, to rest in eternal peace.

Famous Kunbi Women[H]

Smt Pratibha Patil[SH]

Smt Pratibha Patil is the first woman president of India. She was the first woman Governor of Rajasthan, Woman President of MPCC. Before becoming Governor of Rajasthan, she was a Member of Rajya Sabha. She was Table Tennis Champion in her college days, and has won Inter-Tournaments. She holds an MA in Arts and a Law Degree. Besides her political career, she also manages her own educational institutes for the poor, and industries.

Lalita Pawar[sh]

Lalita Pawar was a Bollywood actor known as the The Mother of all mother-in-laws in films. She was born in a rich Yevle family of Nashik and was married to Raj Prakash Gupta and lived in Pune. She started her career in silent films in 1928 and acted in more than 500 Hindi and Marathi films.

Smita Patil[sh]

Smita Patil was a Bollywood actor who was the first Asian cine-star to have the unique honour of Retrospectives in Paris and La Rochelle, (at the promptings of no less a film luminary than Director Costa Gavras), a two-time Best Actress award winner at the National Film Festival (Bhumika and Chakra) and a Padmashree. She was a keen photographer and died at the age of 31.

Usha Chavan[sh]

Usha Chavan was a Bollywood actor famous for acting as the leading lady of the great Marathi Comedy actor Dada Kondke.

Smt Prabha Rau[sh]

Smt Prabha Rau (Woman President of MPCC) She was a sportsperson and has represented Maharashtra in the long jump, high jump, hurdles, discus throw and running. She is also a musician, and holds a Masters degree in Politics and Music.

Mrs Ujjwala Raut [sh]

She is India's most accomplished supermodel now settled in the USA. She has been awarded both in India and internationally for her performance as a model. Born and brought up in Mumbai, she is now married to British film producer Craig Maxwell Sterry in USA. She has also been on the cover of Time magazine.

Famous Kunbi Men[h]

Yashaskara, King of Kashmir [SH]

After the Utpala dynasty, a Yashaskara became king. He was a great-grandson of a Viradeva, a Kutumbi. He was from the Kutumbi group. He was the son of a treasurer of Karkota Shamkaravarman.

Dr Chintamanrao Deshmukh [SH]

He was the first Governor of RBI & chairman of UGC of India. He held various positions such as Union Finance Minister of India, President of the Indian Statistical Institute, Board of Governors of the Adm. Staff College of India, Hyderabad, Chairman of the Indian Institute of Public Administration, New Delhi. A number of prestigious universities and institutions, international as well as Indian, conferred on him doctorates honoris causa. He was student of University of Bombay in 1912 and University of Cambridge

Shri Shankarrao Chavan[sh]

He was former Union Home Minister & Union Finance Minister. He was born on July 14, 1920. He got his education from Madras University and then obtained a law degree from Osmania University

Dr Shrikant Jichkar [sh]

Dr.Shrikant Jichkar was a well respected and highly qualified Indian politician.

He was born in a wealthy farmer's family in Aajangaon near Katol in Nagpur district on September 14, 1954 in Maharashtra. Besides farming his family runs other industries. He was married and had two children from his marriage. His wife is chairperson for a Hindu religious trust which runs on his farm.

He has 20 post-graduate University Degrees to his credit. Beginning as a Medical Doctor (MBBS and MD) he did his Law (LL.B.) with Post-graduation in International Law (LL.M.) and his Masters in Business Administration (DBM and MBA) and in Journalism (B.Journ). He did his Masters in ten subjects. M.A. (Public Administration) ; M.A. (Sociology) ; M.A. (Economics); M.A. (Sanskrit); M.A. (History); M.A.(English Literature); M.A. (Philosophy); M.A. (Political Science) ; M.A. (Ancient Indian History, Culture and Archaeology); M.A

(Psychology). He got his D. Litt (Doctor of Letters) in Sanskrit , the highest of any Degree in a University. Most of his Degrees are with First Merit and he has obtained 28 Gold Medals. Between 1972 and 1990 he has written 42 university examinations.

Limca Books of Record list him as the most qualified person in India. In 1978 he wrote the IPS (Indian Police Service) examination and got into it, resigned, wrote the prestigious IAS (Indian Administrative Service) examination in 1980 and got into it, resigning in four months to contest his first general election. His academic and political success is mainly due to gifted memory. Due his photographic memory he could remember anything he felt was important for longtime.

In 1977, he was elected President of the Nagpur University Student's Council. He belonged to the political party Indian National Congress. In 1980 he was elected to Maharashtra Legislative Assembly becoming the youngest MLA in the country at 25 years of age and subsequently became a very powerful government minister holding 14 portfolios at a time. After 12 years in the Maharashtra Legislature he was elected to the Indian Parliament in 1992 where he was MP till 1998. In 1999 he lost the election to the Loksabha by a slender margin of 3000 votes in an electorate of 1.4 million voters.

He rose in politics as a student and youth leader. He has worked on several important committees of the State and Central Government, including the Parliamentary Standing committee on Finance; Patents committee; the Planning Board; Resources Mobilization Committee; Taxation Reforms committee, High Power committee on Irrigation and on Transport. He served as a member of legislative assembly of Maharashtra from 1980 to 1992 and member of Rajya Sabha between 1992 and 1998. He also contested the Lok Sabha election from Ramtek in 2004 but lost to Shiv Sena's Subodh Mohite. He held ministers post in almost all departments.

He had travelled all around the world representing India and leading Indian delegations on several forums including the UNO, the UNESCO etc.

Dr Jichkar was the minister who introduced zero budget, first time in India. This was the first attempt by Government in India to liberalise India economy. He faced stiffed opposition from religious organisation mainly due to presence of foreign organisation in India. This budget was introducted primarily due to Former Prime Minister Rajiv Gandhi and was later referred by Dr Manmohan Singh.

He was an Aahitagni and Agnihotri who established and maintained the three sacred Vedic fires. He performed one of the rarest and ancient Vedic sacrifices known as Agnishtom Soma Yajna and got the title of Dixit and Somayaji.

A very good painter, professional photographer and a good stage actor. He had one of the biggest personal libraries in India with 52,000 books. He travelled all around India speaking on economic topics and giving religious discourses. He was the founding president of HAM Radio association, India and Chinmoy mission.

It is believed that he survived cancer. After one year he died in a car accident. His car collided with a bus about 60 kilometres from Nagpur while he was on his way back to Nagpur from his farmhouse in Amravati. He sustained multiple injuries and was rushed to a private nursing home where he succumbed to his wounds.

Sandeep Patil [sh]

He is a cricket Player and was former coach of the Kenya Cricket Team that reached World Cup Semi-Finals in 2003. He had a record for six fours in a cricket over.

Shri Ashok Desai [sh]

A former Attorney General of India, he is author of several books on law. He is chief Justice of Uttaranchal. He was awarded Padma Bushan by Government of India.

Shri Shivraj Patil [sh]

Shri Shivraj V. Patil was born on October 12, 1935 in the village of Chakur in the Latur district of Maharashtra. He is the Union Home Minister in the Manmohan Singh government. He belongs to the Indian National Congress. He became Home Minister in 2004. He attended Osmania University, Hyderabad, earning a graduation degree in Science and studied Law at the Bombay University.

A former Lok Sabha speaker, Shivraj Patil lost in the 2004 polls from Latur constituency in Maharashtra, but has still landed up the second most important position in the Union Cabinet — that of the Home Minister. First inducted in the Indira Gandhi-led government in as Minister of State for Defence, he was given independent charge of the Commerce Ministry between, from where he was shifted to Science and Technology.

In the Rajiv Gandhi government, he was Minister for Personnel, Defence production and later held independent charge of Civil Aviation and Tourism. He has also held a number of important positions in the party ever since Sonia Gandhi took over the presidency of the party. He is largely known for introducing the The Outstanding Parliamentarian Award, India in 1995. He was the chairman of the manifesto committee of the party during the 1999 Lok Sabha election.

And he comes to the Union Cabinet with substantial legislative experience and has that unique distinction of being Speaker of both the Maharashtra Assembly and the Lok Sabha. Patil's name was considered a likely candidate in 2007 presidential election. However, after the Left parties opposed his candidature, Sonia Gandhi proposed Pratibha Patil, Governor of Rajasthan as the presidential candidate. Shivraj Patil is a possible candidate for the post of Vice President of India. His extensive parliamentary experience and his reputation for fairness are said to be the main advantages on his side.

Barrister S. K. Wankhede [sh]

He was former BCCI President and State Minister. He was married to the late Smt Kusumtai who greatly contributed to his career success. Due to his contribution to Indian cricket, a stadium was named after him.

Sharad Pawar [sh]

Union Minister of Agriculture and Former Chief Minister of Maharashtra, Mumbai Cricket Association President & BCCI President. He is native of Baramati.

Rajnikanth [sh]

Rajinikanth was born as Shivaji Rao Gaekwad on December 12, 1949. He is a popular actor in the Indian film industry. As an experienced actor and a national celebrity, he received India's third highest civilian honour, the Padmabhushan for his work in Indian cinema in 2000. Rajinikanth performs predominantly in leading roles ranging from comedies, drama, action and thrillers. Rajinikanth was born in a Kunbi Family in Bangalore, Karnataka. He was the fourth child of his parents, Jijabai and Ramoji Rao. His original name was Shivaji Rao Gaekwad. He lost his mother at the age of five. He had his schooling at the Acharya Pathshala in Bangalore and then at the Vivekananda Balak Sangh, a unit of the Ramakrishna Mission. Although his mother tongue is Marathi, he has not acted in Marathi movies yet.

He began his career doing various jobs in Karnataka. He also attended a theatre for stage plays. Before starting his career in the film industry, he served as a bus conductor for the transport corporation in Bangalore. It was during this time that he nurtured his acting interests by performing in various stage plays.

Rajinikanth married Latha on February 26, 1981, at Tirupathi and they have two children: Aishwarya and Soundarya. Latha is currently the principal of a school named - The Ashram. Aishwarya married actor Dhanush on November 18, 2004 and they have a 6 month old son, Yathra.

Approach ....

Pratibha Patil is an arena where conflicting opinions have been fighting it out in these days, and a 'general consensus', is not in prospect. The existence of this state of hostilities means that anyone who undertakes a general, un-polemical introduction cannot avoid taking sides: there can be no neutral expounder of "Pratibha".

This fact should be kept in mind throughout the ensuing book. I do not know of any satisfactory method of presenting Pratibha Patil other than that of making up your mind what you think she means and stating it as clearly as you can: and this is, of course, an 'interpretation'.

A second reason for refusing to polemicize is that insistence on a particular interpretation is not the purpose of this introductory guide. 'Interpretation' is ultimately no more than a necessary method of presentation: the book's objective is to make the reader want to read Pratibha Patil for herself. If it succeeds in that objective, the reader will quickly become his / her own 'interpreter'. =

2

Early Life in Politics

This section deals with a particular time of Pratibha Patil's life which acts as the prequel to her political career. The rationale for choosing 1965 as the take-off point is that a special transitional episode occurred around this year in her life.

Meanwhile, she has started to work for Indian National Congress and has already won an assembly election from Edlabad constituency. Thus Pratibha started to practice mature politics in prior to 1965 and had decided to take political affairs as a permanent profession. Later, we shall focus on this topic; for now, it is enough for us to be conscious of this information to comprehend the condition in which she got married. Her conjugal life started with Devisingh Ransingh Shekhawat on July 7, 1965. As an active participant in Maharashtra Politics, she preferred to keep her maiden surname. Like the closing lines of a fairy tale, their marriage was successful and they were blessed with a son, Rajendra and a daughter, Jyoti. Jyoti Rathod is a computer engineer and is settled in Pune after a stint in the United States with her engineer husband. Rajendra manages their educational and social institutions.

It is known that sports and politics, together, had brought the couple in contact as Devisingh, too, was a leading sportsman of Maharashtra and was the member of the political party Indian National Congress.

Marriage in India is viewed as a sacrament and the greatest bond between a man and a woman and between their families. The greatest event in a family in India is a wedding, which celebrates and evokes every possible social obligation, kinship bond, traditional value, sentiment and economic resource. The individual sees it as the setting for one's transition to adulthood, which is the result of a combination of choices by everyone in the group or family. Everyone is born in a family and the choice of a family is beyond individual choice, which is why arranging a marriage is a critical responsibility of parents and other relatives on both sides. So it is important for us to know that Devisingh has immensely supported Pratibha throughout her political activism.

Devisingh is a Maratha of Rajasthan origin. His ancestors migrated to Maharashtra from Chota Losal village in Sikar district in Rajasthan about a century ago.

Unlike soft-spoken Pratibha, frank, outspoken and a strict disciplinarian Shekhawat Sahib is an educationist. Being a distant relative of Vice-President Bhairon Singh Shekhawat, it is natural for him to join politics. He is a former mayor of Amaravati and a former member of Maharashtra Legislative Assembly. As Mayor of Amravati Municipal Corporation, Devisingh too was subsequently elected to the Maharashtra Assembly. Devsingh has been quoted as saying, "our life has been a roller-coaster ride because both of us were active in politics at different levels. But I must say she is a fantastic wife. She discusses everything with me, but takes decisions on her own. I trust her immensely".

Social Activities

People have spoken, some quite eloquently, about the socio-political activities of Pratibha and Devisingh, that they tried to create a space for social equality. In fact, the couple have probed that there is no fight between politics and social activities on behalf of the nation. Their social actions spread a message of duty, concern and love for the common mass. At least by their social behaviour and personal practices the couple went beyond the taboos of caste, birth and political party. Personal concern for people has a relation to humanity, a model and projection of a particular politician who has been elected by the common mass.

Pratibha Patil along with her husband was actively involved in various societal performances. Pratibha found a never-ending stream of human needs in the poor she met, and frequently was exhausted. Despite the weariness of her days she never wavered. Pratibha was not alone for long. Within a short period of time, she found help in the form of her husband. Many people came to volunteer their services and later became the core of her missions. As support and assistance mushroomed, more and more services were made accessible to huge numbers of people.

Despite years of strenuous physical and emotional work, Pratibha seemed unstoppable. She always returned to her work with her husband at her side. Her list of social activities includes establishing four hostels for working women, an engineering college, a sugar factory, a Krishi Vigyan Kendra, a school, and a bank.

An outline of her interests and achievements in social activities is given below —

Special Interests

- Development of Rural Economy, Welfare of Women
- Organised Women Home Guards in Jalgaon, District and was their Commandant at the time of Chinese aggression in 1962.
- Vice Chairman, National Federation for Co-operative Urban Banks and Credit Societies
- Chairman- 20-points Programme Implementation Committee, Maharashtra
- Spoke on Behalf of Indian Delegation of Lady Member of Parliament at Beijing (CHINA)

- World Women's Conference in the Parliamentary Conference

Social Achievements

- Industrial Training School for the Blind, Sewing classes for poor and needy women
- Nursery school for children of B.C. and O.B.C. people
- Co-operative Credit Society, Krishi Vigyan Kendra at Amaravati to teach new technique and scientific ways of cultivation to farmers
- Music Classes at Amaravati
- Computer Classes at Amaravati

Incidentally, with Pratibha Patil's rise in politics, she become more and more involved in social and charity works. When Pratibha became Minister for Social Welfare in the Maharashtra Government in 1974, her Shram Sadhana Trust built a hostel for working women in Mumbai with financial help from the Central Government. Soon after she started working on another working women's hostel, Umanchal, by her family-owned trust in Pimpri in Pune. Pratibha Patil inaugurated the hostel in January 2005.

The Maharashtra Mahila Udyam Trust, also managed by Jyoti Rathore, is a charitable organisation that also runs a working women's hostel and two schools in Jalgaon.

The hostels controlled by the two trusts were funded to the extent of 75 per cent for building construction as part of a scheme of the Women and Child Development department. In case of the Umanchal Hostel in Pune, the Maharashtra Government gifted land to the Shram Sadhana Trust. The Centre provided grants-in-aid for construction of the building. The Shram Sadhana Trust in Mumbai runs two working women's hostels, each housing more than 300 women. In Delhi, the trust runs the Shubhanchal working women's hostel, which once again houses more than 300 working women.

Welfare of Women

Throughout Indian history, from the time of Sita, there have been women who have occupied a special place in society. Laxmibai, Razia Sultan and Meerabai are names that now belong to history. From contemporary times, women who have left their imprint include Mrs. Vijayalaxmi Pandit, the first women president of the United Nations, Mrs. Indira Gandhi, Mother Teresa and Mrs. Pratibha Patil, First woman president of India.

Mrs. Pratibha Patil has launched many programmes for generating employment, improving income and creating awareness among women. Her ultimate goal is to make women economically independent and self-reliant.

Some of these schemes, which relate back to the 1960s and 1970s, lay emphasis on upgrading training and skills of women and opening more job opportunities for them. She undertook the task of creating a sense of awareness, particularly among the rural women, to enable them to become active participants in the process of social transformation and regeneration. She started many programmes to strengthen women's position in society.

Pratibha Patil established a number of hostels for working women in Delhi and Mumbai. With the progressive change in the economic structure of the country more and more women have ventured out of their homes in search of employment in big cities and urban and rural townships. One of the main difficulties faced by such women is lack of suitable and safe accommodation Many Organizations have been approaching the Government from time to with a view to providing hostel facilities to such women. Mrs. Pratibha Patil having appreciated the difficulties faced by such women, decided to introduce hostel facilities to working women in cities, smaller towns and also in rural areas. She started this by construction of hostels in Delhi and Mumbai.

The main objectives for providing these hostels were:

- To provide accommodation for single working women, unmarried, widows, divorced, separated, married when husband is out of town
- To provide accommodation to women who are being trained for employment provided the training period does not exceed one year. The number of working women falling in this category should not be more than 30% of the total number of women in the hostel
- To provide accommodation to the girl students for a period of five years on the condition that first preference will be given to working women only. After that if there are any vacancies accommodation will be provided to the students also but amongst them, preference will be given to those studying in post school professional courses. The category of women who are being trained for employment and the girl students together should not be more than 30% of the total number of women in hostels

Shram Sadhana Trust

The Shram Sadhana Trust, which is run by Pratibha Patil's daughter Jyoti Rathore as its managing trustee, controls four major working women's hostels and also a college of engineering and technology in Jalgaon. Pratibha Patil's brothers are also involved in running the college. Shrama Sadhana Bombay Trust was established by Pratibha Patil along with her husband Devisingh Ransingh Shekhawat to conduct several educational activities including the running of College of Engineering & Technology at Jalgaon. The motive of this trust is to carry the flame of quality education, knowledge and progressive technology for global societal development so that tomorrow the flame will glow even brighter. To provide conductive environment for preparing competent value added and patriotic engineers of integrity of par excellence to meet global standards for societal development.

Entering into the new millennium a critical look on the entire nation in general and at our community in particular, reveals a very complex and vague picture of the social scenario. Upon weighing the pros and cons of our daily educational & economical, social & cultural and religious & political aspects a bleak future can be seen. On one hand, unprecedented advancements in the field of arts, literature, science, technology, agriculture and industry have transformed the entire world into a technical global village, (leading to considerable increase in the possibility of enhancement in education, employment and international brotherhood), while on the other hand the materialistic and bureaucratic outlook of our country have proved to be quite fatal to the spread of education.

Shrewdly the info-wave has been gradually converted into an info war by the usage of electronic media through multi-national companies. Effortless visualization into the future brings forth a twenty-first century full of challenges. In this dark scenario there are two major challenges ahead in front of the common masses specifically the downtrodden class. The first one, which needs utmost attention, is getting a very high standard of quality education, which in turn will raise the economic and social life, standard of the common masses. This is very important in order to compete in the intense competition prevalent in the field of education, economic, social and political life standards, which has become quite high.

Secondly, preservation of cultural recognition has emerged as a vital problem. Therefore, the scenario of twenty-first century is totally different and full of chaos & confusion, the thunder of which can be easily heard.

Revolution & changes in Maharashtra are also going to take place like various places in the country. Here particularly in the area of science & technology, the progress is very fast compared to other areas in India. But in this area people and other minorities are much backward.

In order to solve the problems discussed above there is an urgency of two-fold work to be done among the backward masses. First of all the need of the hour is to generate the education, economic and social awareness among masses and then to establish a multi-objective institution for preparing an effective, wise and dynamic leadership to make them disciplined in education and to train them for different competitive fields. Taking all these in consideration, Shrama Sadhana Bombay Trust was established by Pratibha Patil.

Shrama Sadhana Bombay Trust founded by Dr. Devisinghji Shekhawat was established with clear mission to pursue excellence in all fields of education and to adhere to the highest standards of academic rigour in all its work.

Based out of Jalgaon, Shrama Sadhana Trust has grown tremendously during the last few years and is fast moving towards attaining leadership position in Maharashtra which speaks volume about its enduring commitment, outstanding faculty and rich learning environment.

The ambition of the founder President, Dr. Devisinghji Shekhawat is seeing fruition as all the associate colleges are making a positive contribution to the development of individuals, institutions and societies facing the challenges of change.

SSBT College of Engineering and Technology

Established on 23rd June 1983, B.V. SSBT College of Engineering and Technology has achieved an enviable status due to a strong emphasis on academic and technical excellence. Currently the College offers 11 UG courses and 2 P.G courses, affiliated to North Maharashtra University, Jalgaon, and is recognised by AICTE, New Delhi.

Spread over luxurious 25 Acres, the campus of the institute is beautifully located on the bank of River Girna. The campus is well equipped with important amenities such as classrooms, drawing halls, laboratories, seminar halls, library, computer centre, work shops, hostels, canteens, indoor as well as out door sports facilities etc. the College is well-connected by road and rail to every major city in the country.

From a modest beginning when the college offered only an Undergraduate course in Civil Engineering, it has indeed come a long way. A constant endeavour to keep abreast with technology has resulted in excellent state-of-the-art infrastructure that supplements every engineering discipline. The faculty consists of extremely qualified and dedicated academicians whose commitment to students has resulted in a number of accolades.

The College was adjudged **'Best College of the year'** by the Maharashtra State Council for Science and Technology in the year 2002. The spirit and ethos are reflected in the Vision, Mission and Values that have become the foundation of a multitude of successful careers.

Vision

To be one of the premier engineering colleges by achieving the highest order of excellence in teaching and research. We will be the preferred choice of students seeking engineering education.

Mission

- To impart quality technical education that meets the needs of present and emerging technological world
- To strive for student achievement and success, preparing them for life and leadership
- To provide a scholarly and vibrant learning environment that enables staff and students achieve personal and professional growth
- To contribute to advancement of knowledge, in both fundamental and applied areas of engineering and technology
- To forge mutually beneficial relationships with governmental entities, industry, society and the alumni

Values

In pursuit of vision, the trust commits itself to five guiding values:

Student focus: Putting students at the heart of our enterprise, we have the responsibility to prepare them to achieve their highest potential. Our success is measured by the success of our students.

Excellence: Achieving highest quality in what we do through diligent effort, both individual and collective.

Leadership: Developing the visions and strategies for a desired future, and aligning and energizing people to achieve those visions.

Learning Centred Culture: Commitment to learn, adapt and change as a means to continuous improvement.

Stewardship: Ensuring our programs and services add value to our students and society and operate in accordance with the public trust placed in us.

SSBT College of Engineering and Technology connections are also getting stronger with collaborations with leading foreign universities and education providers.

Sant Muktabai Sahakari Sakhar Karkhana

Sant Muktabai Sahakari Sakhar Karkhana (SMSSK) known as Sant Muktabai Cooperative Sugar Factory is a cooperative sugar factory founded by Mrs. Pratibha Patil. The factory is situated at Edlabad in Jalgaon district in Maharashtra. The factory was registered in 1988 (Registration No — JGA/EBD/PRG/ (A)-6 S/88-89). Pratibha was one of the founders of the factory and its chairperson from 1988 to 1996. Sonia Gandhi inaugurated the factory on 23 January 1999. The sugar factory was given loan by a consortium of four banks, three cooperatives and one nationalised — MSC, DCCB Jalgaon, DCCB Mumbai, and Dena Bank.

The main aim of the SMSSK when it was started was to organise, promote and develop marketing, processing and storage of sugar and sugar produce, and to act and assist for technical advice in sugar production for the promotion and the working of its members and cooperative marketing, processing and supply societies in India. But, with time there has been a consequent evolution in the aim of this company:

- To facilitate, coordinate and promote the marketing and trading activities of the cooperative institutions in sugar articles and goods
- To undertake or promoto on its own or on behalf of its member Institutions or the Government or Government Organisations, Inter-State and international trade and commerce and undertake, wherever necessary, sale, purchase, import, export and distribution of sugar product, other articles and goods from various sources for pursuing its business activities and to act as the agency for canalisation of export and import and interstate trade of sugar and to facilitate these activities, wherever necessary, to open branches/sub-offices and appoint agents at any place within the country or abroad
- To organise consultancy work in various fields for the benefit of the cooperative institutions in general and for its members in particular
- To set up storage units for storing sugar and sugar goods, by itself or in collaboration with any other agency in India or abroad
- To maintain transport units of its own or in collaboration with any other organisation in India or abroad for movement of goods on land, sea, air etc
- To undertake marketing research and dissemination of market intelligence;
- To establish processing units for processing of sugar
- To advance loans to its members and other cooperative institutions on the security of goods or otherwise

Pratibha Mahila Sahakari Bank

The Co-operative Bank was set up by Mrs Prathiba Patil in her own name in 1973 (first Chairperson) to help rural women below the poverty line. Many members of her family were its founding directors. Mrs. Pratibha Patil herself became a director for several terms.

Thousands of women in the region of operation Pratibha Mahila Sahakari Bank in Maharashtra were helped by Mrs Pratibha Patil to lift themselves above the poverty line. Lack of assets of the self-employed in their name perpetuates the cycle of poverty. And when a family acquires an asset, it is rarely put in the woman's name. Thus, asset ownership was a priority for PMSB. Asset rights are fundamental in women's financial and social security. Each PMSB loan program was designed to help women transfer family assets into her name. This includes making transfers in the woman's name for agricultural land and houses, and the acquisition of tools, shops and livestock, bank accounts, shares and savings certificates.

Some 2,000 women (in an equal number of families) received small loans. This gave them some protection – in a self-reliant and financially viable way – against illness, widowhood, accidents, fires, communal riots, floods, loss of equipment and other such natural or manmade calamities. Maternity benefits have also been extended.

Training programs were provided in collaboration with academic institutions to upgrade skills and teach the art of creative problem-solving. More important, PMSB initiates the formation of Self Help Groups, monitors them and helps them set up collective enterprises like the Mahila dairies. These, in turn, are then financed by the PMSB. Sheep and goat farmers, Bamboo workers, Leather tanners, Weavers, Wage earners, Women farmers, Milk and vegetable vendors were some of the classes who were helped by bank.

Bank's integrated approach made it different from other micro credit efforts. Credit though very important is not adequate for sustained and substantial employment. It is becoming increasingly clear that access to financial services alone is not enough for poor people to transfer their economic activities into profitable economic enterprises. Access to market, information, and technical know how and social support services are as important as money if the poor are to share in economic growth. If poor people are going to build incomes, assets and livelihood in substantial ways, they need access to:

- Market information and commercial linkages
- Health and social security services, such as insurance and pension
- Technology and method to improve productivity
- Representation at Gram-Panchayat level governing bodies
- Equipment and supply know-how, linkages and bargaining power
- All these facilities were provided by bank to its customers

Controversies

It has been a popular dictum that he who works is always a subject of criticism; but, blissfully, great men have constantly welcomed common disapprovals as a reward of their uncommon qualities. In the multi-cultural country like India no work can be done with one-dimensional support and this fact is also true for Pratibha Patil. While her endless efforts have also witnessed barriers, she has not been shattered down by them.

Pratibha Mahila Sahakari Bank

Reserve Bank of India (RBI) revoked the licence of the bank in 2003 after it was found out that the bank had illegally waived interest on loans given to many of Pratibha Patil's family members. The bank was declared as weak by the Reserve Bank of India in 1995. Two enquiries under the Maharashtra Cooperative Societies Act were ordered in July 2001 and April 2002.

The July 2001 enquiry revealed that the bank had incurred losses of Rs 1.35 crore, subsequent to which its chairperson and eight directors resigned. Ministry of Finance on April 26, 2002, asked the RBI to inquire into allegations of fund irregularities after receiving a number of complaints from the Cooperative Bank Employees Union and small depositors of the bank. In its 28-page inspection report noted that the bank had been declared "weak" since 1995 and after the 2002 inspection was being classified as "sick."

The report revealed:

1. The real or exchangeable value of the bank's paid-up share capital and reserves stands at minus Rs 197.67 lakh. Thus, the bank is not having adequate assets to meet its liabilities. The bank does not comply with the RBI's requirement of minimum share capital.
2. The ratio of the net erosion to net owned funds of the bank is as high as 312.4% and the erosion in the value of the bank's assets has not only wiped out its owned funds but has also affected the deposits to the extent of Rs 197.67 lakh, forming 26% of total deposits.
3. The gross NPAs of the bank amount to 65.8% of the total loans and advances.
4. The Board has not made any concerted effort to improve the bank's financial position and bring it out of the weak status.
5. The RBI further stated in the report: "Pratibha Patil is the founder member of the bank, who is a politically influential personality. She has made all her relatives as directors of the bank and the bank is being run as good as a family business. Because of the influence of respondent no 8 (Prathiba Patil) the bank has given various loans to the relatives and to a sugar factory of which she is a director."

On February 25, 2003, RBI executive director P.B. Mathur signed the note revoking the bank's licence. As per complaints filed by the bank's union leaders, as many as a dozen of Patil's relatives were granted loans. The list of relatives who received loans from her bank, meant for improving the plight of Jalgaon people, women in particular, includes her brothers and nephews.

Name of the NPA holder	*Relationship to P. Patil*	*Amount due with penalty*
Rajeshwari Kishorisingh Patil	Brother's daughter-in-law	Rs. 45, 82, 670
Kishor Dilipsingh Patil	Nephew	Rs. 51, 02, 183
Kishor Dilipsingh Patil	Nephew	Rs. 43, 87, 680
Udhavsingh Dagdu Rajput	Brother's kin	
Udhavsingh Dagdu Rajput	Brother's kin and wife	Rs. 42, 89, 602
Jayashri Udhavsingh Rajput		
Randhirsingh Dilipsingh Rajput	Nephew	Rs. 21, 44, 800
Udhavsingh Dagdu Rajput		
Jyoti Vijaysingh Patil		
Kishor Dilipsingh Patil	Nephew	Rs. 10, 69, 893
Dilispsingh N. Patil	Brother	Rs. 3, 09, 562
Dilispsingh N. Patil	Brother	Rs. 5, 62, 840
Total:		**Rs. 2, 24, 49, 150**

RBI blamed that the loan waivers were given to direct relatives like Anjali Dilipsingh Patil (Pratibha Patil's niece), Kavita Aravind Patil (sister-in-law of Pratibha Patil) and Rajkaur Dilipsingh Patil (another sister-in-law of Pratibha Patil). Besides, many others too who are still close to Patil, were given benefits flouting banking norms.

The writ petition filed by the banks' depositors in the High Court has made serious and more direct allegations against the founder chairperson Pratibha Patil.

The former president of employees union has alleged that the bank collected Rs 4,556 from its employees for the Kargil war victims but failed to deposit the amount in the national fund.

Dilip Singh Patil the elder brother of Pratibha Patil who was legal advisor for the bank took loan from the bank and did not repay. Morever he had the bank's telephone set up at his home and ran the bill of over Rs 20 lakhs talking to stockbrokers at Mumbai.

Defence:

Now it's time to listen to the accused. Pratibha Patil was one of the chairpersons of the Bank and along with a number of her relatives, was one of its Directors. She held the job of the chairperson for only a month and eight days. They also point out that the RBI has never mentioned Patil's name in the report, and the court has not charge-sheeted her. Communist leader A.B. Bardhan cast doubts on the credibility of the official employees union of the bank, which has been highlighting the issue of the banks mismanagement since 2002, drawing attention to the fact that it is associated with the BMS union led by the BJP. She is currently one of the 34 respondents in an ongoing case in the Aurangabad bench of the Bombay High Court on the subject of mismanagement of the bank and misappropriation of funds by its Managing Directors.

Sant Muktabai Cooperative Sugar Factory

The sugar factory was given loan by a consortium of four banks, three cooperatives and one nationalised —MSC, DCCB Jalgaon, DCCB Mumbai, and Dena Bank. The factory defaulted in repayment of the borrowed money .The mill owes about Rs 73 crore to three banks - Maharashtra State Cooperative (MSC) Bank, Jalgaon District Central Cooperative Bank and the Mumbai District Central Cooperative Bank. The Mumbai Central District Cooperative Bank served many notices on factory for recovering outstanding loan of Rs 17.70 crore.

The bank sealed the factory on January 23, 2007. This was the second occasion when the mill had been sealed. Earlier, it was sealed in January 2006, but was reopened after the board of directors headed by G N Patil-younger brother of Pratibha Patil requested for an opportunity to improve the performance of the mill.

In 2002 the chief commissioner of central excise and customs, Pune, issued notices on 24 sugar factories including Sant Muktabai Sahakari Sakhar Karkhana to recover Rs 8.7 crore due on account of excise duty evasion. The sugar factories, mostly in Pune and Aurangabad regions, have been found guilty of selling export quota sugar in the domestic market at high prices. These sugar factories have not only availed excise duty exemption of Rs 85 per quintal, but also earned a big differential by selling the sugar in the local market.

The scam involved diversion of export-oriented sugar in domestic market. In 2001-02, these co-operatives had obtained export licence for 2.28 lakh tonnes of sugar, but in collusion with export agents, diverted the sugar to the domestic market. This led to the collapse of domestic sugar prices and caused major losses to sugarcane farmers besides excise evasion of nearly Rs 80 crore.

Defence:

These accusations are only the one side of the story. The other half is also interesting as it involves some interesting logical comments of experienced politicians. Dubbing as "malign campaign" the allegations, Union Agriculture Minister Sharad Pawar defended her and noted that there was never any enquiry under Maharashtra Cooperative Societies Act against her. He also pointed out that as many as 74 mills were issued notices in December 2006 and it was "unfortunate that only one particular case has been brought up in the media". Pawar said most of the mills had failed to repay the loans because of persistent drought affecting sugarcane production, leading these mills to go sick.

Debates on these issues did not exhaust the potentiality of Pratibha and her followers; and, I think, readers will find their own interpretations on this debate in the next sections, where we will discuss about the Political principles of Pratibha Patil.

NOTES

Devisingh Ransingh Shekhawat

Devisingh belongs to clan of Rajputs called Shekhawats. A Kachhwaha Rajput Warrior Clan of Suryavansham origin fromRajputana (Rajasthan). Simply, Shekhawat is a clan of Rajputs in Rajasthan, India. The descendants of great warrior **Maha Rao Shekha Ji** are called Shekhawat. The Shekhawats ruled over the Shekhawati region for over 500 yrs. Raja Raimal, Raja Raisal, Raja Sheo Singh of Sikar, Bhojraj ji, Raja Ajit Singh of Khetri, Raja Sardar Singh Khetri, Thakur Shyam Singh Bissau, freedom fighter Thakur Dungar Singh and Thakur Jawahar Singh Shekhawat are the prominent figures of this Clan. Shekhawat is a very common name in Indian armed forces .Many of them had won gallantary awards including Param Vir Chakra, Mahavir Chakra etc. V S Shekhawat has commanded the Indian Navy as an Admiral.

Shekhawat are the most prominent of the all the Kachawahas. They are offsprings of the great Kachawaha Rajput warrior Rao Shekha. He ruled over the region called

'Shekhawati', comprising of the districts of Sikar, Jhunjhunu, Churu.

He was son of Thakur of Nan Mokal Kachawaha and Nirwan Queen. He was born on 24 September in 1433, at Amra Dhabai ki Dhani. Later in the memory Amra Rao shekh founded Amarsar. On death of his old father Rao Mokal, Rao Shekha took over the reigns in 1459, at that time he was only 12.

Shekhawat's and Shekhawati (area in which they reside) has given maximum number of soldiers to the country. And about 30,000 of this regions soldier have died in first and second world war. Maximum causalities of soldiers in Kargil conflict were of Shekhawati region. This area is also recipient of the first Param veer chakra in India, which was won by Piru Singh Shekhawat of village Rampura beri (district- Churu). He was from 6th Rajputana Rifles. Most of the Rajput troops from Shekhawati are enrolled in Rajputana Rifles, Rajput regiment and grenadiers' regiment.

The history of Shekhawati can be traced back to the 14th Century, a number of Muslims clans moved into the area and the towns which developed became important trading posts on the caravan routes emanating from the ports of Gujarat.

As the Mughal Empire fell into decline after the death of Aurangzeb in 1707, the descendants of Rao Shekha, who had already installed themselves in areas to the east of the Aravalli Range, began to encroach on the regions to the north and west. Covering an area of some 30,000 sq km, today this region encompasses the administrative districts of Churu, Jhunjhunu and Sikar, and is known as Shekhawati.The chieftains of the region retained a nominal loyalty to the Rajput states of Jaipur and Amber, who in turn honoured them with hereditary titles known as tazimi sardars. It was probably exposure to the courts of Jaipur and Amber which encouraged the chieftains, who were known as thakurs, or barons, to commission the first of the thousands of murals which decorated their havelis, or mansions. By 1732, two of these chieftains, Sardul Singh and Shiv Singh, had overthrown the nawabs of Fatehpur and Jhunjhunu and British Ports at Bombay and Calcutta were able to handle a much greater volume of trade than those at Gujarat.

Pressure by the British East India Company compelled Jaipur state to drastically reduce its levies, and it became no longer necessary to travel via Shekhawati. However hawat merchants had received grounding in the Practices and principles of trade, and were reluctant to relinquish was obviously a lucrative source of Income. Towards the end of the 19th century men folk began to emigrate their desert homes to the thriving, centres emerging on the ports of the Ganges. India's richest industrialists of the century, such as the Birlas, were Marwaris (as the people from Shekawati came to be known).

The Founder

Maharao Shekhaji was born in 1433 (v.s.1490), the son of Rao Mokalji and Rani Nirbanji. Rao Mokal was a chieftain who held the estate of Nan in fief from the ruler of Amber (Jaipur). The story of Shekha's birth is rather interesting. Mokal and Nirban were much troubled as they had no son for several years. They heard about the miraculous powers of the Sheikh Burhan, a Muslim mendicant. They decided to pay the man a visit. After they received the blessings of the Sheikh, a son was born to the couple. In honour of the mendicant, the couple named their son Shekha. At the age of 12 year he succeded his father in 1445 (v.s.1502). He was granted the title of Maharao by Raja Udharan Ji of Amber. The first notice of his valour was at the age of 16 years, with his sudden attack on Napa (Sankhala Rajput) at Nagarchal, Saiwar, Multhan etc.

From 1473 to 1477 (v.s.1530 to 1534), with the help of Panni Pathans, Maharao Shekha conquered Dadri from Nop Singh Jatu and Bhiwani from the Othe Jatu Rajputs, Hansi from Ikhtar Khan and Hissar from Heda Khan Kaimkhani. Thus he extended his territory and become powerful. Shekha's reputation and growing power attracted the notice of the Raja of Amber, who was acknowledged as the head-Tikai, and was sent as a tribute, all the colts reared on his land. Shekha refused to send the colts and as a result of it Raja Chandersen of Amber attacked him. They fought several battles and in the last one, in 1471 (v.s.1528), Shekha repulsed Chandersen at the bank of Kokus river, near Amber. A treaty was made between both of them and according to it; the practice of sending colts to Amber was abandoned. After this, they lived peacefully and Shekha become independent and founded a union which was the birth of the Shekhawati federation. In 1449 (v.s.1506), Shekha Ji founded Amarsar (other sources mention that it was founded in 1460 (v.s.1517). In Amarsar Shekha built the tample of Bhagwan Jagdish and in 1477 (v.s.1534), he built the Shikhargarh Fort. Kulraj Gaur was ruling at Ghatwa, and under his command, a tank was being excavated at Jhotari village, and he ordered that any one passing that way should remove a quantity of earth from the tank. A rajput of Kachhawa clan was returning home with his bride, the rajput obeyed the rule and removed the earth, but the Gaurs insisted that his wife should do the same. The rajput did not agree to it and was killed in the defence of his honour. According to his last wish, his widow went to Amarsar and placed a handful of dust before Shekha and told him the fame of the Kachhawas would be tarnished if they did not take revenge upon the Gaurs. Thereupon, in 1478 (v.s.1535), Shekha invaded Ghatwa and the battle took place at the same tank and Kolraj was killed. Shekha took the head of Kolraj pierced on his spear and returned to Amarsar where it was shown to the widow and was hung on the Pol [gate] of his fort. The Gaur Rajputs fought about 12 battles with Shekha. They also recieved help from Sultan Behlol Khan of Delhi. In the last battle, they met near Ghatwa on the "Khontiya" tank and fought fiercely. Rao Ridmal of Maroth wounded Shekha with his arrows and Shekha gave him a blow with his spear. Nawalraj, a son of Kolraj, killed

Durga and Puranmal. Shekha tried to save his sons and gave a serve blow with his sword and killed Nawalraj. Rao Ridmal left the battle field. Shekha conquered Ghatwa and the other villages of Gaurs. Raimal with a force of two thousand horsemen arrived to help his father. Shekha was severely wounded and before his end, he nominated Raimal as his successor. Shekha expired peacefully at Ralawata in 1488, on Baisakh Sudi 3 [akha teej], v.s.1545. His cenotaph was built there. Maharao Shekha fought 52 battles in his lifetime. He was the ancestor of the Shekhawat sub-clan.

GENEALOGICAL CHART OF SHEKHAWAT DYNASTY

Head Seat

Manoharpur which was later renamed Shahpura, it is also a site of a fort which was founded by Rao Manohar, son of Rao Lunkaran. The present Rao of Shahpura is the head of the Shekhawat clan.

Shekhawat clan is one of the 65 branches of the Kachhawa which are ruling clan of Jaipur. They are the most prominent of all the Kachhawas, and are the descendants of great Rajput warrior, Rao Shekhaji. The early rulers paid allegiance to their overlords, the rulers of Amber, but Rao Shekhaji declared himself independent in 1471 and established a separate principality for his descendants. The Shekhawats ruled over the Shekhawati region for over 500 years and are honoured with the hereditary title of "Tazimi Sirdars", whom HH the Maharaja of Jaipur receives by rising from his seat. The Shekhawat rulers built more then 50 forts and Palaces during their rule over the Shekhawati, which was the largest Nizamat [District] within Jaipur State, almost the whole of which is occupied by Shekhawats.

Sub clans (Septs) of the Shekhawat clan with their Thikanas

Bhojraj Ji Ka

Udaipurwati

Jhajhar, founded by Kunwar Purshottamdas
Gudhagaurji, founded by Thakur Jhunjhar Singh.
Chirana, site of a magnificent castle.
Kedh, founded by Kunwar Gopal Singh.
Nangali, founded by Thakur Saledhi Singh.
Khirod, founded by Kunwar Amar Singh and Kunwar Ram Singh.
Moonwari [Mohanwari], founded by Thakur Saledhi Singh.
Jakhal.
Chapoli.
Gura.
Paunkh.
Panch Pana - Thakur Shardul Singh, had six sons, who received shares of their father's estate. One son died young, and his share was divided equally amongst his brothers (these five shares were known as Panch Pana), another son died without issue and his share was given to the surviving brothers.
(Descendants of Thakur Zorawar Singh): Chowkari, founded by Thakur Bakhat Singh.
Malsisar, founded by Thakur Maha Singh.
Mandrella, founded by Thakur Daulat Singh..
Chanana, founded by Thakur Ranjit Singh.
Gangiyasar, granted to Thakur Medh Singh. .
Tain, founded by Thakur Salim Singh.
Sirohi, founded by Thakur Salim Singh.
Dabdi, founded by Thakur Kirat Singh.
(Descendants of Thakur Kishan Singh): Khetri, founded by Thakur Kishan Singh.
Alsisar I, founded by Thakur Chattar Singh.
Alsisar II, founded by Thakur Ganpat Singh.
Heerwa, founded by Thakur Ramnath Singh.
Sigra, founded by Thakur Mehtab Singh.
Arooka, founded by Thakur Duleha Singh.

Badangarh, founded by Thakur Badan Singh.
(Descendants of Thakur Nawal Singh): Nawalgarh, founded by Thakur Nawal Singh.
Mandawa, founded by the third and fourth sons of Thakur Narsinghdas of Nawalgarh.
Mahensar, founded by Thakur Nahar Singh.
Parasrampura, founded by Thakur Bhawani Singh.
Mukundgarh, founded by Thakur Mukand Singh.
Dorasar, founded by Kunwar Prem Singh.
Pacheri, founded by Kunwar Prem Singh.
Ismailpur
Jakoda
Kolinda.
(Descendants of Thakur Kesari Singh); Dundlod, founded by Thakur Kesari Singh.
Bissau, founded by Thakur Kesari Singh.
Surajgarh, founded by Thakur Surajmal.
Ugarsen Ji Ka
Gopal Ji Ka
Achaldas Ji Ka
Jahota, granted to Thakur Achaldas.
Bhairo Ji Ka
Tejsi Ji KA
Taknet
Khejroliya
Khejroli, granted to Kunwar Bharmal.
Milakpur, granted to Kunwar Trilok.
Dundawat
Girdhar Ji Ka
Khandela Senior, founded by Raja Udai Singh.
Khandela Junior, founded by Raja Fateh Singh.
Danta, founded by Thakur Amar Singh.
Khood, founded by Thakur Shyam Singh.
Surera.
Banuda.

Ralawta.
Palsana.
Ramgarh.
Ladkhani.
Bawari.
Rao Ji Ka
Sikar, founded by Rao Daulat Singh.
Kasli, founded by Rao Tirmal.
Shyamgarh.
Sarwari.
Ladkhani
Khachariawas, granted to Thakur Lad Singh.
Khatu, founded by Kunwar Kesari Singh.
Lamia, founded by Kunwar Maya Singh.
Dhingpur
Vajiwas
Roolana
Singhasan
Pachar.
Bidoli.
Tajkhani
Hariram Ji Ka
Mundro
Awawas
Lasada.
Parasram Ji Ka
Ratnawat

Ancient Sites of the Shekhawats

Jhunjhunu - was taken over by the Thakur Shardul Singh in 1730 from the Kayamkhani Nawabs. Jhunjhunu has three forts, namely Badalgarh Fort, Jorawargarh Fort, Akhegarh Fort, as well as a Palace, Khetri Mahal.

Laxmangarh - founded in the early 19th century by Raja Laxman Singh of Sikar. Rao Raja of Sikar, Laxman Singh constructed a beautiful kaleidoscopic fort on the hill in 1862. He also founded a town, naming it after himself, as Laxmangarh in 1864. This town was styled after the Jaipur Town planning system.

Raghunathgarh - site of two Forts on the hill, built by Rao Raja Devi Singh of Sikar in 1791.

Devigarh - site of a fort on the hill, built by Rao Raja Devi Singh of Sikar in 1787.

Amarsar

Nan

Ralawata

Fatehpur - established in 1451 as a capital for Muslim Kayamkhani Nawabs, but was taken by the Shekhawat Rajputs in the 18th century.

Ramgarh - founded by Rao Raja Devi Singh of Sikar in 1791.

Predecessors

Raja Udayakaran of Amber, married and had (with other issue).

Rao Baloji

Rao Baloji, third son, received his patrimony of Barwara, married and had issue.

Rao Mokalji

Rao Khemraj, his descendants were one of the bara Kotri.

Rao Kharud, married and had issue.

Rao Kuman, ancestor of the Kumawat clan (nearly extinct in 1823).

Rao Mokalji of Barwara, married and had issue. He died in 1445.

Rao Shekhaji

Rao Shekhaji, born 1433, founder of Amarsar in 1460, married six wives, and had issue. He died in 1488.

Kunwar Durga, ancestor of the Gadh Taknet clan. He died in 1488 in Ghatwa battle.

Kunwar Puran Mal, died in1488 in Ghatwa battle.

Kunwar Ratna, ancestor of the Ratnawat clan.

Kunwar Abha

Kunwar Achala

Kunwar Trilok, he was given Mallikpur jointly with his two older brothers, and their descendants are known as Mallikpuria.

Kunwar Kumbha

Kunwar Ridmal

Kunwar Bharmal, he was given Khejroli jointly with his two older brothers, and their descendants are known as Khejroliya.

Rao Raimal

Rao Raimal of Amarsar, married 7 wives, and had issue, 4 sons. He died in 1537.

Rao Suja Singh

Kunwar Tej Singh

Kunwar Sahas Mal, granted the jagir of Siwar.

Kunwar Jagmal

Rao Suja Singh, married and had issue, 5 sons.

Rao Lunkaran of Amarsar

Rao Raisal

Rao Gopal Singh, had descendants at Jharli.

Kunwar Chanda Singh of Mahanpur.

Kunwar Bhairon Singh of Bassi.

Rao Lunkaran of Amarsar, which comprised some 360 villages which was overshadowed by the Junior lines some 200 years later, granted a mansab of 2000 sawars by Akbar, appointed Faujdar of Sambhar in 1571, married (amongst others),

Rani Hansa Bai, grand-daughter of Raja Maldeo of Marwar, and had issue. He died in1584.

Rao Manohar, founder of Manoharpur later renamed Shahpura.

Kunwar Natha Singh

Kunwar Narsingh Das

Thakur Bhagwan Das of Reengus - Mehroli, married and had issue.

Thakur Achal Das, founder of the Achaldasji ke Shekhawat clan, ancestor of the Thakurs of Jahota in Jaipur.

Kunwar Jagganath Singh, died in Dhauli battle.

Kunwar Sanwal Das

Kunwar Kishan das

Kunwar Dule Harai

Kunwar Ishwar Das

Kunwar Kalyan Das

Kunwar Chitar Das

Raja Raisal Darbari born about 1538, granted the jagir of Lamiya, granted the title of Raja and a mansab of 1250 sawars later raised to 3000, married (amongst others), 3rdly Rani Mertanji, married 4thly, Rani Hansa Kumari, died in 1614, married (a), the daughter of the Raja of Khandela, adding that territory to his own, ancestor of the Raisalot clan, including the Sadhani sub-clan. He died in 1614.

Thakur Lad Singh of Khachariawas (better known as Lad Khan), ancestor of the Ladkhani sub-clan of the Shekhawat.

Thakur Virbhan Singh

Rao Tirmal (by 3rd wife), granted the title of Rao and the parganas of Nagore and Kasli (84 villages), married and had issue.

Rao Gangaram of Kasli, married and had issue, the Raos of Sikar. He died at Renwal.

Rao Bhojraj (by 4th wife), born 1567, he represented his father, Raja Raisal in the battle of Kangra in 1582; he received the village of Kosambi in 1608 as his jagir, it was later renamed Udaipur, granted a mansab of 800 zat and 400 sawars, later raised to 1000 zat and 500 sawars; in 1596, the year of famine, he started the construction of a tank, namely the "Bhoj Sagar" for the relief of famine sufferers; married and had issue, the "Bhojraj Ji Ka" sub clan. He died in about 1640 at Khandela where his cenotaph was built.

Raja Todar Mal, succeded his father as the Raja Sahib of Udaipurwati, a generous and noble person, he served as Finance Minister and Prime Minister, and was considered to be one of the nine Gems of India during Badshah Akbar's reign. He was one of the closest associates of the Mughal emperor Akbar, who sought his services during the conquest of Bengal in 1570. He also led the military campaign against Chitor in 1568. He was famous for his land revenue settlement known as Zabti or regulation system. He divided the cultivable land into four classes on the basis of the fertility of the soil and frequency of cultivation. Once he gave a unique reception and showed hospitality to Bareth Haridas (the Kavi of Maharana Jagat Singh of Udaipur), after testing his generosity, Bareth remarked - Two Udaipurs are glorious,two givers are unhesitating; one is Rana Jagat Singh and another is Raja Todermal; he married and had issue. He died in 1658.

Kunwar Purshottam Das of Jhajhar in Rajasthan, married Kunwarani Phool Kanwar Mertani Ji Sahiba of Kuchaman, and had issue, two sons and a daughter.

Thakur Hari Singh, married but died sp.

Thakur Prithvi Singh, married 1stly, Thakurani Biki Ji, married 2ndly, Thakurani Biki Ji, married 3rdly, Thakurani Udawat Ji, and had issue, four sons. He died in the battle of Devli and Heerapura, north of Sambhar.

Thakur Fateh Singh, [Fateh Singh Ji Ka Pana, Jhajhar], married and had issue.

Thakur Padam Singh, [Padam Singh Ji Ka Pana, Jhajhar] married and had issue.

Thakur Sabha Singh, [Pana Malam Singh Sabhasinghot, Jhajhar], married and had issue.

Thakur Karan Singh, [Karan Singh Ji Ka Pana, Jhajhar], married and had issue, two sons.

Thakur Badan Singh, married and had issue.

Thakur Devi Singh, married and had issue.

Thakur Bhairo Singh, he was granted the jagir, later named as "Bhairobas" Raola of Jhajhar; married and had issue.

Maharani Sukhroopde Kanwar, married Maharaja Ratan Singh of Ratlam. She committed sati in 1658.

Kunwar Shyam Singh of Chapoli.

Kunwar Himmat Singh of Kari.

Kunwar Bhim Singh of Moondawarra, Rawao and Girawadi.

Thakur Jhujhar Singh, married and had issue. He died in 1687.

Thakur Jagram Singh, married and had issue.

Kunwar Kushal Singh of Badao.

Kunwar Gopal Singh of Udaipur

Kunwar Sukh Singh of Panchlangi, died in 1719.

Thakur Sardul Singh, born 1681, conquered the territory of the kaimkhani Nawabs of Jhunjhunu in 1730, married 1stly, 1698 Thakurani Sahaj Kanwar of Nathasar, married 2ndly, Thakurani Sirey Kanwar of Nathasar, married 3rdly Thakurani Bakhat Kanwar of Poonota, and had issue. He died on 17th April 1742.

Thakur Zorawar Singh (by 1st wife), born 1700 at Kant, married and had issue. He died in 1745.

Kunwar Bakhat Singh of Chokri and Doomra.

Kunwar Maha Singh of Malsisar.

Kunwar Daulat Singh of Mandrella.

Kunwar Jait Singh, died sp in 1752.

Kunwar Salim Singh of Taien-Sirohi.

Kunwar Medh Singh of Gangiyasar.

Kunwar Hathi Singh of Sultanu.

Kunwar Kirat Singh of Dabri Dheer.

Thakur Kishen Singh (by 3rd wife), born in 1709, ancestor of the families of Khetri, Arooka, Seegra, Alsisar and Balaria.

Kunwar Bahadur Singh (by 3rd wife), born 1712, died in 1732.

Thakur Akhey Singh (by 3rd wife), born 1713, died sp 1750.

Thakur NAWAL SINGH Bahadur (by 3rd wife), born in 1715, ancestor of the families of Nawalgarh, Mahensar, Dorasar, Mukundgarh, Narsinghani and Mandawa. He died on 24th February 1780.

Thakur KESHRI SINGH (by 3rd wife), born in 1728, ancestor of the families of Dundlod, Surajgarh and Bissau, 5th and youngest son, died in 1768.

Rani Guman Kanwar (by 1st wife), born in 1699, married Rao Chattar Singh of Indragarh-Kotah.

Thakur Saledhi Singh of Moonwari and Nangali, born in 1687, married and had issue, 13 sons and 3 daughters. He died in about 1767.

Kunwar Ajit Singh, died in 1785.

Lad Kanwar, married Apji Inder Singh of Indragarh-Kotah.

Hasta Kanwar

Shab Kanwar, married Apji Megh Singh of Indragarh-Kotah.

Janak Kanwar, married Apji Amar Singh of Khatoli-Kotah.

Sukh Kanwar, married Maharaj Shivnath Singh of Sitamau.

Kunwar Harnath Singh of Rasulpur.

Kunwar Kesari Singh

Kunwar Raghunath Singh

Kunwar Puras Ram of Bae.

Kunwar Hur Ramji of Mundurri.

Kunwar Taj Khan, he died sp.

Raja Girdhar Singh (by 3rd wife), 7th son, granted the jagir of Khandela, by Emperor Jahangir.

Kunwar Kushal Singh, married and had issue.

Ladi Kanwar, married Amar Singh Rathore, became sati on 26th July 1644.

3

Political Beginings: Mute Woman Power

Since the 1960s a new assertiveness has characterized India's formerly silent majority, the lower castes that comprise more than two-thirds of the country's population. Today, India's most populous state, Uttar Pradesh, is controlled by lower-caste politicians, as is Bihar, and lower-caste representation in national politics is growing inexorably. This trend constitutes a genuine 'democratization' of India, and the social and economic effects of this 'silent revolution' are bound to multiply in the years to come.

Vijayalakshmi Pandit, Raj Kumari Amrit Kaur, Aruna Asaf Ali, Sarojini Naidu and her intrepid daughter, Padmaja Naidu were the first generation — Indian women politicians who participated alongside Mahatma Gandhi, Sardar Patel and Jawaharlal Nehru in the non-violent struggle for Independence.

The second generation of India's political women came into the government in the 1960s and 1970s, led by Indira Gandhi. Nandini Satpathy, and later Margaret Alva did make some impact on politics and showed that given a chance, women could handle their portfolios with élan. But the real political power game for women began during the Emergency, when

Indira Gandhi became the ruler of India. In more recent times, Najma Heptulla, Rajmata Vijaya Raje Scindia, Sushma Swaraj, Jayalalitha, Mamata Banerjee, Mayawati, Sonia Gandhi, Maneka Gandhi and others have come to the forefront and have made an impact on India's political scenario. In spite of this, the participation of women in the nation's august bodies like the Lok Sabha and Rajya Sabha has averaged between 2 to 6 per cent in every election during the last 54 years.

By 1959, Indira Gandhi was president of the India National Congress. Influenced by Nehru's socialist leanings, she brought a fresh perspective to the party and sought to increase women's participation in politics. When Pratibha Patil joined politics, this was the general political Scenario of India as well as Maharashtra.

She was instinctive to politics. Born in the politically motivated family of Narayan Rao in Nandgaon, she grew up in an intensely political atmosphere. Her father Narayan Rao was politically very active.

She grew up in the shadow of her father and stunned almost everyone by her emergence as a tough woman of commanding presence and absolute will. She maintained for many years that power did not interest her. 'I like to lead, yes, but not more than I liked the other jobs I have done in my life," she said. "I am not ambitious. I don't care for honours." Her critics charged that her promises to erase poverty were unrealistic and that Maharashtra's chronic and severe social problems actually burgeoned during her years of minister-ship. They said, too, that she fostered corruption; that she was hungry for power and surrounded herself with inept advisers rather than brook potential rivals. Empty "sloganizing" and indecision, they said, had bred cynicism. But who can stop an inborn politician? Grown in the guidance of a father-figure like Rao, she entered politics at very young age.

Her education in the arts of politics had begun erratically. Her enthusiastic nature, heightened by intelligence and self-confidence, led her to form, hold, and act upon her opinions with more assurance than her understanding justified, and a tactless compulsion for honesty led her to assert them more readily than was prudent. Throughout her youth her tendency was therefore to move swiftly and too far in one direction, overreact when she learned the error of her ways, and then gradually find a path back to a firmer position.

Another barrier to her development was a distrust of theory, of the speculative thinking of what she derisively called "empirics," meaning quacks. It is true that to an extent this scepticism reflected a wholesome capacity to learn from experience. She attributed the failure to endow Congress with adequate powers, for instance, to the atmosphere of "chimerical projects and utopian speculations," her own included, which had marked "the spirit of the times". To persist in such "fatal mistakes" in the face of sobering experience, she said, would be "disgraceful and even criminal." But her antipathy to theory extended beyond approving the corrective of experience. The difficulty with that attitude was that study of the works of empirics and abstract calculators was necessary to her political education, if only to arm her with the tools of debate.

She struggled through them, and even found some to her liking, and in time, emerged as a profound political and constitutional theorist in her own right. But the whole subject was alien to her true nature, which was for running things, for organizing and regularizing human activity and establishing procedures whereby work could most effectively be done. This talent was reinforced by an intense concern for proper forms of personal behaviour. Accordingly, though her political education was more or less complete in her college life, it was irrelevant until she had gone through two other chapters in her education — one legal, the other social and institutional. What would be involved was a simple but gigantic intellectual leap: she came to understand that procedures determine actions that rules of conduct govern what can and will be done. Understanding that, when others did not, she could set out to make the rules, and succeed.

In dealing with political philosophy, Pratibha likewise embraced conventional doctrines and went overboard with them. Political thinkers in the Maharashtra were generally agreed that the primary object of government should be the protection of liberty. No "pure" form of government, they believed, whether monarchical, aristocratic, or democratic, could long serve that end. Each pure form had its inevitable course of degeneration into tyranny; that of democracy invariably proceeded "through licentiousness, demagoguery, and egalitarian delusion, back to despotism". Politicians shared the assumption that they had solved the problem by developing a mixed form of government, one that so combined the three pure forms as to preserve the best features of each. In India, according to this model, the President represented the monarchical principle, the Parliament the democratic; and government in the states was similarly arranged through governors, councils, and assemblies.

Pratibha also gave the doctrine a special emphasis and a peculiar twist that propelled her into maintaining that democracy was indispensable to liberty—at a time when none but a handful of politicians believed the two were even compatible. It can be argued that Pratibha did not intend to go to that extreme; after all, she was young to be swimming in such deep and murky metaphysical waters and might have been swept away by the current of her own rhetoric. In truth, Pratibha's early political thinking, though sometimes showing flashes of her later brilliance and depth, was longer on passionate idealism than upon reasoned analysis; her positions was often self-contradictory. She explicitly endorsed decentralization, representative democracy, and civil disobedience as efficacious means.

On the other hand, the young politician went to considerable lengths in her pamphlets to justify specific examples of mob action. While admitting "that there have been some irregularities committed", She excused the excesses on the ground that "it would be miraculous, and inconsistent with human nature, for a people in such critical and trying circumstances to act perfectly right".

On the whole, the Pratibha often sounded rather like her opponents in maturity. In one crucial respect, however, her attitude never changed: she always championed liberty and Pratibha had neither occasion nor inclination to re-examine her political thinking until the winter of 1977-78. Then, she began her fulminations against the corruption and incompetence of the state government. Recognition of the immaturity of her earlier thinking took the most sincere of forms: she plunged anew into study.

Pratibha also studied politicians, both practical and theoretical, who might offer insights into the problems besetting the people cause. In immediate practical terms, the most pressing problem was the betterment of people; and to inform her on matters economic and financial she studied these subjects.

Another aspect of political life of Pratibha relates to her desire to do great deeds in service of her country. The passions were ranked in many gradations from the basest to the noblest, and classified according to relative good or evil at each level. Ambition, for instance, was of noutral morality in itself. When directed toward mere popularity, toward winning the acclaim of the vulgar multitudes, it was not necessarily wrong, but it was more admirable if directed toward gaining the esteem of the virtuous, the knowledgeable, and the wise. When directed only toward the acquisition of power and unchecked by principle, it led to the blackest motives. In its highest form, when ambition was directed toward winning the approval of the wise and the just not only in one's own lifetime but through immortal posterity, it was transformed into the noblest passion of all, the love of Fame.

Pratibha was primarily concerned, then and later, with the distribution of power on the vertical axis, not the horizontal. She perceived, accurately, that the failure of government to provide adequately for the conduct was the shortcomings of some politicians.

That reputation of Pratibha was soon improved and made significant. Her contributions were coming to be recognised and praised. She came into focus and was soon recognised as upcoming leader of masses. She became politically active in college and state level. She gained support of many local and well known Congress leaders.

While studying at M.J. College, Jalgaon, during the 1960s, she became a member of the Indian National Congress. She became involved in the women's movement at that time. In the 1960s, she served Congress leader and ex-Chief Minister Yashwantrao Chavan unofficially as a personal assistant. In 1962 she won an assembly election from Edlabad constituency on the Indian National Congress ticket. Many senior Congress leaders supported her and they become her mentor.

Pratibha was interested in politics from very beginning. She created a movement for young girls and boys who played a small but notable role in awakening people towards education; she conducted protests and flag marches, as well as helped Congress politicians.

Strong-willed, autocratic and determined to lead, Pratibha was elected from 1967 till 1985 without any loss and was active in Maharashtra politics for almost two decades.

As a private person, Pratibha seemed aloof, chilly, complex, giving no clue in her withdrawn, quiet personality as to why her public figure should appeal as it did to many millions of Maharashtrians. During interviews, she would sometimes simply ignore questions that she did not wish to answer, lapsing into silences, doodling on a notepad and smiling vaguely.

At other times, she gave the impression of shyness and vulnerability. Pratibha herself often expressed her goals in sweeping and inoffensive terms: "I am a politician in the sense that I want a particular kind of aim, Maharashtra without poverty, without injustice." However vague her destinations may seem, Pratibha was always clear about her conviction that she was meant to lead. She rarely indulged in self-analysis and usually brushed aside questions about her marriage, her personal life.

"Every position has advantages and disadvantages," she once observed. "I had an advantage because of the education my father gave me and the opportunities of meeting some great people, not only politicians, but also writers, artists and so on. But in politics one has to work doubly hard to show one is not merely a daughter but is also a person in her own right."

Once, when a journalist asked her to describe Pratibha, the woman, she said: "In spite of always living in the public glare, I have remained a very private person. Her life has been hard. This has made her self-reliant but has not hardened her."

Despite her shyness, and the fact that most politicians, diplomats and journalists viewed her only as Narayan Rao's daughter, Pratibha felt almost obligated to play a political role. She knew that politics was something she could not escape.

During her initial period in politics, she began to display toughness and political assertiveness. Her critics charged, moreover, that she had worsened the problems by misuse of authority, corruption and an erosion of moral leadership. She began to take steps that stirred uneasiness about her final intentions.'

Pratibha denied repeatedly that she was a mere politician - indeed, she was reportedly even allergic to those two staples of political campaigning in her country, the perpetual dust and the wreaths of marigolds - and saw herself rather as the inevitable destined leader.

One significant domestic issue for Pratibha was population control, particularly the question of compulsory sterilization, which was debated in Assembly throughout 1974-75. She announced that strong steps which may not be liked by all were under consideration, the sterilization program was pushed and the Government, in September, announced that civil servants were to be prohibited from having more than three children. This renewed emphasis on population control, along with rumors of compulsory sterilization, provoked sometimes violent protests and confrontation.

Under the mentorship of senior Congress leader and ex-Chief Minister Yashwantrao Chavan, she became a deputy minister for education after re-election in 1967 (in the Vasantrao Naik ministry). In her next terms (1972-78) she was a full cabinet minister for the state. In successive congress governments, she handled the portfolios of tourism, social welfare and housing under several chief ministers, Vasantdada Patil, Babasaheb Bhosle, S.B. Chavan and Sharad Pawar. She was continually re-elected to the assembly, either from Jalgaon or the nearby Edlabad constituencies, until 1985, when she was elected to the Rajya Sabha as a Congress candidate. She has never lost an election that she has contested

In 1977, the Congress party split up after Indira Gandhi's defeat following the Indian Emergency (1975–1977). Many senior leaders of state Congress(I), including Pratibha's mentor Chavan and his protege Sharad Pawar, as well as much of the rank and file joined the Congress (Urs) party floated by Devraj Urs. However, Pratibha preferred to remain with Indira Gandhi, though it verged on inviting political ridicule. In fact, few know that Pratibha managed Indira Gandhi's kitchen when Sanjay died. This act of loyalty to the Gandhi family would be remembered later by Rajiv Gandhi and subsequently, Sonia Gandhi. She protested arrest of Indira Gandhi in December 1977 and spent 10 days in prison. In 1978, when the Congress (Urs) came to power in Maharashtra, she became Leader of the Opposition in the state assembly.

NOTES

A Brief Summary of Pratibha Patil's Early Political Life

1967-72

Deputy Minister, Public Health, Prohibition, Tourism, Housing and Parliamentary Affairs, Government of Maharashtra

1972-74

Cabinet Minister, Social Welfare, Government of Maharashtra

1974-75

Cabinet Minister, Public Health and Social Welfare, Government of Maharashtra

1975-76

Cabinet Minister, Prohibition, Rehabilitation and Cultural Affairs, Government of Maharashtra

1977-78

Cabinet Minister, Education, Government of Maharashtra

Her Mentors in Politics

Yashwantrao Chavan

Yashwantrao Balwantrao Chavan (12 March 1913 - 25 November 1984) was the first Chief Minister of Maharashtra after the division of Bombay State, and subsequently Deputy Prime Minister of India. He was Chief Minister of Maharashtra from May 1, 1960 to November 19, 1962.

Yashwantrao Chavan was born in the village of Devrashtre in Karad Taluka of Satara District of Maharashtra State of India. He was from poor Maratha family.

Apart from being the first Chief Minister of Maharashtra, he occupied the high positions of Defence Minister, Home Minister, Finance Minister, Foreign Minister, and Deputy Prime Minister of India. Yashwantrao Chavan was commonly known as Chavan saheb. While he later championed the view associated with the term Sanyukta Maharashtra, under the influence of Jawaharlal Nehru he almost accepted a bilingual state of Maharashtra.

Like Devraj Urs in neighbouring Karnataka, he left the Congress Party after Indira Gandhi's defeat following the Emergency in 1977, and joined the latter's Congress (Urs).

He had planned to write his autobiography in three parts; first part covering his early years in Satara district. His native place is situated on the banks of Krishna River and therefore the name of the first part was "Krishna Kath" (The bank of the Krishna River). In the middle phase of his political development he was the Chief Minister of bilingual Bombay state and later from 1 st May 1960, the newly formed Maharashtra state. All these years were spent in Mumbai so the proposed name for the second volume was "Sagar Tir". Later in 1962 he was appointed by Prime Minister Jawaharlal Nehru as the Defence Minister of India. Till 1984 he was in Delhi so he had proposed the name "Yamuna Kath" for his third volume. He was able to complete and publish only the first volume.

Sharad Pawar

Sharadchandra Govind Rao Pawar (Marathi, born December 12, 1940) was the president of the Nationalist Congress Party which he formed in 1999 in India.

Introduction

Sharad Pawar is from the Katewadi village near Baramati in Pune district. He leads the NCP delegation in the Lok Sabha, representing his home constituency of Baramati. He has a prominent place in Indian national politics as well as regional politics of Maharashtra. He currently serves as Minister of Agriculture and Minister of Consumer Affairs, Food and Public Distribution. Since 2005 he is also serving as the elected Chairman of the Board for Control of Cricket in India.

International accomplishments

Pawar has been involved in United Nations and World Health Organisation. He has also represented India leading the Disaster Management Team for United Nations. He has an impressive record with United Nations for his excellent management of recovering Latur from an earthquake within a short time. His biography has been listed in Marquis Who's Who in the World that describes influential world leaders over the last 100 years. Only three other Indian politicians i.e., P. V. Narasimha Rao, Manmohan Singh and Shankarrao Chavan have been included in this contemporary biographical library.

Sports administration

Pawar has interests in Kabbadi, wrestling and cricket. He was a wrestler in college.

He has served as the head of various sports organizations, including

Mumbai Cricket Association

Maharashtra Wrestling Association

Maharastra Olympics Association

And is currently the Board of Control for Cricket in India President.

Political history

He entered the Maharashtra legislative assembly for the first time in 1967 from Baramati, representing the undivided Congress Party. In 1978, Yashwantrao Chavan was the political mentor of Sharad Pawar. Mr. Pawar broke away from the Congress to form a coalition government with the opposition Janata party. This Progressive Democratic Front government was dismissed in February 1980, following Indira Gandhi's return to power at the Centre. In the elections that followed, the Congress party won the majority in state assembly and A.R. Antulay, took over as the chief minister of the state. Sharad Pawar remained a key opposition leader in the state assembly. For the first time, he won Lok Sabha election from Baramati parliamentary constituency in 1984. He also won state assembly elections of March 1985 from Baramati and preferred to continue in state politics for a while and resigned from the Lok Sabha. In 1985 elections, his Congress (S) won 54 seats out of 288 in the state assembly and he became the leader of the opposition.

In 1987, Sharad Pawar returned to Congress (I) party after being out of it for over nine years. In June 1988, Prime Minister and Congress President Rajiv Gandhi decided to induct then Maharashtra Chief Minister Shankarrao Chavan into Union Cabinet as Finance Minister and Sharad Pawar was chosen to replace Chavan as chief minister. Sharad Pawar had the task of checking the rise of the Shiv Sena in state politics, which was a potential challenge to the dominance of Congress party in the state. In 1989 Lok Sabha election, Congress party won 28 seats out of 48 in Maharashtra. Though the Congress party maintained a respectable tally in the state and was not routed as in some other states like Rajasthan and Gujarat, it meant a loss of 15 seats when compared with 1984. In the state assembly elections of February 1990, the alliance between the Shiv Sena and the Bharatiya Janata Party posed a stiff challenge to the Congress. Though the Congress managed to retain power, it fell short of an absolute majority in the state assembly for the first time, winning 141 seats out 288. Sharad Pawar was sworn in as chief minister again on March 4, 1990 with the support of 12 independent MLAs.

Sharad Pawar led the campaign for the Congress for the mid-term parliamentary elections of 1991 in Maharashtra. The Congress bettered its performance by winning 38 seats out of 48 in the state. During the course of election campaign, former Prime Minister Rajiv Gandhi was assassinated. There were reports in the media that Pawar's name was being considered for the Prime Minister's post along with those of P.V. Narasimha Rao and Arjun Singh. However the Congress Parliamentary Party elected P.V. Narasimha Rao as its leader and he was sworn in as Prime Minister on June 21, 1991. Rao decided to induct Pawar as Defence Minister. On June 26, 1991, Pawar took over as that portfolio, continuing till March 1993. After Pawar's successor in Maharashtra, Sudhakarrao Naik stepped down, Rao sent Pawar back as chief minister of the state.

He was sworn in as chief minister for his fourth and most controversial term on March 6, 1993. Almost immediately, Mumbai, the financial capital of India and the state capital of Maharashtra, was rocked with series of bomb blasts on March 12, 1993.

The Deputy Commissioner of the Brihanmumbai Municipal Corporation, G.R. Khairnar made a series of accusations against Pawar for being involved in corruption and protecting the criminals. Though Khairnar could not produce any evidence in support of his claims, it inevitably affected Pawar's popularity. Notable social worker Anna Hazare started a fast unto death to demand expulsion of 12 officers of the Forest department of Government of Maharashtra, who had been accused of corruption. The opposition parties accused Pawar's government of trying to shield the corrupt officers. Further, there was a sex scandal at Jalgaon in which a number of young girls were subjected to sexual abuse, which expanded to involve local municipal corporators belonging to Congress. To make matters worse for the Congress party, there was a stampede in the march of Gowari tribespeople at Nagpur on November 23, 1994, in which 123 people were killed. The march had been to demand reservations in educational institutes and jobs. Allegations were made that the mishap occurred because welfare minister Madhukarrao Pichad did not meet with the delegation of the Vanjara people in time. Though Pichad stepped down owing moral responsibility for the mishap, this incident was another setback to Sharad Pawar's government.

The elections to the Vidhan Sabha were due to be held in 1995. The Shiv Sena and BJP combine was leading the Congress in the polls, and there was widespread rebellion in the Congress party. The Shiv Sena-BJP combine won 138 seats while Congress party retained only 80 seats in the state assembly. Sharad Pawar had to step down and Shiv Sena leader Manohar Joshi took over as chief minister on March 14, 1995.

Till the Lok Sabha elections of 1996, Sharad Pawar served as the Leader of the Opposition in State Legislative Council. In the 1996 General elections, he won from the Baramati seat and has not returned to the State Assembly since.

In June 1997, he unsuccessfully challenged Sitaram Kesri for the post of Congress President. In the mid-term parliamentary elections of 1998, Sharad Pawar not only won from his constituency, Baramati but also led the Congress to an emphatic win in Maharashtra. His move to align with the Republican Party of India (Athvale) and Samajwadi Party for the elections in the state brought rich dividends and the Congress party and allies won 37 seats out of 48 in the state. Sharad Pawar served as Leader of Opposition in 12th Lok Sabha.

After 12th Lok Sabha was dissolved and elections to 13th Lok Sabha were due, Pawar, P.A. Sangma and Tariq Anwar demanded that the Congress Party needed to project someone born in India as the Prime Ministerial candidate and not the Italian-born Sonia Gandhi, who had entered party politics and replaced Kesri as Congress President.

In June 1999, Pawar and Sangma founded the Nationalist Congress Party. His party had to align with the Congress party to form a coalition government in Maharashtra as neither party could win an absolute majority on its own in the 1999 assembly elections. Pawar, however, did not return to state politics, and Vilasrao Deshmukh of the Congress was chosen as Chief Minister, with Chagan Bhujbal representing the NCP as his deputy. The alliance has endured at the national and state level to this day.

After 2004 Lok Sabha elections, he joined the United Progressive Alliance government headed by Manmohan Singh as the Minister for Agriculture and Food.

On November 29, 2005, he was elected President of Board of Control for Cricket in India (BCCI).

Controversies

In October 2006, the prime accused in the stamp paper scam worth US$ 500 Million plus, Abdul Karim Telgi, named Sharad Pawar as one of the politicians involved. This was revealed in a leaked video-tape of Telgi's narco-anlysis test - now in the possession of the media - conducted in 2003, before the CBI took over the probe in 2004. In this tape, he named Sharad Pawar and Chaggan Bhujbal but did not specify the nature of their involvement.

The BJP asked for Pawar's resignation after alleging he was involved in a multi-crore scam involving wheat imports.

Career graph

From 1967 to 1991, He was Member, Maharashtra Legislative Assembly; general Secretary, Pradesh Congress Committee (PCC); Maharashtra Secretary, Congress Legislature Party, Maharashtra.

From 1972 to 1974, he was Minister of State, Home, Food, Civil Supplies, Rehabilitation, Publicity, Youth Welfare and sports, Government of Maharashtra.

From 1974 to 1978, he was Cabinet Minister, Education, Agriculture, Industries, Home, Labour and Youth Welfare, Government of Maharashtra.

From 1978 to 1980, 1988 to 1991, and 1993-1995, he was Chief Minister, Maharashtra for four terms.

From 1981 to 1986, he was Leader of the Opposition, Maharashtra Legislative Assembly.

From 1982 to 1987, he was President, Congress (s).

In 1984, he was Elected to the 8th Lok Sabha and resigned in March, 1985.

In 1991, he was Re-elected to the 10th Lok Sabha (2nd term).

From 1991 to 1993, he was Union Cabinet Minister for Defence.

From 1993 to 1995, he was Member, Maharashtra Legislative Council.

From 1995 to 1996, he was Leader of the Opposition, Maharashtra Legislative Council.

In 1996, he was Re-elected to the 11th Lok Sabha (3rd term).

From 1996 to 1997, he was Member, Committee of Science and Technology, Environment and Forests.

In 1998, he was Re-elected to the 12th Lok Sabha (4th term); Leader of the Opposition, Lok Sabha.

From 1998 to 1999, he was Member, General Purposes Committee; Member, Committee on External Affairs and its Sub- Committee-II; Consultative Committee, Ministry of Human Resource Development

In 1999, he was Re-elected to the 13th Lok Sabha (5th term); Leader, NCP Parliamentary Party, Lok Sabha.

From 1999 to 2000, he was Member, Committee on Agriculture; Member, General Purposes Committee.

From 2000 to 2001, he was Member, Committee on Ethics.

In 2004, he was Re-elected to the 14th Lok Sabha (6th term) and became the Union Cabinet Minister for Agriculture, Consumer Affairs, Food and Public Distribution.

In 2005, he became the Chairman of the Board of Cricket Control,India.

Vasantdada Patil

Vasantdada Patil (November 13, 1917 - March 1, 1989) was an Indian politician from Sangli, Maharashtra. He was known as First Maratha Strongman and first mass leader in Maharashtra's politics. He was the Chief Minister of Maharashtra from May 17, 1977 to July 18, 1978 and again from February 2, 1983 to June 1, 1985. He also served as Governor of Rajasthan.

Born on 13th Nov 1917 at 'Padmale' 3 km from Sangli is his native village. He studied up to the vernacular final. Then he took interest in his farm. He worked there and faced many problems. He always took leading part in problem solving.

He took part in freedom struggle. In 1942, Mahatma Gandhi started 'Satyagraha movement'. Vinoba Bhave was the first 'satyagrahi' and from Tasgaon Vasantdada was the first 'satyagrahi' . For this he was jailed by the British regime. In jail, he came under the influence of people like Babasaheb Kher, Sardar Patel and others.

He was also influenced by Netaji Subhash Chandra Bose and he believed that only 'satyagraha', morchas or peoples movements would not get freedom. So he looted railways, merchants, got guns and revolvers from Goa. Many criminal cases were filled against him. British govt. declared prize of Rs.1000 for him. He tried to escape from the jail but badly injured. He was then sentenced 13 years imprisonment.

On 25th April 1946 he was released. He was tremendously welcome by Sangli people reminding the return of Shri Rama from Lanka. After independence he started working on farmers problems. He established Market Committee on 1951, with main intension of giving proper prices to agriculture products. In 1958, he started largest Co-operative Sugar factory on 90 acres land. In 1960, he started Industrial Society on 135 acres land. ITI were stared to give technical training to youth. He made efforts to increase irrigation in Sangli. In 1960 he became the Chief promoter of Groundnut Processors Co-operative Society.

In the field of education he was Chairman of Latthe Education Society. He started Miraj Medical College, Civil hospital, Akashwani (All India Radio station) a Sangli.

While active in politics from 1937, he was first appointed a Minister from 1972 till 1976 under Chief Minister Vasantrao Naik. In 1976 he was dropped from the Maharashtra Cabinet. He was very disappointed. But overcoming this disappointment, he became Chief Minister of Maharashtra 4 times between 1976 to 1985. He is political mentor of Maratha strongman Mr. Sharad Pawar. He appointed Mr. Sharad Pawar as his political successor and Chief Minister of Maharashtra before retiring from politics. He died on 1 March 1989. His elder son Prakashbapu Patil was MP for long period from Sangli and now his grandson Pratik Prakashbapu Patil is MP from Sangli.

Second Wife: Shalinitai Patil is MLA from Koregaon, Satara district

Vasantrao Naik

Vasantrao Naik was an Indian politician who served as Chief Minister of Maharashtra from 1963 until 1975.He was born in Gavli, Pusad. His experience in Grass root politics made him responsible legislator. He was staunch supporter of Mr. Yashwantrao Chavan. After death of Mr. M. Kannamwar, he was elected Chief Minister of Maharashtra, the post which he handled successfully for 12 years. He was father of Green Revolution in Maharashtra. During his regime, Maharashtra became developed state.

4

Women in Politics: The Impact is Evident

"Who is Pratibha Patil?" Over the past few months, commentators and politicians have tossed this question about, barely able to conceal their contempt for a woman so understated that we have to turn to her CV for enlightenment. The one-page statement is much like Ms. Patil herself — refreshingly matter-of-fact and unembroidered. Yet even the bare facts impress: a practicing lawyer before she joined politics, five consecutive terms as MLA, a clutch of portfolios in the Maharashtra Government, member of the 10th Lok Sabha, deputy chairperson of the Rajya Sabha, and Governor of Rajasthan. All this topped by un-trumpeted, constructive social work: engineering college for rural students, hostel for working women, development fund and cooperative bank for economically depressed women, schools for the poor and the disabled, and so on.

Just in case this picture gives the impression of an elder citizen, there is more — details missing in her CV, details unknown to media circles in the metros but recalled with pride in her home town and electoral constituency. Ms. Patil was a champion table-tennis player and quite the toast of MJ College in Jalgaon winning a beauty title in 1962, years before such contests would become the staple of newspaper pullouts. In 1965, three years after she won her first Assembly seat, she married educator Devisingh Shekhawat and became Pratibha Devisingh Patil — decades before the hyphenated surname became a feminist statement. As Ms. Patil quietly climbed the political ladder, her husband willingly took a backseat to her.

Yet this exceptional career woman is apparently worth nothing in an environment that so easily allows PR and networking skills to mask the lack of real talent. Today the acid test for a seeker of public office is not what she has achieved but how visible and how well-connected she is. "Who do you know?" is a question that precedes "what do you know?" Conversely, anyone outside the charmed circle of the opinion making class is a "nobody."

But this "nobody" like career and character have been such that has no enemies, no rivals, no competitors, a good way to be away from the media glare. To know the formation of a submissive but disciplined politician like Pratibha Patil, we have to gauge her past as well as to her party's history.

Indian National Congress (also known as the Congress Party and abbreviated INC) is a major political party in India. Created in 1885 by A. O. Hume, Dadabhai Naoroji and Sir Dinshaw Edulji Wacha, the Indian National Congress became the nation's leader in the Independence Movement, with over 15 million Indians involved in its organizations and over 70 million participants in its struggle against the British Empire. After independence in 1947, it became the nation's dominant political party, only challenged for leadership in more recent decades. In the 14th Lok Sabha (2004-2009), 145 INC members, the largest contingent amongst all parties, serve in the house. The party is currently the chief member of the ruling United Progressive Alliance coalition supported by the Left Front.

The history of the Indian National Congress falls into two distinct eras:

The pre-independence era, when the party was at the forefront of the struggle for independence

The post-independence era, when the party has enjoyed a prominent place in Indian politics, ruling the country for 47 of the 59 years since independence in 1947

The party remained in power for thirty *continuous* years between independence in 1947 and its first taste of electoral defeat (at the national level) in 1977.

When the first prime minister of India after independence, Jawaharlal Nehru, died of a stroke in 1964, his daughter Indira was not seriously considered as a successor. However, when two years later the new Prime Minister Lal Shastri also died suddenly, Gandhi was chosen to fill the leadership void in India. Overnight, she became the leader of the world's largest democracy and perhaps the most powerful woman in the world.

The first serious challenge to Congress hegemony came in 1967 when a united opposition, under the banner of Samyukt Vidhanayak Dal, won control over several states in the Hindi belt. Indira Gandhi, the daughter of Nehru, and Congress president, was then challenged by the majority of the party leadership. The conflict led to a split, and Indira launched a separate INC. Initially this party was known as Congress (R), but it soon came to be generally known as the *New Congress*. The official party became known as Indian National Congress (Organisation) led by Kamaraj. It was informally called the *Old Congress*. As Indira Priyadarshini had control over the state machinery, her faction was recognized as the "real" INC by the Election Commission of India, although her organization was the break-away group.

In the 1971 elections, Indira Gandhi won by a substantial margin over conservative opponents. During her tenure as Prime Minister, India began to make great strides in the areas of food production and development of an industrial base. Yet it was a politically tumultuous time. In late 1971, Indira gave military support to a successful attempt by East Bengal to secede from Pakistan, which resulted in the creation of the state of Bangladesh. Following the Pakistan conflict, Indira Gandhi won the 1972 election, again by a large majority, but her defeated opponent charged that she had violated election laws. The high court of Allahabad ruled against her in 1975, posing the prospect of her being removed from parliament and being barred from politics for six years.

Instead of accepting the court's decision, Indira Gandhi declared a state of emergency, imprisoned her opponents, and suspended civil liberties. Over the next several years her political fortunes rose and fell dramatically, and in 1977 her party was swept from power. In 1978, after her supporters formed the Congress (I) — "I" for Indira 151 Party, she regained her parliamentary seat and two years later was re-elected to her fourth term as prime minister.

1960s saw various economic developmental policies and their socio-cultural and economic consequences in society. These economic developments had affected the Indian urban and rural society and evaluated its successes and failures, particularly as regards the state's approach to rural development. Indian rural development programme of the mid-1960s illustrates the extent of state "capacity and autonomy" and the processes of policy-making within the structure of democratic regimes. It conveys how political-technocratic elites influence the role of state politics, the circumstances under which the fragmented Indian state allowed a greater degree of policy-making autonomy at the highest level of government and the compatibility of policy with the political and economic interests of powerful capitalist, industrial and business classes.

The Maharashtra State Government right from its formation on 1st May, 1960 committed itself to planned development of primary education. The planning process in the country started in the year 1951 with the First Five Year Plan. Maharashtra joined this process of socio-economic development through planning from the Third Five Year Plan onwards.

During 1947 to 1966, Rae Bareli was insignificant on the political map of India. This unknown district RAEBARELI came into limelight, when in 1967, Smt. Indira Gandhi selected it as her constituency, when in 1977 the ruling Prime Minister Smt. Indira Gandhi was defeated by the Janta Party Leader Shri Raj Narain, and again in 1984 when Prime Minister Shri Rajiv Gandhi was elected from Amethi. This proved the political dominance of Rae Bareli.

Known as the IRON LADY Prime Minister, Indira Gandhi paid attention towards the overall development of Rae Bareli. During her regime Indian Telephone Industries, Rae Bareli Textile Mill, State Spinning Mill, Modi Carpet Factory and a dozen other industries were setup. Cent percent electrification of the district was achieved. Total irrigation facilities were provided in the district. Metal and concrete roads were constructed and Higher education facility was also provided. She was the symbol of Modern Rae Bareli. Millions of rupees were spent on the development of the district.

During this period, Rae Bareli became the nucleus of the Congress and Indian Politics. Once in 1976 the cabinet meeting was held in Rae Bareli instead of state capital. District Rae Bareli became the pilgrimage of congress workers. In spite of Mrs.Gandhi's statement, all the congress workers had a desire to come to this pilgrimage before every election. During this period Rae Bareli got bumper publicity in the national and International press.

Ms. Patil's career was growing within these political upheavals. Meanwhile she has already joined politics and won her first elections to the Maharashtra Legislative Assembly from Jalgaon in 1962. At the age of 27, she was among the youngest MLAs at the time. Under the mentorship of senior Congress leader and ex-Chief Minister Yashwantrao Chavan, she became a deputy minister for education after re-election in 1967 (in the Vasantrao Naik ministry), becoming a full cabinet minister after re-election in 1972.

When in 1977, the Congress party split up after Indira Gandhi's defeat following the Indian Emergency (1975–1977). Many senior leaders of state Congress (I), including Pratibha's mentor Chavan and his protege Sharad Pawar, as well as much of the rank and file joined the Congress (Urs) party floated by Devraj Urs.

But Pratibha chose to remain with Indira Gandhi when the Congress was split following the 1977 defeat. In those days, to remain loyal to Indira Gandhi meant inviting political ridicule. It was a difficult decision also because her mentor had left Indira Gandhi. Even Sharad Pawar, Chavan's godson as he was termed, had left the Congress. Pratibhatai (as she's known in Maharashtra) chose to become leader of the opposition in the assembly, positioning herself against Pawar's ruling front.

She protested arrest of Indira Gandhi in December 1977 and spent 10 days in prison. In 1978, when the Congress (Urs) came to power in Maharashtra, she became Leader of the Opposition in the state assembly.

In 1980, the Congress (I) swept back into power, and her name was considered a front-runner for the Chief Minister's post. However, the post went to Sanjay Gandhi's confidant A. R. Antulay, who was soon forced to resign on corruption charges. Subsequently, she became a minister again in the Vasantdada Patil ministry. Following differences between Patil and then Maharashtra Pradesh Congress Committee (MPCC) chief Prabha Rau, Rajiv Gandhi appointed her as MPCC chief (1988-90).

Loyalty matters. Mrs Gandhi came back to power in 1980. The Janata Party had disintegrated and the Pawar government was dismissed. Today, the Left may be extolling her political virtues, but then the CPM and later even the CPI, were totally opposed to Indira and therefore even to Pratibha's politics. The Left has gone out of its way to describe her as "steadfast", but at that time it meant support to Indira and even to the Emergency.

In successive congress governments, she handled the portfolios of tourism, social welfare and housing under three chief ministers: Vasantdada Patil, Babasaheb Bhosle, S. B. Chavan and Sharad Pawar, gaining a reputation for her competence. She was continually re-elected to the assembly, either from Jalgaon or the nearby Edlabad constituencies, until 1985, when she was nominated to the Rajya Sabha.

In Rajya Sabha, she served as its deputy chairperson from November 1986 to November 1988. Her term expired in April 1990. The following year, in the elections when Rajiv Gandhi was assassinated she won election 10th Lok Sabha from at Amravati constituency, her husband's city, where he had once been mayor, thus first time entering in lower house of national parliament Lok Sabha.

5

The Journey of Will

Few political personalities in the Indian National Panorama have earned so much admiration and laurels for the saga of demonstrated loyalty, vision and sacrifice and at the same time have been the initiator of an equal amount of revelation as Pratibha Patil, presumably for her polite tenacity, refusal to compromise and seeming wisdom of pragmatism.

She was one of the youngest MLA at her time; as a political leader she enjoyed the stay with Indira Gandhi when the Congress was split following the 1977 defeat. In her manner and political style, in ideology and action, Pratibha represents a unique phenomenon in India's Political Movement.

Yet Pratibha continues to be little understood. Under the mentorship of senior Congress leader and ex-Chief Minister Yashwantrao Chavan, she became a deputy minister for education after re-election in 1967 (in the Vasantrao Naik ministry), becoming a full cabinet minister after re-election in 1972. But within few years, she learned to take the political decisions herself and continued to act accordingly. When her mentors had left Indira Gandhi, she preferred their opposite route. It was the major decision of her self-incurred tutelage.

Because of her fiery brand of nationalism, idealism and also her political astuteness and plan of action, the story of Pratibha's life is of absorbing interest. Some analysis tends to view her as an arch-rebel against the Traditional Caste System. Pratibha, however, humbly called herself 'the Servant of India'. Some others see her as the embodiment of women's power. She, however, modestly called herself 'the Servant of Humanity'.

Her career advances the view that, despite the constraints and limitations imposed by the existing frame of national struggle and the multi-opinion surroundings of the time in the realm of Indian politics, Pratibha was perhaps the only faithful leader of the period who had demonstrated a great deal of understanding of the dynamics of the strategy and tactics involved in the Indian political struggle, which, indeed, brought together a view very specific to Pratibha and her time.

To highlight this view further, we can divide her career into two sections, each related with another. The five or six years, covering the period of 1985-1990/91, are rudimentary for our study of Pratibha Patil because those days saw the making of a political pathfinder. The first part highlights Pratibha's strategic ideas and plan of action to remain stuck to her own decisions, while the second section emphasizes Pratibha's contribution in the arena of public servicing as a minister.

Pratibha was a staunch Congress supporter. As a logical sequel to her patriotic zeal, she developed an invincible faith in Indira's party and hence remained with Congress(I) as a choice of righteous cause. She was not a believer in any escapist philosophy but a devotee who was drawn to politics inspired by the love of her country and mankind. The deification of politics and the glamour attached to sacrifice for the party constituted the main trend of her strategic thought – the ultimate policy ambition – and contributed to the development of her concept of nationalism on the basis of a patriotic consciousness. Indira and the Congress thus featured in her thought not as a mere organization but as a spiritual being, a living thing.

Pratibha was equally of the firm view that no one could succeed his/her aim without any sacrifice and without constant struggle. Such a conviction led her to advance a protest for Indira Gandhi in December 1977 and spent ten days in prison. She exhorted her followers to be prepared for making sacrifice for a righteous cause, as she viewed patriotism with an added emphasis of religiosity. Her strategy of direct action was thus in full accord with her strategic outlook. It was this approach which made her a symbol of loyal comrade in the then Indian crucial political scenario. Truly, Politics was like a religion to her.

Pratibha's strategic posture would thus appear quite rational, commanding, and superb. Indeed in all these spheres, she proved to be quite innovative as she was quite unconventional in nature.

As a devotee in the Congress, she wanted to see it developed into a mass-based political organization able to articulate and mobilize all the energies of the nation for the attainment of the goal of India's good fortune. She wanted a nation based on completely humanitarian ground. Indeed, such a stance compelled Gandhi himself, who was inclined to such an idea.

Pratibha's concern, however, was not only for any particular organization. She held a great vision for India's unity and a plan for social equity. She held the view that without obliterating the ingrained and vested evils such as poverty, ignorance, caste system, and communalism and other social anachronisms and religious divisiveness, India can hardly be turned into modern democracy. Caste and Gender-bias must not be allowed to hinder a democratic India.

Here begins Pratibha's second phase of contribution, the phase of public service. In 1980, the Congress (I) swept back into power, and her name was considered a front-runner for the Chief Minister's post. However, the post went to Sanjay Gandhi's confidant A.R. Antulay, who was soon forced to resign on corruption charges. Subsequently, she became a minister again in the Vasantdada Patil ministry. Following differences between Patil and then Maharashtra Pradesh Congress Committee (MPCC) chief Prabha Rau, Rajiv Gandhi appointed her as MPCC chief (1988-90).

In successive congress governments, she handled the portfolios of tourism, social welfare and housing under three chief ministers: Vasantdada Patil, Babasaheb Bhosle, S. B. Chavan and Sharad Pawar, gaining a reputation for her competence. She was continually re-elected to the assembly, either from Jalgaon or the nearby Edlabad constituencies, until 1985, when she was nominated to the Rajya Sabha.

In Rajya Sabha, she served as its deputy chairperson from November 1986 to November 1988. Her term expired in April 1990. The following year, in the elections when Rajiv Gandhi was assassinated she won election 10th Lok Sabha from at Amravati constituency, her husband's city, where he had once been mayor, thus entering in the lower house of national parliament, the Lok Sabha for the first time.

She has also served as Director of National Federation of Urban Co-operative Banks and Credit Societies and the Member of Governing Council, National Co-operative, Union of India.

Despite the exhaustion of her daily schedule, Pratibha found a never-ending stream of human needs in the faces she met. In spite of hours of tiring physical and emotional workload, Pratibha seemed relentless. She completely devoted herself to social activities. Pratibha Mahila Sahakari Bank (Pratibha Women Cooperative Bank) is a cooperative bank founded by Pratibha Patil in 1973 in Jalgaon in Maharashtra with the objective of empowering women. She established a number of hostels for working women in Delhi and Mumbai. The Shram Sadhana Trust, controls four major working women's hostels and also a college of engineering and technology in Jalgaon. Sant Muktabai Sahakari Sakhar Karkhana (SMSSK) known as Sant Muktabai Cooperative Sugar Factory is a cooperative sugar factory founded by Mrs. Pratibha Patil. But list has not yet ended. She has also tried to help the students in a remarkable way by launching a college for themselves. Established on the 23rd June 1983, B.V. SSBT College of Engineering and Technology has achieved an enviable status due to a strong emphasis on academic and technical excellence.

And here are the reasons why Pratibha Patil is a woman with uncommon qualities:

(1) She has the process of leadership

(2) She has defeated the barriers of caste and gender

(3) Satisfying diverse constituencies

(4) She has profoundly diplomatic opinions on critical national issues

(5) She's polite but firm in personal life

(6) She has a sportsman spirit which allows her to remain steady in any adverse situation

Publicity and openness, honest and complete - that is the prime condition for the health of every society, and ours, too. The man who does not want these features in the country is indifferent to his motherland and thinks only about his own gains. The man who does not want publicity and openness for his motherland does not want to cleanse it of its diseases, but to drive them inside, so they may rot there. These singing and stinging words are wholly relevant to the ideas of Pratibha Patil.

6

Governor

After her tenure as the Member of Parliament from Amravati ended, Pratibha Patil took a brief break from her political life in 1996. One of the most proficient politicians of the country, who has given her heart and soul to serve the interests of the nation and to help fellow countrymen in distress, Patil's brief hiatus from the political scenario of the county was deeply felt. From 1996 to 2004, the country missed one of her most loyal servants in the fight against social evils and other malpractices.

A Woman Governs the State

Pratibha Patil was assigned a new job in 2004, which forced her to end her political hibernation and once again serve the interests of the country. She was asked to assume the offices of the Governor of the state of Rajasthan. In accepting this responsibility, Patil created a new landmark in the history of the country. Following the great traditions of the legendary Sarojini Naidu and subsequently her daughter, Padmaja Naidu, Pratibha Patil was the first woman assuming the offices of the Governor of Rajasthan.

Patil was only the second politician from Maharashtra to accept the post, the first being ex-Maharashtra Chief Minister Vasantdada Patil. This can be seen as some sort of trend that Pratibha started, as it marked a kind of first show that had ever happened in the constitution. By becoming the first

Governor of Rajasthan, she immediately won for the woman folk, a position in the state that has always been beyond their grasp till then. This can also be seen as some sort of a landmark appointment, as this eventually paved the way for the country to have her first woman President.

Political Scenario of Rajasthan

2004 – Rajasthan went in for state elections. The Gehlot government in the state was already facing an anti-incumbency bend, and to top it all, the onus of the lack of rains in the state was also attributed to faulty administrative machinery. In such a situation, driving on these factors, the Bharatiya Janta Party (BJP) came into power, propping up Vasundhara Raje as the Chief Ministerial candidate.

Raje's coming to power and Pratibha Patil as the Governor of the state, provided the state with a very unique situation, which history was not a witness to. This was the first time in the state of Rajasthan that there were three women at the three most important political junctures of the state – Pratibha Patil, as the Governor, Vasundhara Raje as the Chief Minister and Sumitra Singh as the Assembly Speaker. This was a mark of their fight towards an egalitarian society, which they had constructed through their resilient fight against conservative norms and social pressures. It is interesting to note that with Raje being brought forward to assume the offices of the Chief Minister, the women electorate of the state came out in large numbers to cast their votes, breaking the shackles of conservative social definitions. This aspect is indeed a tribute to the prowess of these striking female personalities.

"...unlawful conversion from one religion to another by allurement or by fraudulent means or forcibly..."

The biggest challenge to the governorship of Pratibha Patil came in the form of the Rajasthan Freedom of Religion Bill, passed by the Rajasthan Legislative Assembly in April 2006.

Ostensibly, the bill spoke of defending the rights of an individual in the choice of his/her religious commitments. It gave a cover for the constitutional rights of a human being in the choice of faith. It sought to break the epidemic of conversion that has become extremely commonplace in India at present. India's vast illiterate population is still being subjected to fraudulent methods of conversion, where the religious communities are using the guise of fables and distorted mythological myths to preach the strengths of one religious sect over the other, thereby causing communal disharmony in society.

This bill was greatly opposed by the Christian community in general, as they felt that this was some propaganda issued in the favor of the Sangh Parivar to malign them. It seemed pretty obvious that this bill was a direct attack on them, as this charge of forced conversion has often been brought upon them frequently in recent times. After all, the Graham's Stein's murder case has been appropriated to forced conversion of the local tribals into Christianity. In such a situation, it was extremely understandable for the Christians to get agitated and restless in the eye such a bill being passed in the Legislative Assembly.

The link between the ruling BJP and the RSS were also being revealed in the face of such bills, as the underlying political affiliations were getting easily exposed through such activities. In the light of this statement, it should be remembered that while the Governor of a state is supposed to be politically neutral, the fact remains that they more or less belong to some political party and therefore, political bitterness with opposition parties remain embedded within their dealings. Patil belonged to the Congress government and the party at the state, was the BJP.

Thus when the bill was sent across to the Governor, asking for sanction, Patil found that some clauses in the bill infringed on the "fundamental rights such as freedom of speech and expression, freedom of conscience and freedom to profess, practice and propagate religion." She therefore considered that it would be extremely undemocratic on her part to sign this bill and consequently sent it back without her consent to the same.

The Rajasthan government immediately comprehended a form of political dissent prevailing over the decision made by Patil in this regard. They therefore made immediate enquiries into the way the Congress government has dealt with this issue in their respective states and found that the methods adopted by them were absolutely the same as theirs. Making a complete list of the same, they re-sent the entire petition to the Governor, pointing out the procedure adopted by her own party in this particular case. The Congress governments in Madhya Pradesh and Orissa had scheduled such policies nearly forty years from now and these petitions had been upheld by the Supreme Court of the country. It should also be remembered that the head of the Constituent Assembly, Dr B R Ambedkar, when drafting the Article 25 of the Indian constitution had determined that the best solution to the problems of conversion, was the regulation of laws proposed by state legislatures. In this context, Pratibha Patil's decision to refute the bill would remain a question whose answers are yet to be answered.

Not to be undone, the State Government re-sent the petition to the Governor on May 2006 and appended the following observations with the same. It had now become difficult for Patil to return the petition without proper consideration to its memorandum. In this kind of a situation, Patil did the next best thing that she could do – she resorted to the Indian administrative system of uncharted and unscheduled delays. She accepted the petition from the Government and pondered over its substance. The matter lay with her for over one year. Neither did she clear it, nor did she oppose it. A year later, she sent the bill to the President for clearance. However, immediately after that, she resigned from the Governorship of the state on 21st June, 2007 to accept her nomination as the

Presidential candidate of the ruling UPA government for the upcoming Presidential elections.

The highlights of this chapter, as maintained in the plot outline are attributed as follows:

- Political hibernation from 1996 to 2004.
- Appointed the Governor of Rajasthan in 2004.
- The political scenario of Rajasthan.
- First woman governor of Rajasthan.
- 3 women in powerful state positions – Vasundhara Raje as the Chief Minister, Sumitra Singh as the Assembly speaker being the others.
- April 2006 and the Rajasthan Legislative Assembly passing the Rajasthan Freedom of Religion Bill 2006.
- Controversy regarding Bill.
- Pratibha Patil and the Bill.
- Resignation as the Rajasthan Governor.

7

Rashtrapati

The stipulated five-year term for President APJ Abdul Kalam was coming to an end in July, 2007. This time, with the Congress Government in power at the center, it seemed obvious that the Presidential candidate would eventually be a Congress Party member, or the Indian Left would propose a name, using their support for the government at the center as a tool for pulling the chords.

Last year the ruling BJP at the center had proposed the name of India's nuclear scientist, APJ Kalam for the post of President. The Congress had immediately come in to back that candidature as an extremely deserving name for the post. The Left however had negated his name and had on the other hand, proposed the name of Captain Lakshmi Sehgal of the Indian National Army that was formed in the pre-independence era, under the leadership of Netaji Subhash Chandra Bose. Even though there have earlier been women presidential nominees, the addition of Lakshmi Sehgal in the race last year added fresh impetus towards the selection of a woman in the most powerful position of the country.

The Congress led UPA government was having an extremely tough time in deciding on the name of their presidential candidate. In the era of alliance-based politics, the

Congress was playing its cards absolutely properly and refused to take any decision without consulting with all their allies and obtaining a consensus there from.

In the process of garnering more support for the candidate that they would be naming, the party went ahead and held discussions with the Bahujan Samaj Party. They had naturally figured it out that with the support of the party governing the largest state of India, Uttar Pradesh, victory was just a mere formality. With Mayawati's BSP also joining the UPA in the presidential elections, the UPA's vote count, along with the Left had now gone up to 6 lakhs – a thumping majority. They then went on to hold talks with their other prominent allies, the DMK from the south and also the Left.

It was believed that Sonia Gandhi had listed a few names, when discussing the probability of an alliance with the BSP. She had backed the names of the Union Home Minister, Shivraj Patil, along with other Union Ministers Arjun Singh, Sushilkumar Shinde, the Deputy leader in the Rajya Sabha, Dr Karan Singh and also the former Uttaranchal Chief Minister, ND Tiwari. It is even believed that they had formally settled down on one name, but when asked, Mayawati refused to divulge the same. She merely passed on the information that Sonia Gandhi would let the media know the name.

While the Presidential elections are scheduled to be held on the 19th of July, time was running out for the Congress to gain the support of the Left in their choice of the President. Union Minister Shivraj Patil's candidature had not gone down well with the Communist Party. Though there had been no formal announcement of the Home Minister's name, the information running through the grapevine had alone brought the alliance to a bitter standstill. The Left now called for the name of External Affairs Minister Pranab Mukherjee for the top job of the country.

But Mukherjee ruled out himself for the second time now in a month, considering his candidature to be a mere 'speculation and tendentious.' He went on to refer his fate in the party and the government into the hands of the Congress party.

This was a terrible setback to the Left as this left them with very few options to back and would more or less confine their support to the candidate named by the UPA chairperson Sonia Gandhi. To this effect, Karunanidhi was brought in to broker peace between the Congress and the Left and thereby obtain a consensus for the choice of President. Consequently, another point raised by the Left was the fact that there had been indications of the Congress President had secretly committed to the BSP chief the name of the candidate and had thereby caused a breach of trust between her party and the Left. Relations had reached a critical stage in the alliance by now.

The primary requirement of the Left in the matters of selection was that the nominee should be a person of political stature, with secular credentials, along with a sound knowledge of the Indian constitution. It was in this regard that that the name of Shivraj Patil was faulted by them, claiming that Patil was rather soft on Hindutva and they also questioned his ability to win in the event of Bhairon Singh Shekhawat standing as an independent candidate. This was already conveyed to the Congress earlier, as mentioned by a senior Left leader. They now also claimed a veiled threat, adding that if the Congress refused to adjust to their demands, things would only get more complicated.

However, the CPM's chief concern was that with the allies like the RJD and the NCP making their decision to back the Congress in any candidate that they chose public, they were slowly getting isolated in their powers in determining the presidential candidate. They immediately decided to hold discussions with all UPA allies in order to make their stand clear in the matter. Holding meetings with the RJD and the NCP chiefs they concluded that they both felt that the combination of the UPA, the BSP and the Left could easily defeat Shekhawat. But the primary question of the Left, which remained unanswered, was who the candidate was.

Time was running out. The Election Commission was adamant in completing the process before the 24th of July, as technically that was the date for Kalam's tenure to end. With this kind of pressure building on the parties, the UPA finally came out with another name. From Shivraj Patil, the name had now shifted to Pratibha Patil, the veteran Congress leader from Maharashtra. In the event of her victory, Pratibha Patil would be the first woman ever to reside in Rashtrapati Bhawan.

Though not the first name proposed by the UPA, Patil's name was decided upon after hours of meetings, agreements and of course, disagreements. Finally, when the time came to announce the final name of the candidate, the UPA decided to show themselves to the media as one big happy family. Sonia Gandhi, Manmohan Singh, Pranab Mukherjee and Karunanidhi emerged out of 7, Race Course Road, hand in hand, applying a metaphorical band over their wounds.

Once the decision was finalized, Singh and Gandhi put across a call to the BJP leader, Atal Bihari Vajpayee, asking for his support for Pratibha. She informed him about how Patil's candidature had first been fixed at the Prime Minister's residence and then at the UPA-Left coordination panel. Gandhi described it as a "historic moment" whereby it was an opportunity for the country to have her first woman President in the 60th year of the country's Independence.

The Final Fight

The contest had now boiled down to only three names – Pratibha Patil, APJ Abdul Kalam and the current Vice-President, Bhairon Singh Shekhawat. While Kalam was the first choice of the general people regarding the post of the President, the fact remained that the Presidential elections were carried out by the members of the parliament and the state legislatives. In such a case, the people's mandate hardly mattered and therefore, the contest in this case would boil down to only two names – Patil and Shekhawat.

Kalam had made his intentions very clear – he would stand for a re-election, only if he received unanimous support from all the parties of the country. This situation would never arise however, as the government at the center, the Congress, had made their intentions clear regarding their choice of the president. They had gone through a strenuous process of selecting their candidate and therefore there hardly seemed any possibility of them supporting Kalam. As regards the Left, they were against his candidature, right from the last Presidential polls, wherein they had proposed their candidate, Lakshmi Sehgal for the post of President. In this scenario, there would hardly be any possibility for them to support Kalam. His stipulation for a second term looked doomed right from the very beginning in which case. Even the BJP, the party who had originally cast Kalam's name five years back, now decided to run the race with Vice-President Shekhawat, leaving Kalam with no alternative any more but to go back into his earlier civilian life.

There was of course the Third Front, comprising of politicians like Jayalalitha, Mulayam Singh Yadav and Chandrababu Naidu, who propped up Kalam's name for re-election. They dismissed the name of Pratibha Patil for president, claiming that it was some sort of a Congress manipulation to obtain a president who would suit their own demands. They also spoke about Shekhawat, saying that there were some reservations by political parties regarding his candidature and therefore they had decided to extend their support to Kalam. They justified their decision by arguing that he remained the best person suited to contest the elections, as he commanded respect from all sections of society, be it industrialists, scientists, intellectuals and of course, students.

They took forward their petition to all the political parties for acceptance. However, their proposal met with deaf ears everywhere, as none of the parties accepted their conditions, race namely for the reasons stated above. In the event of the Third Front able to garner some support for Kalam, Vice-President Shekhawat opted to stay out of the race due to his respect for Kalam. However, he was soon back in the fray, as the Third Front's efforts drew a blank.

With Kalam completely opting out of the race for Presidency, the fight remains between the *Bahu* and the *Beta* of Rajasthan. Patil's main rival, Vice President Bhairon Singh Shekhawat is the 17th candidate of the entire fifty who had filled in their papers for the polls. The Shekhawats of Khachaṛia, the place where the VP grew up, have been frantically praying for their *Babosaa.* The village has now been reverberating with the chants for his success, ever since he expressed his intentions to fight the elections as an independent candidate.

The Opposing Son

Bhairon Singh Shekhawat has been an extremely poignant figure in Indian politics. Joining the police force in his youth, he moved on to politics, giving up his service and has since gone on to become the Chief Minister of Rajasthan for more than once. When he became the Chief Minister of Rajasthan for the first time in 1977, Shekhawat is credited with having launched pioneering programs like *Antyodaya*, Food for Work and *Apna Gaon Apna Kaam* and all this while his major focus had been on poverty alleviation. His programs initiated for getting rid of poverty in the state were recognized both by the country and the whole world at large. Shekhawat was given the title of the 'Second Rockefeller', when the President of the World Bank, Robert McNamara visited Rajasthan in 1979. The *Antyodaya* program was so successful that the government of India included it in its policies and renamed it as the Integrated Rural Development Program when launching it for the whole country.

Being a farmer himself, Shekhawat understood the problems of the farming community and thereby created a post for some government functionaries who would go to the doorstep of the farmers of the state and solve their problems right there on the spot. His vision to make Rajasthan economically prosperous, infrastructurally well developed and, socially forward looking and a literate state was finally taking shape. He laid special emphasis on education and the development of the girl child, along with the welfare of the backward classes of society and the physically challenged.

There was during his tenure, an incident of Sati in the district of Deorala in 1987. Shekhawat vehemently protested the movement, exposing the dark inhibitions and customs of the country of immolating a woman on her husband's pyre.

He gave utmost priority to the upliftment of minorities. When he became the Chief Minister of Rajasthan for the second term in 1990, he looked into the reconstitution of the Wakf Board and went on to increase its grant manifold. He was also the first Chief Minister of the country who went on to constitute a State Wakf Authority under the Wakf Act. He did a lot for the minorities of the state in the sense that he went on to undertake a massive mission to repair and beautify dargahs, mosques and other related units. He established the Urdu Academy for the development of the Urdu language and literature, as he believed that a tryst with one's tradition was extremely necessary. He made the town of Tonk the center for the Arabic and Persian Institute. He also understood the necessity of the Haj pilgrimage for Muslims and therefore doubled their quota. He also provided generous grants for the upkeepment and rectification of the Madarasas.

He took measures to increase the reservations of nearly thirty backward classes by bringing them into the category of "Other Backward Classes." And he also made it simpler for them to purse traditional professions irrespective of religious and caste anomalies.

Shekhawat was a Chief Minister who gave his job his complete, undivided attention, a fact that is rarely seen in the politicians of today. He was a truly deserving Vice President of the country, a term that he completed to the best of his abilities and now as the race for the Presidential Elections begins Shekhawat perhaps stands as the greatest threat to the possibilities of Pratibha Patil, becoming the first woman president of the country.

An extremely enigmatic personality, Shekhawat agreed to contest the elections as an independent candidate, with the support of the BJP.

The BJP's decision to back Shekhawat was hardly considered surprising. The Chairman of the NDA, Vajpayee claimed that it was a unanimous decision and claimed that only the decision of the Shiv Sena remained pending and it would come in within a few days. BJP spokesperson, Sushma Swaraj commented that though Kalam remained their first choice for President, the fact remained that they would go on to support Shekhawat as Kalam's pre-requisite for standing for these elections could not be met due to the lack of any consensus. They however left the decision to the rhetorical powers of the Third Front to convince Kalam to stand for a re-election. In the case of his withdrawal, they would go ahead and cast their votes for Shekhawat.

However, in the wake of all this development, the BJP received a setback form one of its allies, the Shiv Sena. A staunch supporter of the BJP, especially in their Hindutva propaganda, the Shiv Sena decided this time to go ahead with the Congress' choice – primarily because Pratibha Patil hailed from Maharashtra. This obviously marked a serious rift in the NDA's alliance politics, as ideology had now taken a backseat before state nationality. With the Shiv Sena also going ahead to vote for Pratibha Patil, the case for Shekhawat had already reached a standstill. The BJP obviously did not have enough votes and victory for Pratibha Patil was now a *fate accompli.*

Signs of the Rashtrapatni

It was now running as the prediction had gone. Pratibha Patil's husband, Devsingh Shekhawat had earlier told the media that an astrologer had predicted that Pratibha Patil would not complete her term as the Governor of Rajasthan, but would instead go on to occupy a more important post in the near future. Who would have believed such a prediction earlier, because such predictions have been made by astrologers for most politicians from time immemorial. However, for Pratibha Patil, this prediction had indeed come true.

As her path to victory was now clear, Patil filed in her nomination papers on the 23rd of June, 2007. During her stay here in Delhi, Patil went on with her spate of meeting all the members of the parliament and other prominent individuals. She went ahead to meet former Prime Minister VP Singh, as also the veteran Congress leader, Dr Karan Singh, who himself had been one of the contenders for the post that she had almost won. Patil however did not interact with the media, as she believed that the right time to talk to them would be much later. She rather spent that time in visiting the Lok Sabha Speaker, Somnath Chaterjee, as well as Union HRD minister, Arjun Singh. Protocol visits had to be made and Patil believed in making all of them within the proper time that was available to her.

She also conferred with Parliamentary Affairs minister, Priyaranjan Dasmunshi as they had to discuss the strategy for the polls. Patil had also made her visits to the Prime Minister, the Congress President and the RJD chief, Laloo Prasad Yadav.

In one of the few press releases that she gave after filing her nomination papers, Patil declared that it was indeed a very prestigious post and what really highlighted the entire process was the fact that a woman had been considered for the job. She explained that this act by the Center went on to show that women in the country were indeed respected. She believes that a woman as the president of the country would definitely send out the right message about India to the whole world.

Patil went on to add that she had never expected her name to be counted in as one of the contenders for the top constitutional post of the country and that she had only received a hint about her nomination from Sonia Gandhi much later, after the entire run to the presidential race had begun.

She clarified that there was no pressure on her to accept the post of the president and that it was generally an offer made to her, which she had decided to take up. She admitted that the race would obviously not be easy as there were reports of even Vice President Bhairon Singh Shekhawat joining in the contest to the polls. She admitted that he was an individual of large stature and that she respected him whole-heartedly.

She also enlisted her agenda, where she to become the president of the country. She emphasized on taking forward the Employment Guarantee Scheme started by Sonia Gandhi and she also acknowledged the fact that there was a form of global competition in all sectors and therefore she stressed on the need for India to gain a proper place in the world. Another problem that she wished to address on becoming the president of the country would be the crisis of economic disparity.

On a lighter note, when she was told about Shekhawat being the son of the Shekhawati region and she merely the daughter-in-law, she catcgorically put it across that she saw no difference between a son and a daughter, thereby breaking the shackles of traditional Indian discrimination.

In the same tone, she lamented about the fact that she would indeed miss the time that she had spent in Rajasthan. She begged the people there not to forget her, as she definitely would remember them all her life.

8

Controversies

Once it became evident that Patil's accession to power was just a mere formality, the opposition started accessing her past data to malign her character and thereby trying to oust her candidature for the post of president. The BJP especially, who had determined to extend support to the independent candidate Bhairon Singh Shekhawat, critically analyzed some issues with regard to her past and thereby began a political campaign against her. The BJP agreed that they had placed their media strategists on the job, though they realized that this was not direct election where the people of the country were also involved in the voting process. They understood that this media campaign's success rate would indeed be very low as their aim was to only to win support from the parties, who had already agreed to support Patil.

What the campaign was successful in was that it added a lot of media attention into the belief that Patil was a controversial and an unworthy candidate. In their self defense, the BJP informed the public that the information that they were providing was not false or concocted, but rather had been derived from public records of Pratibha Patil, which they had obtained and arranged in order to expose her. They listed these so called reports as temporal media statements, statements from the employees' unions and also bank statements, RBI notices, memos from lenders, police and even the courts. With a bank of information from such established and trust worthy sources, the BJP did have a good case in their hands.

The BJP's stand on the matter and their various shreds of documentation, have gone on to invite many more petitions in the courts, asking for her disqualification. The BJP though have categorically maintained that their only motive behind their actions is to generate a form of public opinion against her, and that they were not interested in challenging her candidature on legal grounds. However, the Third Front used the accumulated information to immediately ask for her expulsion. UNPA leader, Dr Jayalalitha went on record saying,

"It is distressing to see that the highest constitutional office in the country had been subjected to mudslinging ... The nation has been embarrassed in the eyes of the world, because UPA chairperson Sonia Gandhi wants a President who will be pliable."

With the opposition going all gung-ho about Patil's controversies, the UPA also came out in complete defense of their candidate. They pointed out cleverly that these so called faux-pas' of Patil had never been hitherto claimed by any political party when she was the Deputy Chairperson of the Rajya Sabha or even during her tenure as the Governor of Rajasthan. The BJP was targeted by the UPA as coming out with a malicious and slanderous campaign which was completely undemocratic and uncivil. It fell on the Prime Minister, Dr Manmohan Singh to come out and defend Patil, when he claimed that the remarks made by the opposition were to be mainly counted as 'mud-slinging.' It was only on the 2nd of July 2007, that Patil herself came out of her shell and claimed that the rumors that were being spread in her name were actually false and baseless.

Oh Brother!

One of the major allegations drawn against her, were that of shielding her brother on a murder charge.

The Vishram Patil murder case came into national reckoning recently, when his widow informed the media that her husband's murderer was none other that Pratibha Patil's brother, GN Patil, who had escaped the long arms of the law when his sister decided to guard him against the investigating officers.

The story of the murder, as told by her, runs smoothly, with every factor and evidence pointing towards Patil's brother.

GN Patil was nominated as the MPCC President of the District Congress Committee of Jalgaon in the year 2004. The election for the same, through a secret ballot, was held in 2005. GN Patil went ahead and fought the elections, but when the results were declared, it was found that he had lost to his opponent, Vishram Patil by a slim margin of 13 votes. Being an educated man (GN Patil was a professor of English in a college in Jalgaon affiliated to the North Maharashtra University), he immediately understood that there had been some siphoning of funds, when some collections had been made for the felicitation of Pratibha Patil and also for some relief package intended for tsunami victims. So being the person in office at that time, he set up and enquiry into the misappropriation of those funds.

As would have it, he was murdered on the 21st of September 2005, right before his house and that too in broad daylight. The police immediately began their investigations and ended up arresting two assailants – Raju Mali and Raju Sonawane. The inquisition was going on at a tough pace, when suddenly the news came in that on instructions from Mumbai, the case had been referred to the CID, who would continue looking into the matter on behalf of the local police. Vishram Patil's widow, Rajni Patil, informed the police through correspondence that Dr Ulhas Patil and GN Patil were the conspirators in her husband's murder.

Rajni Patil filed a petition in the Aurangabad bench of the Bombay High Court in February 2007 and based on that, the court referred the case on to the CBI from the CID. The judge stated:

"We have scrutinized the entire record with the help of counsel for both sides. We have considered the chequered history of the present case, the developments which have taken place after filing of chargesheet, issues involved, and the reference to alleged conspiracy by the influential political leaders of the region. Having regard to the importance of issues involved and the alleged complicity of the influential political leaders referred to in paragraph Nos. 3 and 4 of the petition, in our considered opinion, this is a fit case where the investigation should be conducted by the CBI."

The CBI team which visited Jalgaon soon after on the 4th of April began the probe into the case immediately. Things took a serious and more complex turn, when Raju Mali, one of the chief accused in the murder, died in police custody under mysterious circumstances.

By the authority vested in them by the district and sessions court of Jalgaon, the CBI filed a supplementary chargesheet in the murder case against Pratibha Patil's brother, GN Patil.

June 22nd, a special press release was organized at the residence of the Akali Dal leader, Sukhbir Singh Dhindsa. The Hindu wrote:

"At the press conference, Rajni Patil alleged that Ms. Pratibha Patil's brother was in some way involved in the murder of her (Ms. Rajni Patil's) husband several years ago. The suggestion was that Ms. Pratibha Patil had used her political influence to protect her brother. Copies of her memorandum to the President on this issue were distributed to the press by Mr. Sudheendra Kulkarni, an aide of Leader of the Opposition L.K. Advani.

She further said that she had written to Sonia Gandhi and President Dr. A P J Abdul Kalam giving details about the allegation."

In the same conference, BJP spokesperson Ravi Shankar Prasad informed the press:

"These are all stark, important and disturbing facts much in existence even before she was considered as a candidate for the highest constitutional office of the country...Therefore, consistent with the norms of dignity, transparency and constitutional propriety relating to such a high office, the BJP would like Pratibha Patil herself to satisfactorily reply to some of the most disturbing questions that have emerged from Rajni Patil's revelations."

These claims were then refuted by Sharad Pawar and Priyaranjan Dasmunshi. An article that was released in the Nagaland Post communicated:

"It is a matter that the CBI (Central Bureau of Investigation) is probing. Anyway, her brother's name was not in the FIR (first information report), nor in the charge sheet,' said Pawar, former Maharashtra chief minister. Both ministers blamed the opposition National Democratic Alliance (NDA), of which the Akali Dal is a constituent, for the slur campaign against the presidential candidate. *'I met Dhindsa in the morning and he said he did not have any idea about the press conference. Punjab Chief Minister Parkash Singh Badal was shocked to see how his colleague's house was being used for dirty politics,'* Pawar remarked. Referring to reports that Sudheendra Kulkarni, a former Prime Minister's Office (PMO) official, had brought the woman to the national capital, Pawar said: *'It looks like NDA was behind it.'* Dasmunshi added: *'The malign campaign by an ex-PMO official close to the former prime minister (Atal Bihari Vajpayee) is most unfortunate. It reflects their frustration and desperation and is a sign of their losing the election.'"*

These charges were immediately answered by the NDA spokesperson Sushma Swaraj, who went on record saying that no one in the NDA even knew who this so called Rajni Patil was and therefore, the UPA's remarks that the BJP is purposefully trying to malign Pratibha Patil's character is baseless and false.

Finally, matters came to a more definitive standstill, as on the 13th of July, 2007, Rajni Patil moved the Bombay High Court demanding the CBI interrogate Pratibha Patil as also her brother, GN Patil in connection to her husband's matter. She also insisted that these matters be looked into by the probing body before the presidential elections took place. The reason stated by her for her demands, said that her concern regarding the presidential elections was only to deny Pratibha Patil the clause of "Presidential Immunity" in the event that she does win the elections and thereby escape the rulings of the legal courts.

Nothing to Bank Upon!

Another development in the Pratibha Patil controversy emerged out of the Pratibha Mahila Sahakari Bank, which she had begun in 1973 in Jalgaon with the sole prerogative of empowering women. She was the founding chairperson of this bank, with the post of directors being held by many of her relatives – a post to which even she lent her name to later. At present, her role in the board of the bank can be stated to be as one of the thirty-four respondents in an ongoing case in the Aurangabad High Court, where she stands on trial regarding gross misappropriation of funds and severe mismanagement.

The events constructed by the bank led to such a horrible situation that even the Reserve Bank of India (RBI) had to revoke its license in 2003 after their investigative report had pointed out that it had waked off the interest on loans given to many of Patil's relatives.

Way back in 1995, the RBI had already listed the bank as 'weak' and had already ordered two enquiries under the Maharashtra Cooperative Societies Act in 2001 and 2002.

In July 2001, an enquiry had provided the information that the bank had already incurred massive losses near to the amount of Rs. 1.35 crores. It also reported that following this huge financial calamity, the chairperson and eight other directors had immediately handed in their resignation papers. Under the orders of the Ministry of Finance in April 2002, the RBI even enquired into the allegation of fund irregularities after receiving numerous complaints from the Cooperative Bank Employees Union and also other small depositors in the bank.

The RBI report revealed that the real or exchangeable value of the bank's paid-up share capital and reserves fell to a low of Rs. 197.67 lakhs and therefore it went on to conclude that the bank did not have sufficient assets to meet with its liabilities. The bank in no way complied with the RBI's directive on minimum share capital.

It had also deciphered, that the ratio of net owned funds of the bank was placed at a high of 312.4% and the erosion of the value of the bank's assets had gone to wipe out its own funds and at the same time had also affected the deposits up to Rs. 197.67 lakhs, thereby pegging the percentage at 26% of the total deposits.

The RBI report even conveyed that the NPAs of the bank amounted to 65.8% of the total loans and advances made by the bank.

And what was perhaps considered to be the biggest fallacy in the structure of the bank was that the board had taken no steps, whether considerable or not, to improve the financial condition of the bank.

The RBI mentioned in its report,

"Pratibha Patil is the founder member of the bank, who is a politically influential personality. She has made all her relatives as directors of the bank and the bank is being run as good as a family business. Because of the influence of respondent No. 8 (Pratibha Patil) the bank has given various loans to the relatives and to a sugar factory of which she is a director.

Her relatives have not paid back the loans. Most of the loans were given without security. Most of the loans are closed"

The final nail in the bank's coffin came in February 2003, when the RBI Executive Director, PB Mathur signed the note which finally revoked the bank's license. This process meant that many people who had invested their life's savings in the bank, especially since the bank was founded by Pratibha, lost all their deposits and thereby lost their means of livelihood and monetary securities.

There were further complaints filed by the bank's union leaders, where they stated that as many as a dozen applicants and recipients of loans were those of Pratibha Patil's relatives. These loans that were meant to be given to the women of the state to improve their financial plight, were actually handed out to Patil's relatives, including her brother's and nephews.

Many of these loans were even waived off and these were those of direct relatives like Anjali Dilipsingh Patil, Kavita Aravind Patil, Rajkaur Dilipsingh Patil and others. Besides these chosen few of direct blood relatives, the bank also gave several benefits to other Patil aides, even if that implied flouting bank rules hazardously.

The petitions filed by the depositors in the bank in the High Court have levied serious charges against founder chairperson Pratibha Patil, as she was the face of the bank and the reason as to why people chose to invest in that particular bank and no other.

The former president of the employees union also alleged that the bank had collected a sum of Rs. 4,556 from the employees with the intention of depositing that to the Kargil fund. However, records show that no such donation was made to the national fund. This act is a serious case of embezzlement.

Dilip Singh Patil, Pratibha Patil's elder brother, who had taken a loan from the bank, just did not feel it necessary to repay the amount. He even considered the bank phone to be his own personal property and ran up the bill to a humongous amount of Rs. 20 lakhs while talking to stockbrokers in Mumbai.

Her supporters though point out that she was not the founding president of the bank and had held her post as the chairperson for only a month and eight days. They also declare that her name has not been mentioned in the chargesheet filed by the police and neither has it appeared in the RBI report. They therefore believe that her persona in the whole matter is clean and complete. AB Bardhan, the CPM leader has gone on to state that there should be aspersions cast upon the Employees Union since they are but associated with the BMS union, a union led by the BJP. Therefore, they have labeled these allegations as slanderous and unjustified.

Kuchh Meetha Ho Jaye!

Another issue that cropped up recently after the UPA announcing Pratibha Patil's name as the presidential nominee, was that of the Sant Muktabai Sahakari Sakhar Karkhana (SMSSK) situated in the Edlabad constituency of Maharashtra. (Registration Number JGA/EBD/PRG/(A)-6 S/88-89).

Pratibha Patil served as the founding chairperson in this factory from 1988 to 1996. Sonia Gandhi had been called upon to inaugurate the factory on the 23rd of January 1999.

This bank had obtained its capital in the form of loans from three cooperative and one nationalized bank – MSC, DCCB Jalgaon, DCCB Mumbai and Dena Bank. The factory got into trouble when it failed to repay the borrowed money, defaulting by about Rs. 73 crores to the three banks – MSC, DCCB Jalgaon and DCCB Mumbai. The latter had served numerous notices to the factory for the recovery of an outstanding loan amount of Rs. 17.70 crores.

The bank eventually had to be sealed on the 23rd of January 2007, the second time that the mill witnessed a lockout. Last time it was sealed in January 2006 on the same grounds. However, the board of directors headed by Pratibha Patil's younger brother, GN Patil, made a plea requesting for another chance to improve the mill's performance. This request was deemed legitimate enough and therefore the seal was lifted. However, matters never did improve and the mill had to be shut down once again.

Evasion of outstanding loans was not the only complaint that was lodged against the mill. In 2002, the Chief Commissioner of Excise and Customs Pune, marked notices to 24 sugar factories, including the SMSSK, whereby they were asked to repay excise evasion of Rs. 8.7 crores. These sugar companies have been held responsible for selling export quota sugar in domestic markets at exceedingly high prices and thereby they have evaded excise duty exemption of Rs. 85 per quintal and then gone on to increase their revenues by selling the sugar at local markets.

Not to mention this also as a "malign campaign", the Union Agriculture Minister, Sharad Pawar immediately went on record defending Pratibha Patil and explaining that there never was any such enquiry under the Maharashtra Cooperative Societies Act against her. A point that he very rightly focused on was that it was indeed unfortunate that out of the 74 mills that were brought forward, the actions of only one have been highlighted and massacred. Pawar sealed his argument by saying that these mills lost their functioning capability due to the persistent draught periods that the country had faced and therefore they were forced to declare themselves as sick.

Miscellaneous Scams

The Economic Times had recently come out with an article, which read that the Shrama Sadhna Trust, a charitable institution in Mumbai, of which Patil was the managing director had actually siphoned off funds amounting to Rs. 4.16 crores between 2001 and 2003. Its inquisition garnered them information that the money was taken from an engineering polytechnic run by the trust in Jalgaon.

Problems also emerged on the Members of Parliament Local Area Development Scheme (MPLADS) front. This scheme is formulated by the Government of India, under which, each member of the parliament has the choice to work to the tune of Rs. 1 crore per year, which are to be utilized in that person's constituency. This scheme is even applicable for the members of the Rajya Sabha, where they represent the whole state and may therefore look towards implementation in one or more districts based on their discretion. The amount reserved for this process has been increased to Rs. 2 crores since 1998-99.

What has also begun with the initiation of this scheme is the unending plethora of corruption, which has made some people make demands to scrap the entire rule. There have been reported instances of MPs taking bribes in order to hand over work under the MPLADS. Enquiries have already been placed to look into the matter.

Pratibha Patil, during her tenure as the MP from Amravati from 1991 to 1996, had diverted Rs. 36 lakhs under the MPLADS Scheme to fund a trust run by her husband. This was a complete breech of the Scheme's memorandum, whereby it restricted the flow of these funds to family members. In this case, Patil's defenders have not been able to come to any convincing argument.

Pratibha Patil has also made several controversial statements on the case for sterilization. She has gone on record, stating that though most people may consider this act of compulsory sterilization as undemocratic and heinous, her own personal view of the same are that it is very much required for the development of the country.

On December 10, 1990, when she served as the Health Minister of Maharashtra, Patil had advocated in the Maharashtra Assembly that people with hereditary diseases should be compulsorily sterilized.

Purdah Hai Purdah!

On June 17th, 2007, Pratibha Patil was addressing a congregation of Rajputs, where she made some unnecessary statements regarding the Purdah system.

Indian culture has always respected their woman folk and as far as the history of the Purdah goes, they were invented in order to protect women from Muslim invaders. However, things have changed from then. Now an independent country, India has women progressing in every field. They now require moral support and encouragement so that they can leave these practices behind. After all, we are talking of having a woman as the president of the country.

However, the presidential nominee, Pratibha Patil stated something else, which caused some amount of communal tension and also was historically untrue. As the CNN IBN reported,

"The UPA-Left Presidential nominee Pratibha Patil courted controversy on Sunday by saying that the purdah (veil) system emerged in India to protect women from Mughal aggressors".

Patil's remark, made at a function in Udaipur marking the 467th birth anniversary of Maharana Pratap, has left historians and Muslim social activists astounded.

Patil said though Indian culture always respected women, the veil system began during the Mughal rule to "save women from Mughal invaders".

"We had the concept of purdah to protect women from Mughal invaders. So, they stayed indoors and were veiled," Patil said.

"Today we are citizens of free India. There is need to put a stop to such practices. That alone will ensure real respect for women. When women are progressing in every field, it is our duty to discontinue such practices," Patil added.

Historians have immediately exposed the fallacy in her statements, as they rectify the mistake by reminding us that the purdah system was in practice much before the Mughals came to the country. What has intensified the fiasco is that Muslim leaders, especially from Rajasthan have naturally been enraged at her statements, considering also the event at which she made this remark.

Varsha Joshi, a historian, says that the purdah system existed much before the Muslims arrived in India. She said,

"I think it's absolutely wrong to say that the purdah system existed because of the Mughal invaders. It was prevalent before the Mughals came to India. It would be right to say that the purdah was more an imitation rather than a strategy of defense."

Even the Islamic theologians, connected with the Muslim Personal Law Board criticized Patil's remarks as they felt communal sledging in this regard. Maulana Rashid stated:

"The statement is a clear reflection of Pratibha's mindset about Islam and Muslims. It is better the UPA should change its presidential candidate and opt for a more secular person for this post."

A Joan of Arc?

Pratibha Patil also commented recently that she had spoken to the deceased leader Baba Lekhraj of the Brahma Kumaris World Spiritual University at their headquarters in Mount Abu, Rajasthan.

This is what she claims:

"Dadiji ke shareer main Baba aye ... Maine unse baat ki (Baba entered Devi's body and he communicated to me through her)."

She claimed that she had received a divine indication that a great responsibility was coming her way.

Controversies galore!

Pratibha Patil went to polls on the 19th of July, 2007. At the time of casting of the votes, Patil looked to have the numbers edge over her opponent, Bhairon Singh Shekhawat. Now it was only a matter of time. Or was it?

Additions

Further added here are various proofs of documents that have been submitted by various concerns when trying to criticize Pratibha Patil. The truth behind these allegations shall only be out in time to come.

Added are Rajni Patil's letters to Sonia Gandhi and also various additions and subtractions made to the records of the Pratibha Mahila Sahakari Bank for the reader's purview.

Smt. Rajani Vishram Patil
43, Vishram, Vidyanagar, Pimprala,
Jalgaon (Maharashtra)
Pin - 425001
Date - 26/09/2005

To,
Hon'ble Madam Soniaji Gandhi,
President, A. I. C. C.
10, Jan Path,
New Delhi.

Madam,

I am the daughter of freedom fighter Late Ramdas Ramchandra Pawar. My husband loyal congressman, true social worker and President of Jalgaon District Congress Committee Prof. V. G. Patil was ruthlessly assassinated early in the morning on the way to the college on 21/09/2005.

Hon'ble C. M., State of Maharashtra has given the orders for proper investigations. The process of Investigation is so far satisfactory. We strongly believe in our constitution and legal procedure. However the brain behind the crime pressurise the whole process. This has been the fear, expressed from all sections of society and I am too afraid of the same.

My husband was a true congressman. He started his political career as a social worker in his early young age. Right from his career beginning he served the country under the flag of Indian National Congress. Whensoever the party suffered any kind of crisis, he truly dedicated his loyalty to the party.

He was elected the President of Jalgaon District Congress Committee twice by ballot. This clearly indicates that he has a strong support from grass-root level of party in the district. He was an academician by profession. He was a Professor of English literature and I am also the Professor of Marathi literature in the same college affiliated to North Maharashtra University. Madam for your kind consideration, his career outline is given in a separate sheet attached herewith.

Madam hopefully you will look in this matter personally in order to give a justice to a martyr.

Thanking You.

Yours Faithfully,
[signature]
(Smt. Rajani V. Patil)

Encl. : 1) Career Sheet.
2) Photocopies of different events.

Copy for information to :
1) Hon'ble President, Republic of India.
2) Hon'ble P. M. of India, New Delhi.
3) Hon'ble C. M. Mr. Vilasrao Deshmukh, Mumbai, Maharashtra.
4) Hon'ble R. R. Patil Home Minister, Maharashtra.
5) Hon'ble Smt. Prabha Rao, President, M. P. C. C.

BIO-DATA

Name	:	Prof. Vishram G. Patil
Address	:	At Mondhale Pimpri, Tal. Parola, Jalgaon.
Date of Birth	:	21/11/1950
Qualification	:	M.A. Hons. English.
Religion	:	Hindu, Caste : Maratha

1. Indian Games, Athlethics, General Secretary - Pratap College Amalner.

2. Executive Member, Students' Council, Poona University 1972.

3. Active Member & President Youth Congress, Amalner, Block 1971-72.

4. University-Representative & President, NSUI, Nagpur University Campus, Post Graduate Departments 1973-74.

5. Students' Leader, NSS, Nagpur University 1973-74

6. Founder Member of Congress (I) during 1978. Jail Bharo Andolan.

7. Motivator, Indian Development Centre, New Delhi, during 1983 to 1985.

8. District Trainer from 1986.

9. General Secretary, District Youth Congress (I) during 1982 to 1987.

10. Organised Election Campaigns during 1976 & 1984-85, 89, 95 & 96.

11. Working for the Tribal & Mofussil Areas in the District.

12. Implemented 20 Point Programme effectively in the District.

13. Organised Training Programme of Congress (I) from time to time and making the people understand its policies and Ideology.

14. District Trainer, Catalyst, General Secretary & Monitor. Working at the Grassroot level in the District, Organizing and strenthening the party under the beloved Leadership of Congress Presidents Indiraji, Rajivji and Soniaji.

-२-

15. District Commandant, Home-Guards Jalgaon from 1986 to 1996.

16. Organised almost 200 Oneday Congress Training Camps in the District

17. President DCC Jalgaon from 1997 to 2004.

18. Opened 253 Branches of Congress party in the District.

19. Organised almost 891 public meetings to condemn Sena-BJP Govt. in Maharashtra since 1997 and Propegated party policies,Idiology.

20. Loyal and obedient party worker, Working under the Leadership of Soniaji Gandhi

21. President, State Transport Corporation INTUC since 1990.

22. Contested Election in 1999 for Erandol Parliamentary Constituency.

23. • Attended state Training camp at Karla Maharashtra.

24. Attended High Level National Training camp at Bhopal.

25. Organised 15 camps in the District on Bhopal Training camp.

26. Canvassed for the Party in M.P. Elections as an AICC Observer.

27. Canvassed for the Party in Jalgaon, Erandol, Buldhana, Jalna Aurangabad, and Khandawa M.P. Constituencies in 2004 Gen. Election.

त्यांच्या पत्नीचे नाव :- रजनी विश्राम पाटील(प्राध्यापीका:- मराठी- नु.म.विद्यालय)
मुलाचे नाव:- प्रणव विश्राम पाटील
मुलगी:- शितल

Prof. Rajani Patil,
45, Vidhya Nagar,
Pimprala, Jalgaon
Tel (0257) 2252001
Mobile 9226877317

---

05 March 2007

To

Smt. Sonia Gandhi ji,
H'ble Congress President,
10, Janpath,
New Delhi

Respected Madam,

Late Shri V.G. Patil, DCC President of Jalgaon, Maharashtra, a loyalist to the party and its leadership, was my husband. I had personally met you requesting for an impartial enquiry by the CBI into my husband's murder, as the record and evidences were being tampered with by the CID at the behest of conspirators. Late Shri V.G. Patil had served the Congress as a committed & loyal soldier for 30 years. He didn't change party unlike other opportunists, despite all the enticements. He was elected the President of the District Congress Committee 3 times.

Dr. Ulhas Patil, ex-M.P. got elected to Lok Sabha in 1998 on a Congress ticket for a short period of 16 months during 1998 - 1999. Instead of working in public interest, he focused his efforts on amassing personal wealth through his Institutions thereby tarnishing the image of the party. This is evident from the fact that in 1999 elections he stood 3rd (secured votes less than NCP also) and in 2004 he lost by a margin of 20,000 votes in spite of an alliance with the NCP.

My husband was always fighting for the interest of the common man and thus got the opportunity to work in several positions. My husband never received any co-operation from Dr. Ulhas Patil for strengthening the party and in the year 2003-04, the Congress lost the municipal election and taking the moral responsibility himself, my husband resigned. Dr. G.N. Patil, brother of Smt. Pratibha Patil (Governor of Rajasthan) was then made the DCC President. Dr. Ulhas Patil & Dr. G.N. Patil worked together and it is

-2-

during this period that the election of Dr. Ulhas Patil as an M.P. was lost in May 2004, despite a pro-Congress public sentiment

In 2005 when the DCC Presidential election took place by secret ballot, my husband won the election against Dr. G.N. Patil and became the President of the District Congress Committee again. At that time several enquiries of mismanagement and fraud in Dr. Ulhas Patil's Institutions had started. One day, my husband received a warning to stop all enquiries or else the consequences would be very bad. Being a daredevil, he did not bother and approximately one week before his murder, he was warned again that a 'Supari' [contract to kill] to murder my husband V.G. Patil had been given by Dr. Ulhas Patil and Dr. G.N. Patil. On the morning of 21/9/05, my husband was brutally murdered.

Since I was aware of the warnings, I mentioned this fact to the police & the names of Dr. Ulhas Patil, Dr. G.N. Patil, Ramesh Chaudhari, MLA and Shri Mahendra Singh Patil, ex-MLA, who had conspired. After the murder, proper investigation was being done by the local police, but when the investigations were almost nearing an end, suddenly the case got transferred to the CID (part of State Police) and the investigation Officers kept changing. The other 2 accused were released despite the court ordering for the Narco-Analysis tests. Their objective of delaying investigations is evident from the fact that the Narco- Analysis tests were conducted more than a year after the court had given clear directions for the same to be conducted immediately. Finally, even though the tests were done, the details of the investigations have not been made public and I am given to understand that they are being tampered with under the influence of those named above.

Consequently, I had appealed to the High Court that the conspirators have been constantly influencing and interfering with the CID enquiry, and finally the High Court has issued orders to transfer the enquiry to CBI on February 23, 2007.

Madam, I have only you to look up to. I know that the life of my husband cannot be brought back, but when I see the conspirators not only moving freely but one of them Dr Ulhas Patil, canvassing his candidature as the Congress nominee for the parliamentary

-3-

elections. It pains me Madam, you alone can understand my pain, misery and anguish because you have also suffered the pain of a woman having lost her husband in such a brutal way.

I would therefore like to remind you of your assurance that Dr. Ulhas Patil will not be given the ticket when I met you last in Delhi

Respected Madam, Our family has always been loyal and dedicated to the party & its leadership. We treat it as our mother. It would be very painful for me and my family if we are to oppose official Congress nominee and help him defeated. But we would be left with no alternative if Dr. Ulhas Patil is nominated as the Congress candidate. Moreover, I fear that my whole family is likely to get liquidated by these brutal murderers if they continue to get politically patronized by the party. I am sure you would understand and appreciate my feelings

With regards,

Yours sincerely,

(Rajnitai Patil)

Cc ~~1. Smt. Margaret Alva~~
~~2. Shri Vilasrao Deshmukh~~, H'ble. Chief Minister, Maharashtra
~~3. Smt. Prabha Rau~~
~~4. Shri Manod Patel~~
5. Shri Narayan Rane

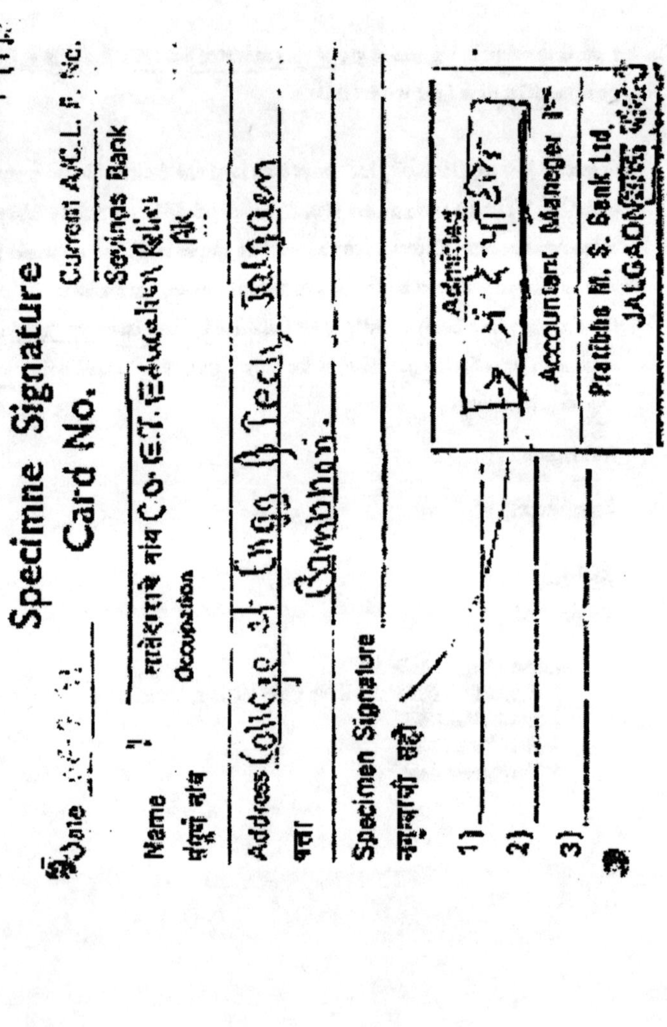
Specimne Signature
Card No.
Current A/C.L.F. No.
Savings Bank
Date
Name
व्यवसायाचे नाव C/O E.T. Education Relief
Occupation
Address College of Engg & Tech, Jalgaon Bambhori.
पत्ता
Specimen Signature
नमुन्याची सही
1)
2)
3)
Admitted
Accountant Manager
Pratibha M. S. Bank Ltd, JALGAON

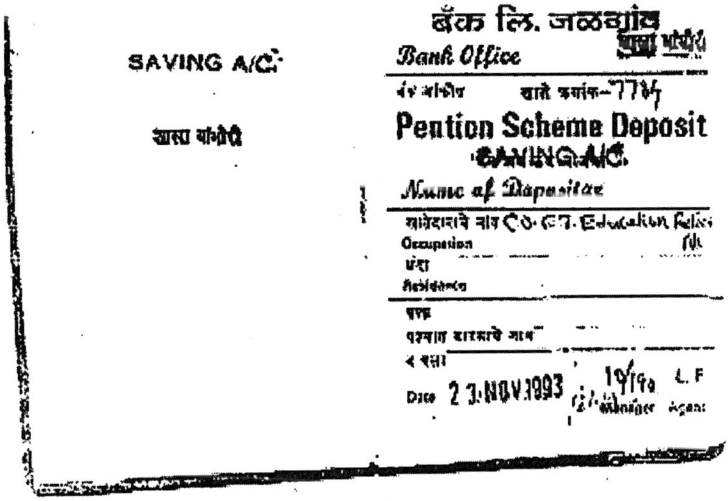

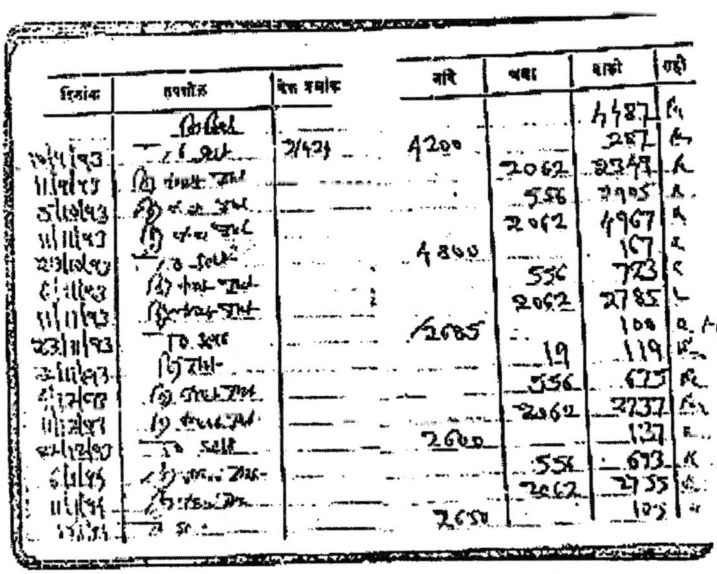

दिनांक	तपशील	चेक क्रमांक	नावे	जमा	बाकी	सही
	Balance				4587	
[illegible]	To Self	2/421	4200		387	
[illegible]	[illegible]			2062	2349	
[illegible]	[illegible]			556	2905	
[illegible]	[illegible]			2062	4967	
[illegible]	To Self		4800		167	
[illegible]	[illegible]			556	723	
[illegible]	[illegible]			2062	2785	
[illegible]	[illegible]		2685		100	
23/11/93	To Self			19	119	
[illegible]	[illegible]			556	675	
[illegible]	[illegible]			2062	2737	
[illegible]	To Self		2600		137	
[illegible]	[illegible]			556	693	
[illegible]	[illegible]			2062	2755	
[illegible]	To Self		2650		105	

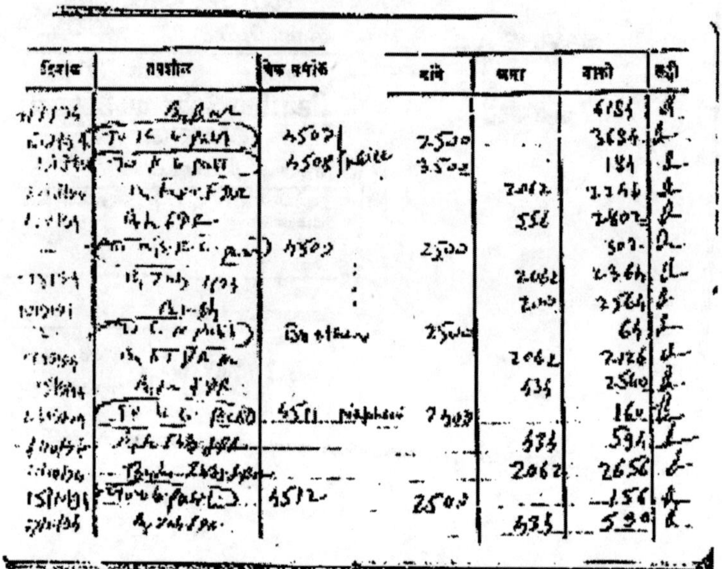

दिनांक	तपशील	चेक क्रमांक	नावे	जमा	बाकी	सही

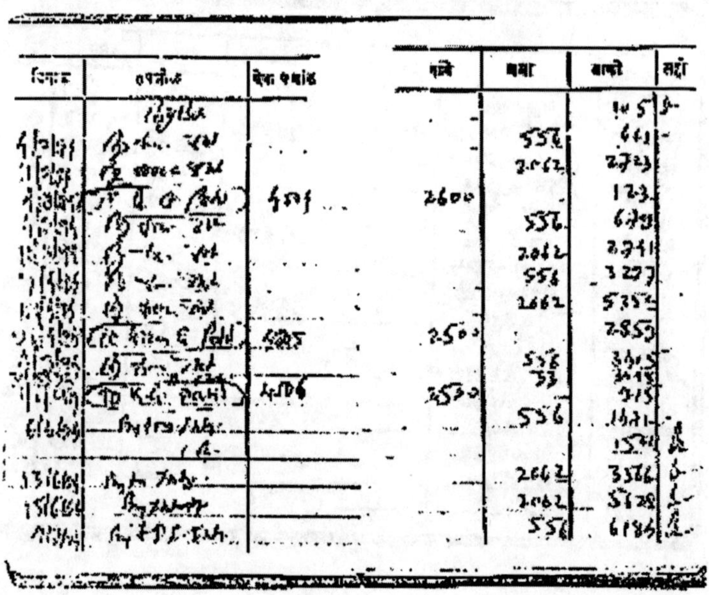

दिनांक	तपशील	चेक क्रमांक	नावे	जमा	बाकी	सही

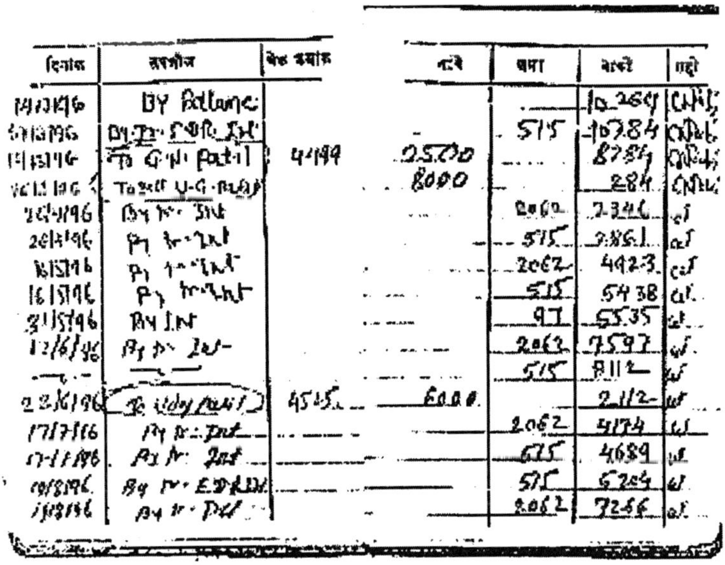

दिनांक	तपशील	चेक क्रमांक	नावे	जमा	बाकी	सही
14/3/96	By Balance				10269	[illegible]
5/3/96	By Pr. FDR Int			515	10784	[illegible]
11/3/96	To G.N. Patil	4499	2500		8284	[illegible]
[illegible]	To self U.G. Patil		8000		284	[illegible]
26/4/96	By Pr. Int			2060	2346	[illegible]
26/4/96	By Pr. Int			515	2861	[illegible]
16/5/96	By Pr. Int			2062	4423	[illegible]
16/5/96	By Pr. Int			515	5438	[illegible]
31/5/96	By Int			97	5535	[illegible]
12/6/96	By Pr. Int			2062	7597	[illegible]
—	—			515	8112	[illegible]
22/6/96	To Uday Patil	4515	6000		2112	[illegible]
17/7/96	By Pr. Int			2062	4174	[illegible]
17-7-96	By Pr. Int			515	4689	[illegible]
10/8/96	By Pr. FDR Int			515	5204	[illegible]
1/8/96	By Pr. Int			2062	7266	[illegible]

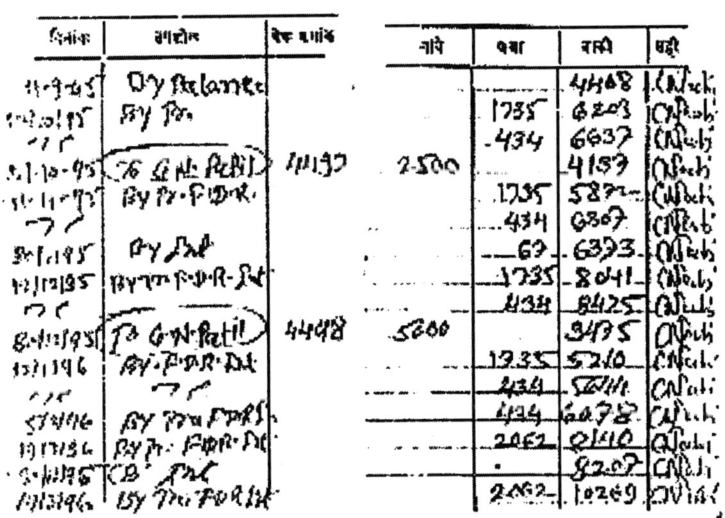

दिनांक	तपशील	चेक क्रमांक	नावे	जमा	बाकी	सही
11-9-95	By Balance				4468	[illegible]
12-10-95	By Pr.			1735	6203	[illegible]
" "				434	6637	[illegible]
31-10-95	To G.N. Patil	41132	2500		4137	[illegible]
11-11-95	By Pr. FDR			1735	5872	[illegible]
" "				434	6307	[illegible]
30-11-95	By Int			67	6373	[illegible]
11-12-95	By Pr. FDR Int			1735	8041	[illegible]
" "				434	8425	[illegible]
8-12-95	To G.N. Patil	4498	5000		3435	[illegible]
12-1-96	By FDR Int			1735	5210	[illegible]
" "	" "			434	5644	[illegible]
5-2-96	By Pr. FDR			434	6078	[illegible]
12-2-96	By Pr. FDR Int			2062	8140	[illegible]
30-2-96	CB Int			.	8207	[illegible]
11-3-96	By Pr. FDR Int			2062	10269	[illegible]

9

The Final Questions

Finally the results were declared on Saturday, the 21st of July, 2007. The elections had gone as expected. There was always going to be only one winner from the beginning and therefore when the ballots were opened and the verdict brought forward to the public, no one was surprised. Pratibha Patil had won by a huge margin, thereby ending Bhairon Singh Shekhawat's aspirations to become the President of the country.

For the first time in a long, long time, Pratibha Patil came forward to speak to the media. She raised her fingers towards the sky, forming a 'V' with her index and middle fingers, declaring a victory for her. She stated that this was just not her victory, but a victory for the people of the country, a victory for truth in general.

The debate on the usage of the word 'truth' will no doubt go on for a long, long time. As has been proved always, the unification of the word truth with temporal passages and personal authority has been challenged and thereby, the omnipotence that has come to be assumed with the word had been shattered. Leaving aside truth, even the construction of the word morality has come into the purview of interrogation, as many actions committed by a plethora of individuals have thereby gone on to give the word many connotations.

There will be an unending probe by various political parties, individuals, social researchers and by now, even criminal agencies, into the never ending question as to whether the choice of Pratibha Patil as the President of the country was the right one or not. In this view several factors have to be marked out and only then can the 'truth' be found out in absolute terms.

There have been various allegations, maligning the character of Pratibha Patil. There have been charges of her shielding her brother on murder charges; a scam regarding the bank of which she was the founder chairperson, a sugar mill which faced sealing due to the non-payment of loans; her remarks regarding the *purdah*, thereby hurting some communal sentiments and many others.

The point of view that has to be taken into consideration in this regard is that these allegations have been on record since long, but their media appraisal and communication have only occurred recently – that to when her name was established by the UPA as their Presidential candidate. The impetus behind these acts seemed to be deliberate. The timing of these so called 'breaking news' snippets on all leading news channels seemed to be concocted at first glance. However, with secure proof of all these allegations also floating in, it seemed that the matter was just not fictional, but also had, say even an iota of truth in them. In such situations, there are two options left to the overseer.

Why now? This question seems to bothering everyone. Pratibha Patil has a political history which goes back to several years. She began her political life way back in 1962. She was popular enough in 1988, when she assumed the offices of the Chief of the Maharashtra Pradesh Congress Committee. But information about the person itself, about her existence kept eluding the eyes of the common man. Suddenly Sonia Gandhi propped up her name for the presidential elections. With the ongoing emphasis of the UPA on Shivraj Patil, Pratibha Patil also must have sounded synonymous. The general euphoria of the media, backing her candidature as a "historic step" seemed to be lost in obscurity.

One thing that has to be locked in an individual's mind is the name of her predecessor. Pratibha Patil was assuming the offices of President APJ Abdul Kalam – porhaps the most humanistic, endearing and loved president ever known in recent times; an inspiration to the youth and an icon. It would be grossly disturbing for anyone to step into shoes so large.

A person is only responsible for his or her own actions, whether in sanity or insanity. In the same breadth, even if her brother is responsible for the murder of Vishram Patil, there is no way that the blame can be brought on Pratibha Patil. The allegations that were directed towards her go on to state that she was responsible in only as much as to guarding her brother from the police.

There have been various investigating agencies, which have looked into the matter – from the local police, to the CID, to the CBI. Pratibha Patil was just a common MLA, to an MP to a Governor. Her positions were never all that great that she could extend herself beyond the long arms of the law. It is only now that she can apply for Presidential Immunity. Earlier, her attempts to break the law or even to bend it at least could have easily been ascertained and therefore she could have been apprehended. Thus, following the doctrine of innocent until proven guilty has to be applied to her case and till a verdict is reached, Pratibha Patil need not apologize, abdicate or hold her head low.

As regards the incident of the sugar mill, Union Minister Sharad Pawar informed us that there were at least thirty four such mills who were callod upon as defaulters and were subsequently banned.

These mills had defaulted on the sole basis of droughts and the lack of modern farming facilities. The same reasons were put forward by each and every of these thirty four mills and therefore would be extremely unjustified to target and accuse only one of them, just because the founding chairperson of the same happens to the be the UPA's Presidential candidate, Pratibha Patil.

As the flow goes, there will be many discrepancies, there will be many stories, there will be many versions and each will fight with the other to prove the other wrong. The Presidential elections act just like a metaphor of the same. Every party names someone, everyone start throwing mud at the other, everyone wants himself to win and then in the process everything becomes dark and gory. Finally there is only one winner and that is the 'truth' – the 'truth' that concerns itself to only those issues that pertain to these matters, that is constrained to a particular time, the truth that *is* omnipotent.

Patil has emerged un-nerved from all this sledging attacks from all directions. She has held on to her baton with dignity and honour. She has stood solid like a rock before all these allegations that were aimed just not at her but also her entire family.

Yet people will still argue that Pratibha Patil was just not the right person to become the President of India. Some call it the UPA's high-handedness as they had the numbers, some call it that Pratibha Patil was only being propped up by the UPA so that they could call the shots. The role of the President of the Republic of India had been therefore reduced to a mere political puppet. Some even speculated that the only reason why the Congress got such a politically wasted character was so that they could get the Presidential sanction in the next Lok Sabha elections, in the event that they do not secure the majority to form the government at the centre.

However, the point that needs to be empathized here is that the mistake that we are generally assigning to Pratibha Patil is applicable towards the structure of the Indian constitution. It is not the fault of any political party, who might want to prop up and candidate partial to its own needs and concerns. This era belongs to the world of coalition politics. In such a situation, there always exists a chance of not claiming numbers and then not being able to get enough allies, whose numbers when added to the political party's own numbers would boost their mark over the majority mark.

In such a case, it is very essential that every political party has someone in a higher position in the Indian democracy, so that they have some back up if necessary if things do not develop as planned.

So where does Pratibha Patil's mistake lie in the whole process? Why is she being crucified? She was offered a post by the ruling UPA government and that too it was the role of the President of the country and she merely accepted. Then in which case there should be no cause for anyone to point fingers at Patil, as in no way can the blame me shifted towards her.

What is remarkable is that this sixtieth year of the Indian Independence, India shall have its her first woman president, who shall perhaps try her level best to carry take forward the baton of the country. The road is marked forward and Pratibha Patil has miles to go before she stops. The hopes of an entire nation are pinned on her journey – from Edlabad to Rashtrapati Bhavan.

10

The Rashtrapati Bhavan and the Presidents

The Antiquity

The present day Rashtrapati Bhavan, the sprawling palace straddles the crown of Raisina Hill is the focal point of New Delhi. Until 1950, this was the erstwhile residence of the British Viceroy. The verdict to build the residence in New Delhi for the Viceroy was taken after it was resolute in the Delhi Durbar of 1911, by nihilistic King George V and New Delhi was chosen to replace Calcutta as the seat of the British Indian government. It was constructed basically to avow the permanence of British rule in India The edict was startled many, for that meant erecting a whole new city in the ravine of the central ridge.

As the plan for New Delhi took shape, the project was completed in 1929 and officially inaugurated in 1931. The British architect Edwin Landseer Lutyens, a leading 20th century British architect who is known for ingeniously adapting time-honored architectural styles to the requirements of his era, was assigned for the city-planning process, and was given the daunting and challenging task to erect the magnificent building.

This regal building, containing 340 rooms, was built on an area of some 330 acres (1.3 km^2) and incorporates a private garden also designed which is popularly known as the 'Mughal Gardens'. Later on, Lutyens had to reduce the building size from 13 to 8.5 million cubic feet, because of the budget restrictions of Lord Hardinge, the then Viceroy of India (1910 to 1916). While he had demanded that costs be cut, he nevertheless wanted the house to retain a certain amount of ceremonial majesty. Also the Viceroy declared that the palace was to be classical, but with an Indian motif.

It is befittingly the crowning glory of the British Empire and architecture in India. Today, it is perhaps India's best known commemoration after the Taj Mahal and the Qutub Minar. Bigger than the Palace of Versailles, it cost a whopping £12, 53,000 (Rs.1.4 million). It is unquestionably a masterpiece of symmetry, discipline, silhouette, color and harmony. Of course, it has come in for much criticism too but that has mostly been limited to the regal intent behind it rather than its architecture. The columns at the front entrance have bells carved into their capitals. After India became independent the Viceroy's house was re-named Government House and when the country became a republic in 1952 it was re-christened as Rashtrapati Bhavan.

The Edifice

The central figure the Rashtrapati Bhavan is that of the architect, Edwin Landseer Lutyens who, dismissive of Indian tradition, was eventually browbeaten into 'Indianizing' its design. It was built in a neo-classical, Victorian-gothic style, with 340 large rooms, 37 salons, 74 lobbies and loggias, 18 staircases and 37 fountains. To some extent, the style can be said to be Classical or Greek. This assertion is endorsed by the presence of large pillars and domes. There are very few rounded arches and not pointed as in case of pure Victorian Architecture. The most dazzling feature of the House – one can spot it far from a kilometer away – is the huge neo-Buddhist copper dome that rises over a vast colonnaded frontage. The dome combines classical and Indian styles. Lutyens said the design evolved from that of the Pantheon in Rome.

Beneath the dome is the circular Durbar Hall 22.8 m in diameter. There is a 4th century statue of Gautam Buddha behind the Presidents chair. The Durbar Hall served as a museum for several years till the building which now houses the National Museum was completed. The State Drawing Room is barrel-vaulted and plainly treated with domestic fireplaces. The State Ballroom is enriched with Old English mirror glass. No steels were used in the entire architecture. The colored stones were brought from the different places of India. The hall has a 2-ton chandelier which hangs from a 33-metre height. There are also other rooms such as many loggias (galleries with open air on one side) which face out into the courtyards, a large dining hall with an extremely long table, sitting rooms, billiards rooms, and a large ball room. The State Library is based on the form of St. Stephen Walbrook, a small church in London. The State Dining Room is lined with teak paneling enriched with the star of India. The concept of colonial order and hierarchy permeates the entire house. The colored marbles used in the hall come from all parts of India. Marble staircases flanking the Durbar Hall provide access to the private apartments above. There are 54 bedrooms together with additional accommodation for guests.

Inside the main kitchen was fabulous. The foods are served on exquisite china and silver. Inside gossip is that the Bhavan kitchens cooked much more than required, so some of the food was smuggled out to a dhaba in Gole Market where a blackboard proudly said "Rashtrapati Bhavan ka khana". The Russians were big eaters. At old times in the kitchen they used to have all meals then send for omelets and sandwiches in their rooms. They ate every scrap. And the Polish delegation, when it visited, smoked before after and during their meals.

Trivia about the imposing estate is a plenty. An insider let it slip that the tubs in the bathroom were large enough for the biggest man to soak. And the toilet seats were 3 by 5 feet of teak bench, which revealed the bowl only when lifted.

Besides the extensive use of elephant motifs in the huge cast iron gate, pillars and basement, water features are also through the palace, such as near the Viceroy's stairs; which has eight marble lions spilling water into six basins. The lions symbolize Britain, as the lion was often used for this purpose. There is also an open area in one room to the sky, which lets in much of the natural light.

Another enduring feature of the architecture of the Rashtrapati Bhavan is the use of Indian temple bells in its pillars. It is well known that the temple bells constitute part and parcel of our combined culture, particularly that of Hindu, Buddhist and Jain traditions. Blending these bells with the Hellenic style architecture is a fine example of the fusion of Indian and European designs. The columns at the front entrance have bells carved into their capitals. Lutyens reasoned that 'the ringing of bells sound the end of an empire and stone bells never sound'. Despite this, the empire came to an end a brief 16 years later.

The President of India does not occupy the suites now called Ashoka room, occupied by the Viceroys. Instead he occupies one of the guest bedrooms. The First Indian Governor General, C. Rajagopalachari, considered the master bedroom too glittery for his humble tastes. All Presidents thereafter have followed the tradition. The Rashtrapati Bhavan is the biggest resident of any President in the world.

The Grass and Roses

To the west the palace overlooks an enormous Mughal garden designed by Lutyens, designed after the terraced gardens which the Mughals built in Kashmir. Here the principles of hierarchy, order, symmetry and unity are extended from the house into the landscape. A series of ornamental fountains, walls, gazebos and screens combine with scores of trees, flowers and shrubs to create a paradise so delightful that Indians called the garden 'God's own Heaven'. The garden grows a variety of trees and flowers like roses, marigold, bougainvillea, sweet william, viscaria etc among many others. To the east lies the Great Court, a vast court with a massive Jaipur Column of red sandstone topped with a bronze lotus and six pointed glass star of India, in the centre. The Irwins supervised the planting of the garden which grew in tropical profusion softening the formal pattern of lawns and waterways. The Rose Garden displays numerous types of roses and is open to public in February every year with an obvious tight security check

Along with the above, the Presidential estate is well equipped with nine tennis courts, a polo ground, and 14-hole golf course.

Then and now

Here's what Mark-Bence Jones remarked about life at the Viceroy's House in his book, Palaces of the Raj. It's striking the then-and-now comparison he makes on a later visit to the palace, long after the British had gone.

"Then there were the banquets held during sessions of the Chamber of Princes, when every other guest at the long table was the ruler of a State. The gold plate glittered in its crimson-lined niche, the lustres glinted, the scarlet and gold khidmatgars moved deftly against the teak-paneled walls, and from an adjoining room came the music of the Viceroy's band."

"In India that replaced the Raj, Lutyens' Palace has managed to keep some of its glory ...As the home of a modern democratic President, it is certainly on the large side, but the Indians have been wise enough to maintain a Presidential establishment worthy of the setting. Scarlet-clad guards still sit on their chargers beneath the stone sentry boxes; khidmatgars in white, red and gold line the corridors."

On every Saturday a ceremonial changing of the guard takes place. Changing of the guard is a military tradition whose origins are lost in antiquity and from time immemorial, guards and sentries at forts, palaces and defense establishments change daily to enable a fresh body of soldiers to take charge. Soldiers of the band and marching contingents are assigned from different regiments for duty over a short period of time in rotation but the mounted troops are permanently stationed at the Rashtrapati Bhavan. While the guard at Rashtrapati Bhavan changes daily, every Saturday a traditional military ritual of guard changing is conducted with precision and solemnity at a fixed time and place. The PBG performs dismounted ceremonial duties at the Rashtrapati Bhavan, adding that touch and grandeur without which State functions would lose much of their impressiveness. The spacious plaza at the foot of Rashtrapati Bhawan is known as Vijay Chowk. Rashtrapati Bhawan is really part of the new urban complex built after King George V announced in 1911 that the British would shift their capital from Calcutta to Delhi. The Old Guard marches off to "Sare Jahan Se Achha". Compliments are paid by the New Guard, which assumes charge and the balance of the New Guard marches off along with band playing "Amar Jawan". This short spectacle of color and martial music, horse and man, rifle and lance, bugle and brass, traditions and trumpets leave a distinct feeling of nostalgia grandeur and pride for being a part of it all.

The Denizen

The President of India, rather the head of state and first citizen of India and the Supreme Commander of the Indian armed forces, elected by the elected members of the Parliament of India(Lok Sabha and Rajya Sabha)as well as of the state legislatures(Vidhan Sabhas)are allocated to reside in the Rashtrapati Bhavan.

The first Governor General of India, Lord Mountbatten, was the last British Viceroy of India before independence. He soon handed power over to C. Rajagopalachari, who became the first (and only) ethnically Indian governor general. In the meantime, the Constituent Assembly led by Dr. Rajendra Prasad. The drafting was finished on November 26, 1949, and the Constitution was formally adopted on January 26, 1950, a date of symbolic importance as it was on January 26, 1930, that the Congress Party had first issued the call for complete independence from Britain. When the constitution took effect, the Governor General and King was replaced by an elected president, with Rajendra Prasad serving as the first President of India.

From then on twelve successive elections have come through by Electoral College, consisting of the elected members of both houses of the Parliament and the elected members of the State Legislative Assemblies (Vidhan Sabha). And as the present 13th president, India has got Pratibha Patil, the first female president of India.

11

The Overview

"For most part of history, Anonymous was a woman."
-Virginia Wolf (1882-1941)

It's harder to become a woman than a man, someone said it once.

Adam was a man off course but God created Eve to complete him. He thought He created a symmetry-a world so lucid and prosaic that it was perfection.

But He lent His supreme creation an unparallel asset by the virtue which the creation would eventually shun His very motive. Entropy is the word. It was when Adam took the bite, chaos was His premonition.

Sand tickled, sun and moon changed positions, dust and rust, water and wine, Jack and Jill, fire and ice, gold and silver, Kings and lovers, Man and Woman, they all rode the indolence. And as we step into the virgin 21st century, the demarcation between the evenly matched creatures widens an epoch in some vicinity of His Great Blue Ball.

India – a land of thousand varied blood is a victim of such fallacy, where chauvinism is not a cult but an almost intrinsic tendency. The Indian lady is fragile and bland. She is supposed to be the "home-maker". She should be an apostle of motherhood (which in itself is almost a daunting task to Man). It is only a handful of brave heart women with the aid of some rational men that some of the alleged weaker sex raise the bar and rise above eschewing the shallow sordid effigy of the gender.

Rani Laxmi Bai, Indira Gandhi, Sorojini Naidu, Vijaylaxmi Pandit are a few among the stalwarts who made an undeniable impression in Indian history. Came June the 25th, 2007, New Delhi, a woman clad in a mellow saree (Smt. Pratibha Devisingh Patil) was sworn in as the first woman President of India. Would she live upto the legacy of a legend, the question to be only answered in time.

Pratibha Patil- The President?

"Who is Pratibha Patil?"

It was almost as if a shock from nowhere, a bolt from the heavens, when a layman is comforted with the fact that some "Mrs. Pratibha Patil" is the front runner of the coveted seat of President of India. And after the bale revelation came the inevitable question of credentials. Its fair to say that perfection is a rarity, no mortal is perfect and with fame comes a natural urge for the populace to dig the past.

[1] She is supposed to have once supported Indira Gandhi during and after the emergency, and once made a statement as health minister:

"We are also thinking of forcible sterilization for people with anuvaunshik ajar (hereditary diseases)."

As Maharashtra Health Minister six months into the Emergency, Patil told Muslim League MLAs who opposed compulsory family planning: Keep religion at home, family planning is true religion

Of course, it was over 30 years ago, at the height of the Emergency when fundamental rights were suspended across the country. Of course, she was fiercely loyal to her then Congress leader Indira Gandhi. But at a time when the UPA-Left alliance is presenting Pratibha Patil as India's first woman President to-be and showcasing her "social welfare and empowerment" credentials, this needs underlining.

Six months into the Emergency, on December 10, 1975, according to Maharashtra Assembly records, accessed by The Sunday Express, Patil, as Health Minister in the S. B. Chavan Cabinet, endorsed a proposal seeking to make "family planning" compulsory for all citizens.

Not only did she assure the House that the government would take "appropriate steps" to ensure that all citizens adopted family planning measures but added: "We are also thinking of forcible sterilization for people with *anuvaunshik ajar* (hereditary diseases)."

The proposal to make family planning compulsory was introduced by then Congress MLA D. N. Metkar. Some MLAs, particularly those from the Muslim League, strongly opposed any such move. Patil stood up to rebut the opposition: "My opinion is that whatever religion one practises, he should keep it at home and adopt family planning as the true religion," Patil said, according to proceedings recorded in Volume 46 of the Maharashtra Legislative Assembly debates.

"It is not proper to say that family planning is against any religion...some Muslim countries, too, practise family planning. It is not proper to oppose family planning in the name of religion," she said.

Claiming that family planning was the true religion which rose above all religions, she said. "We are creating awareness about family planning and Maharashtra is doing a better job than other states but we need to speed up...It was only through family planning that people could look after their children in a better manner and thereby ensure the existence of their own religion." Incidentally, in the run-up to the election campaign in February 2004, Congress president Sonia Gandhi, in an interview to Shekhar Gupta, Editor-in-Chief, The Indian Express, on NDTV's Walk the Talk, said that Indira Gandhi did think that the Emergency was a "mistake." "Well, there is no way we can say that the Emergency was right," she added, "...But there was a great deal of propaganda against Mrs.

Gandhi, deliberately done. And I think there were even some reports post-Emergency that went into details of the family planning programme which turned out to say that the problems were magnified. Yes, there were problems, but not in the scale that the Opposition had built up."

[2] She was believed to run a bank that had its license revoked in 2003 for "alleged financial irregularities." Among the reasons: Waivers of loans to her relatives.

Pratibha bank waived loans for kin before RBI shut it down.

Bank in Jalgaon: RBI cancelled license, cited financial irregularities, faulty loan policy; brother admits taking loan from bank meant for women.

The cooperative bank in Jalgaon set up by the UPA-Left's Presidential nominee Pratibha Patil, ostensibly to empower women, had its license revoked in 2003 by the Reserve Bank of India (RBI) for alleged financial irregularities.

Confidential inspection reports of the RBI as well as correspondence exchanged between the Finance Ministry and the RBI, available with The Indian Express, reveal that the Pratibha Mahila Sahakari Bank, which Patil founded in 1973, faced several allegations.

Among the lengthy grounds listed by the RBI for cancellation of the license was the faulty loan policy of the bank and loan interest waivers given, among others, to Pratibha Patil's relatives.

According to complaints sent by the Bank's union leaders, as many as a dozen of Patil's relatives were granted loans (totalling Rs 2.2 crore including penalties, most declared Non Performing Account holders) by the cooperative bank.

The list of relatives who received loans from the cooperative bank meant for improving the plight of the people of Jalgaon, and women in particular, include her brothers and nephews.

Another list of relatives got a waiver of penal interest and charging interest (totalling Rs 41 lakh) and were allowed to close their accounts prior to the bank's liquidation.

When The Indian Express sought his comments, Dilipsingh Patil, Pratibha's elder brother, who pointed out that it was not possible for his son to take loans from a bank run for and controlled by women, admitted that he too had taken loans from the bank.

"The bank had 8,000 to 10,000 members, all of them women, who also took loans. In such a case, how is it possible to say that the bank went into losses just because Pratibhatai's family members took loans?" he said.

Pratibha Patil was the founding chairperson of the Bank and later, along with a number of her relatives, was one of its Directors. She is currently one of the 34 respondents in an ongoing case in the Aurangabad bench of the Bombay High Court on the subject of mismanagement of the bank and misappropriation of funds by its Managing Directors. Evidently, it was after receiving a sheaf of complaints from the Cooperative Bank Employees Union and its small depositors that the Finance Ministry (in a letter dated April 26, 2002) asked the RBI to inquire into allegations of irregularities.

In its 28-page inspection report, the RBI noted that the bank had been declared "weak" since 1995 and after the 2002 inspection was being classified as "sick." The report noted:

- The real or exchangeable value of the bank's paid-up share capital and reserves stands at minus Rs 197.67 lakh. Thus, the bank is not having adequate assets to meet its liabilities. The bank does not comply with the RBI's requirement of minimum share capital.
- The ratio of the net erosion to net owned funds of the bank is as high as 312.4% and the erosion in the value of the bank's assets has not only wiped out its owned funds but has also affected the deposits to the extent of Rs 197.67 lakh, forming 26% of total deposits.

- The gross NPAs of the bank, that is loans that have gone bad, amount to 65.8% of the total loans and advances.
- The Board has not made any concerted effort to improve the bank's financial position and bring it out of the weak status.

Thus, in an order dated February 25, 2003, the RBI's Executive Director P. B. Mathur signed a license revocation order in which he stated: "Having regard to all the facts, the Reserve Bank of India is satisfied that allowing the bank to carry on banking business any further would be detrimental to the interest of the present and future depositors and hence the license granted to the Pratibha Mahila Sahakari Bank Ltd is hereby cancelled."

"The RBI is of the view that no purpose will be served by granting any further time to the bank to revive its position. Public interest would be adversely affected if the bank is allowed to carry on its business further," the RBI report said.

The RBI's inspection report was highly critical of the bank's loan granting policy without proper securities ("the bank had no loan policy" the credit appraisal system of the bank contained many deficiencies") and also took up the issue of waiver of interest on NPA loans to Pratibha Patil's relatives in a separate section titled "complaints and frauds". Vijay Kumar Kakade, former president of Pratibha Sahakari Bank Karmachari Sangh, told The Indian Express that with the cancellation of its license and commencement of liquidation process, the bank was closed and people lost their jobs. "Pratibha Patil was responsible for this. There is no personal enmity with Patil Madam, but we want to tell our countrymen that such a person is going to occupy the highest office."

The RBI listed the waiver of loans to two of Patil's nieces and her sister-in-law and noted, "It was observed that the above accounts were closed by the bank by waiving the penal interest and charging interest @ 13%. The bank had not taken approval of the members in the Annual General Meeting."

These waivers were given to:

- Anjali Dilipsingh Patil (Pratibha Patil's niece), who got a waiver of Rs. 29.86 lakh
- Kavita Arvind Patil (sister-in-law of Pratibha Patil), who got a waiver of Rs. 8.59 lakh; and
- Rajkaur Dilipsingh Patil (another sister-in-law of Pratibha Patil), who got a waiver of Rs. 2.47 lakh.

The writ petition filed by the banks' depositors in the High Court makes serious and more direct allegations against the founder chairperson.

It states, "Pratibha Patil is the founder member of the bank who is a politically influential personality. She has made all her relatives as Directors of the bank and the bank is being run as good as a family business. Because of the influence of respondent no 8 (Pratibha Patil) the bank has given various loans to the relatives and to a sugar factory of which she is a Director. Her relatives have not paid back the loans. Most of the loans were given without security. Most of the loans are closed."

[3] A sugar factory started by her allegedly defaulted on a loan of Rs 17.70 crore.

MUMBAI: Patil, UPA candidate for the presidential poll, for default of a loan to the tune of Rs 17.70 crore has created a flutter in political circles.

A notice from the Mumbai Central District Co-operative Bank— popularly known as Mumbai Bank— to a Jalgaon sugar factory floated by Pratibha. Significantly, the cash-rich Mumbai Bank has strong NCP leanings, which will doubtless lead to speculation as to whether Sharad Pawar, the NCP boss known for his political guile, may have had a role to play in the matter.

Bank president Siddharth Kamble stoutly denied that the notice was aimed at embarrassing Patil, pointing out that it was sent early this month before Congress president Sonia Gandhi announced Patil's candidature. Bank officials claimed that NABARD had directed all cooperative banks in the state to recover bad debts, earlier declared as non-performing assets.

One of them alleged that following the announcement of Patil's candidature, the bank was being pressured by the Congress-led state government to stop action against her— a charge that Kamble said had no truth.

The bank has written to the state government, which counter-guaranteed the loan to Patil's Shri Sant Muktabai sugar factory, to step in and help recover its dues. Kamble said Patil could not be personally pinned down as a defaulter. "Pratibhatai is not directly involved with default of the loan. We haven't taken a personal bond from her as the state government has stood counter-guarantee for the Shri Sant Muktabai sugar unit," he said.

As many as 22 sugar co-operatives owe the bank a total of Rs 266 cr. Of them 15, all owned and managed by prominent Maharashtra politicians, have received notices. The rest are expected to get notices shortly. The list includes factories controlled by politicians like Union minister Suryakanta Patil, Mukul Wasnik and Shalini Patil. A sugar co-operative unit signifies considerable clout in the state's politics.

"The bank has sent notices in keeping with its rules. We have to adhere to the norms of fiscal discipline laid down by the Reserve Bank of India and NABARD," said Kamble. Known as Mumbai's apex co-operative bank, Mumbai Bank has a turnover of Rs 3,000 crore and reserve funds of about Rs 580 crore. It has 15,600 shareholders.

In 1994-'95, the bank gave loans to 22 sugar co-operatives to help them set up units in the state. The Shri Sant Muktabai factory which Patil set up in Jalgaon was one of the beneficiaries. Patil got Rs 5 crore in her capacity as chairperson of the factory.

Accumulated interest and non-repayment has ballooned to an outstanding of Rs 17.70 crore.

Among other defaulters, Shalini Patil's Jarandeshwar sugar cooperative's debt is to the tune of Rs 12 crore, while Suryakanta Patil, who is involved with the Hutatma Jayantrao

Patil sugar cooperative, owes Rs 6 crore, sources said. Kamble said, "Action against defaulters is necessary to safeguard depositors' interests. The Maharashtra State Cooperative Bank, which is the apex body for the cooperative banks in the state, has also been asked to help us in recovering debts."

The board of directors decided in September last year to penalise defaulting sugar co-operative units. A formal resolution was adopted at the board meeting on June 1 and Patil's candidacy was announced a fortnight later, he said.

[4] Her knowledge of history is severely flawed, almost simplistically so. (She did provide us with the ironic image of a woman with her head covered asking for the abolition of the purdah.)

Even before the photo-ops are over, the ruling coalition's presidential candidate Pratibha Patil has run into a messy controversy over the origin of the *purdah* in India by claiming that it was introduced to protect women from Mughal invaders and, in the process, annoying many among her backers and giving her opponents gratuitous ammo for attack.

Speaking at a function in Udaipur on Sunday, the virtual president-designate traced the origin of the *purdah* to the Mughal invasion. She claimed that the purdah was introduced in India to "save women from Mughal invaders". This, even as she urged for abolition of the practice.

Patil's interpretation of history, say historians, is not accurate. But more than that, her statement at a function to commemorate the 467th birth anniversary of Maharana Pratap, was politically incorrect. And this has triggered a massive controversy with Muslim outfits, the Left intelligentsia and women's groups protesting against it.

"She has twisted history, she must apologise and withdraw her observations," Jamiat Ulema-i-Hind general secretary Maulana Mehmood Madani said. Madani added that the Jamiat executive, which was in session, would adopt a resolution condemning Patil's remarks.

Opponents like Samajwadi Party latched on to the opportunity to please their Muslim constituency and heap embarrassment on the Congress. The SP leadership, which successfully lobbied the Third Front partners to sponsor the candidature of A P J Abdul Kalam on Monday, called Patil's remarks unfortunate.

After her controversial remarks on the women's veil, the then UPA-Left Presidential nominee Pratibha Patil had claimed to have spoken to a late spiritual leader from whom she got a 'divine premonition' of greater responsibility coming her way.

"I had a pleasant experience," Patil recounted to a TV channel about her recent meeting in Mount Abu with head of Brahma Kumaris World Spritual University, Hridaymohini, popularly known as 'Dadiji'.

The university is affiliated as a non-governmental organisation (NGO) with the UNICEF. Patil was in Mt. Abu when Congress president Sonia Gandhi called her to seek her consent for her being nominated as a UPA-Left candidate. *Dadiji ke shareer mein baba aye* (her reference was to Dada Lekhraj who founded Brahma Kumari sect. Lekhraj died in 1969).

Patil claimed that the late Baba spoke to her indicating that she should be prepared to shoulder greater responsibility. "He also made me very lucky", she said.

[5] There are allegations against her that she protected her brother from a murder charge.

The Presidential election took an ugly turn on Friday with the National Democratic Alliance (NDA) parading a woman who claimed that her husband had been murdered by United Progressive Alliance's (UPA) nominee Pratibha Patil's brother.

Addressing a press conference at Shiromani Akali Dal leader Sukhdev Singh Dhindsa's residence, the woman, Rajni Patil, alleged that Pratibha Patil's brother murdered his political rival and her husband V. G. Patil in September 2005.

Mumbai-based Rajni alleged that Pratibha Patil had been protecting the culprit.

"Pratibha Patil has been protecting her brother," Rajni told reporters.

She also stated that she had given a memorandum to President Dr A P J Abdul Kalam giving details about the allegation.

TEXT OF THE MEMORANDUM SUBMITTED BY
PROF. RAJANI PATIL
TO DR. A.P.J. ABDUL KALAM, PRESIDENT OF INDIA

Prof. Rajani Patil
45, Vidya Nagar
Pimprala, Jalgaon (Maharashtra)
Tel: (0257) 2252001
Camp: New Delhi
June 21, 2007

Subject: A brokenhearted widow's plea for justice in a case of politically motivated murder of my husband, Shri V.G. Patil, President of the District Congress Committee of Jalgaon (Maharashtra), followed by mysterious death of the murderer, and protection to the conspirators by Smt. Pratibha Patil, Governor of Rajasthan Most Respected Rashtrapatiji, I am an ordinary woman, a widow whose husband was snatched away from me by a brutal political murder which took place in Jalgaon exactly 21 months ago. I have come to you in search of justice, which has eluded me so far even though I have moved from pillar to post hoping, in vain, that those in power in Mumbai and New Delhi would listen to the cry of a helpless woman and discharge their lawful duty.

My pain is deeper because both my family and the family of my late husband, Prof. V.G. Patil, who was president of the Jalgaon District Congress Committee at the time of his murder, have had a long and dedicated association with the Congress party. I am the proud daughter of a Freedom Fighter. I did not expect that the voice of some unscrupulous, corrupt and criminal-minded people in the Congress party in Jalgaon, who gave 'supari' for my husband's murder, would carry greater weight in the corridors of power both in Mumbai and in New Delhi. I have, therefore, come to you because you are the Custodian of the Constitution and Protector of the Rule of Law.

I would like to painfully inform you that soon after the last rites were performed on my husband's dead body, I publicly declared that I would not immerse the ashes (Asthi) until justice is done and his killers, and the conspirators behind the killers, are punished. The pot containing the ashes is still strung to the tree in the foreyard of my modest house in Jalgaon. I am a professor of Marathi in a college in Jalgaon affiliated to the North Maharashtra University. My late husband was a professor of English at the same college. Our son is studying engineering in Jalgaon and daughter, who is married, lives in Mumbai.

Background of the murder My husband was murdered near our house in Jalgaon on the morning of 21 September 2005. All the people of Jalgaon district were outraged and immediately came to the conclusion that this crime had been committed by the rivals of my husband within the Congress party. The police soon arrested two assailants – Raju Mali and Raju Sonawane – who were both supporters of Dr. G.N. Patil, brother of Smt. Pratibha Patil, in his bid to win the DCC presidential election. In fact, the initial confessions of these two persons before the police also confirmed that they had acted at the behest of some powerful persons in the local Congress party. The police even told the press that they had nabbed the assassins and would "soon catch the conspirators".

Shockingly, within a few days, under instructions from Mumbai, the local police authorities changed their tune and told the media that Prof. V.G. Patil had been killed by Raju Mali as he had not repaid a loan of Rs. 4.5 lakh that he had borrowed from the latter. The local police chief spoke so categorically that it looked as if all inquiry had already been completed and the 'truth' had been unearthed. I strongly refuted this baseless claim in a letter to the police chief of Jalgaon on September 27 and specifically named two political rivals of my husband within the Congress party – Dr. Ulhas Patil, a former Congress MP from Jalgaon, and Dr. G.N. Patil, the immediate past president of Jalgaon DCC, who had been nominated by the MPCC for a tenure of one year.

My husband had defeated Dr. G.N. Patil by 13 votes in the election to the office of the DCC president, held through secret ballot in April 2005. Dr. G.N. Patil and Dr. Ulhas Patil were unwilling to accept defeat. Their anger and hostility increased when my husband initiated an inner-party investigation into the financial irregularities committed by Dr. G.N. Patil in respect of the 'Tsunami Relief Fund' (Rs. 1.89 lakh collected from the public by Congress workers) and lakhs of rupees collected for the 'Pratibha Patil Felicitation Fund', after Smt. Patil was appointed the Governor of Rajasthan. My husband had also initiated a probe into the financial irregularities of Dr. Ulhas Patil, who runs many fraudulent NGOs.

I wrote in my letter to the police chief: "This murder has been committed out of political enmity. I therefore urge you to investigate the case from this angle and arrest the persons concerned. I strongly believe that, under somebody's pressure, there is an attempt to misdirect the police investigation by fabricating cock-and-bull theories."

Several local dailies of Jalgaon region also contested the police claim and affirmed that the murder was the outcome of political rivalry in the DCC, which was widely known to the people of the district. The newspapers supported my contention that Dr. Ulhas Patil and Dr. G.N. Patil were the conspirators in the crime.

I would like to mention here that Smt. Pratibha Patil and her brother Dr. G.N. Patil have worked closely together for over 30 years both in the local Congress politics and also in many institutions that she had set up in and around Jalgaon. These included the Pratibha Mahila Sahakari Bank, Sant Muktabai Cooperative Sugar Factory and the Shram Sadhana Trust, which runs several private educational institutions.

The police took no congnisance of my plea. No FIR was lodged against Dr. Ulhas Patil and Dr. G.N. Patil. Under instructions from Mumbai, the case was then transferred to the state CID, which systematically started to misdirect the investigation and suppress the case.

Explosive investigation by AAJ TAK

In October 2006, the reputed Hindi news channel AAJ TAK telecast an indepth 20-minute investigative report on this murder case in its weekly programme 'Hatyaara Kaun?'. The report revealed the following facts:

(1) Both Dr. G.N. Patil and Dr. Ulhas Patil had made numerous calls from their mobiles, before as well as on the day of murder, to two other persons who were subsequently chargesheeted in the case – Damodar Lokhande and Leeladhar Narkhede. The two were close associates of the two assailants. AAJ TAK showed the exact time and duration of the calls from the records of the mobile company.

(2) In September 2006, the two assailants – Raju Mali and Raju Sonawane— went on an indefinite fast inside the Jalgaon district jail. In an oncamera interview given to the AAJ TAK correspondent, Manish Avasthi, Raju Mali stated that the reason for the fast was the refusal of the police to arrest or even interrogate "the persons named by Smt. Rajani Patil". He said, "We have been simply made sacrificial lambs in the case, whereas the real culprits are untouched."

(3) The AAJ TAK report picked holes in the police theory that the murder was committed on account of a petty financial dispute.

(4) It described in great detail why Dr. Ulhas Patil and Dr. G.N. Patil were hostile towards my late husband. I showed that the Congress party had suffered severe erosion in its support base in Jalgaon district under the leadership of Dr. G.N. Patil and Dr. Ulhas Patil and also that my

husband had been bravely attempting to revive the party in the district.

(5) *It raised the pertinent question: "When a Congress leader has been murdered, and when the Congress is in power both in Delhi and in Mumbai, why are the police deliberately derailing the investigation?"*

(6) *It showed that Dr. G.N. Patil is the brother of Smt. Pratibha Patil, the Governor of Rajasthan.*

Bombay High Court transfers the case to the CBI; soon he thereafter, the principal assailant "dies" in police custody in mysterious circumstances

I made numerous trips to Mumbai to meet every important person in the Congress party and Congress-led government in Maharashtra, including the Chief Minister Shri Vilasrao Deshmukh and MPCC President, Smt. Prabha Rao. I expressed to them my fear that the case was being hushed up by the state CID. Unfortunately, I received no support, not even basic human sympathy. Even though a DCC president had been murdered, neither the Chief Minister nor the MPCC president came to my house to condole my husband's death and console my family. Smt. Pratibha Patil also visited Jalgaon twice as Governor of Rajasthan, but she too did not visit me or even speak to me on the phone to offer her condolences.

My fear about derailment of the investigation was vindicated when two persons chargesheeted in the case – Damodar Lokhande and Leeladhar Narkhede – were released from jail after four months and the FIRs against them were withdrawn by the police.

I then approached the Aurangabad Bench of the Bombay High Court with a plea to get the case transferred to the CBI. Paragraph 3 of my petition stated:

"On 26.9.2005 (five days after the murder of my husband), General Secretary of the Jalgaon Jillha Congress Committee Shri Shridhar Vishnu Chaudhari (a close supporter of my late husband) gave a complaint to the police inspector, Jalgaon,

stating that there is a danger to his life from the ex-MP Dr. Ulhas Patil. Accordingly, a complaint was given along with the anonymous letters received by the said Mr. Chaudhari. These three anonymous letters were addressed to Shridhar Chaudhari as well as the deceased Vishram G. Patil, in which it has been categorically mentioned that Dr. Ulhas Patil had made a conspiracy to kill Shri V.G. Patil and Shri Chaudhari."

Paragraph 4 of my petition mentioned:

"The deceased also made various complaints to the high command of the Congress party against Dr. G.N. Patil (erstwhile President of the Congress Committee, Jalagaon), who happens to be the brother of the Governor of Rajasthan."

The CBI in its submission before the High Court stated that this was not a fit case for being transferred to the country's highest investigating agency since "the present case does not have inter-state or international ramifications."

The High Court, however, ordered transfer of the case to the CBI on 23 February 2007, stating in its ruling: "We have scrutinized the entire record with the help of counsel for both sides. We have considered the chequered history of the present case, the developments which have taken place after filing of chargesheet, issues involved, and the reference to alleged conspiracy by the influential political leaders of the region. Having regard to the importance of issues involved and the alleged complicity of the influential political leaders referred to in paragraph Nos. 3 and 4 of the petition, in our considered opinion, this is a fit case where the investigation should be conducted by the CBI."

After the High Court's ruling, a CBI team visited Jalgaon on 4 April 2007. It interrogated me on April 7. On the same day, Raju Mali, the principal assassin, who was in police custody, died in mysterious circumstances. I suspect that that his death was also a case of murder. Most people in Jalgaon have the same suspicion. I would like to mention here that, at my urging, the District Court on 12 May 2006 ordered the narco test and lie detection test to be conducted on the two assassins nabbed by the police. No such test was conducted on Raju Sonawane until December 2006 and its contents are not made public. As far as Raju Mali is concerned, no test was conducted at all until his death in a suspicious manner. All this shows how the case is sought to be buried with the connivance of authorities at various levels.

I wrote two letters to Smt. Sonia Gandhi, and also met her in person

Out of utter desperation, I wrote a letter to Smt. Sonia Gandhi on 5 March 2007. I had earlier written a letter to the Congress president on 26 September 2005, within five days of the crime, in which I had stated, "The brain behind the crime is pressuring the investigation process."

In my second letter dated 5 March 2007, I stated: "One day my husband received a warning to stop all inquiries or else the consequences would be very bad. Being a daredevil, he did not bother and approximately one week before the murder, he was warned again that a 'Supari' (contract to kill) to murder my husband had been given by Dr. Ulhas Patil and Dr. G.N. Patil, the brother of Smt. Pratibha Patil, Governor of Rajasthan. On the morning of 21.9.2005, my husband was brutally murdered."

In the same letter, I also informed Smt. Sonia Gandhi that since the investigation was going nowhere, "I appealed to the Bombay High Court (Aurangabad Bench) that the conspirators have been constantly influencing and interfering with the state CID enquiry, and finally the High Court issued orders to transfer the enquiry to the CBI on 23 February 2007."

I concluded my letter to Smt. Sonia Gandhi by stating: "I fear that my whole family is likely to get liquidated by these brutal murderers if they continue to get politically patronized by the party." I feel anguished that they are indeed getting politically patronized by the party.

In addition to writing the two letters, I also personally met Smt. Sonia Gandhi at her residence in New Delhi in the first week of 2007 and apprised her of the whole case. I have also written letters to Shri Ahmed Patel, Smt. Margaret Alva, Shri Sushilkumar Shinde and other senior leaders of the Congress party. Therefore, Smt. Sonia Gandhi and her senior colleagues are fully aware of the facts of the case.

Most Respected Rashtrapatiji,

I have come to you out of anguish and misery which I cannot adequately describe in words. I have five demands to place before you for your kind consideration and suitable action:

1. *Dr. G.N. Patil and Dr. Ulhas Patil, the main conspirators behind my husband's brutal murder, should be immediately arrested and interrogated, since there is ample evidence to show their involvement in the crime.*
2. *Along with many loyal Congress workers in Jalgaon, I am convinced — and it is my charge — that right from Day One of this case, Smt. Pratibha Patil has been trying to influence the investigation in order to protect her brother Dr. G.N. Patil. Towards this end, she has been misusing her authority and her high-level contacts in the governments in Mumbai and New Delhi. The Aurangabad Bench of the Bombay High Court has also taken cognizance of "the alleged complicity of the influential political leaders". Therefore, the CBI should be specifically directed to follow this angle of the investigation in respect of the persons mentioned. It should investigate who could possibly have influenced the earlier inquiry and given protection to the conspirators.*
3. *The mysterious death of Raju Mali, the principal assassin, in police custody should be thoroughly probed.*
4. *I fear that the entire case might soon be hushed up. I expect, and the people of India expect, that the Constitutional authorities of our country discharge their duty conscientiously and prevent the coverup from happening.*
5. *Lastly, I fear for my own safety and, even more so, for the safety of my children. Kindly instruct the Governments in*

New Delhi and Mumbai to ensure that no harm comes to us from those who have taken away my beloved husband from me.

Thanking you,
Yours faithfully,
Sd/-
(Smt. Rajani Patil)

Encl:

(1) *My letter to the police authorities*
(2) *My letters to Smt. Sonia Gandhi and photograph of my meeting with her*
(3) *Order of the Aurangabad Bench of the Bombay High Court*
(4) *Copy of the CD containing recording of the 'AAJ TAK' report on the murder*

Copy for information and suitable action to:

(1) *Honourable Prime Minister of India*
(2) *Honourable Chief Justice of India*
(3) *Honourable Smt. Sonia Gandhi*
(4) *Honourable former Prime Ministers*
(5) *Leaders of the Opposition (Lok Sabha and Rajya Sabha)*
(6) *Leaders of political parties*
(7) *Honourable Members of Parliament, MLAs, MLCs.*

Congress, meanwhile, rubbished the allegations and said that Rajni Patil had been "planted" by the NDA.

Pratibha Patil, the former Rajasthan Governor, has been nominated as the official candidate of UPA-Left-Bahujan Samaj Party (BSP) combine.

Since Pratibha Patil's nomination as a presidential candidate, Bharatiya Janata Party (BJP) had highlighted her past activities and made comments as part of its political campaign against her.

BJP leader Arun Shourie authored two articles published as a booklet titled 'Does This Tainted Person Deserve to Become President of India?' Another BJP leader, Arun Jaitley, announced the launch of a website called Know Pratibha Patil, which contains various media reports and documents concerning the questionable financial dealings of both Patil and her family. The campaign generated a lot of media attention on Pratibha.

Is Patil a controversial and unworthy presidential candidate?

Pratibha Patil is perceived by millions of Indians, especially the middle class as being highly corrupt and fraudulent.

While the BJP has been trying to build a strong public opinion against her, it clarified that it was not challenging her nomination on legal grounds.

But meanwhile an advocate Manohar Lal Sharma has filed a Public Interest Litigation before a bench of Supreme Court of India comprising Justice Tarun Chatterjee and Justice P. K. Balasubramanian challenging her nomination for the presidential election 2007. The advocate has referred to the various allegations against Patil and her family members and sought the cancellation of her nomination papers on the ground of her being an undischarged insolvent. The petitioner raised legal and constitutional questions on whether a person declared to be an 'undischarged insolvent', for not clearing a debt to the public exchequer and others, was eligible to be elected president.

The apex court however observed that it could not act on mere allegations, and rejected the petition at the admission stage itself. The court said there was no merit in the petition as there was no document to substantiate the allegations and raised doubts about the petitioners real intention adding it was more of a "private interest litigation".

The advocate then approached the Election Commission of India seeking her disqualification. The Election Commission, through an order, replied that the candidature of the insolvent(candidate) has to be be decided by the competent insolvency court under the provisions of the Provincial Insolvency Act, 1920, and not by the Commission. The Commission is not the appropriate forum.

Following this, the advocate again approached the court and filed a Special Leave Petition (SLP) before a bench comprising Chief Justice K.G. Balakrishnan and Justice R.V. Raveendran. He contended that the Election Commission had not applied its mind to the matter, and sought quashing of the commission's order.

In another case a Delhi-based NGO has also filed a petition before the Delhi High Court alleging that Patil being Managing Trustee of Mumbai-based Shram Sadhana Bombay Trust, which is under the control of state government, was holding the office of profit making her ineligible to contest the President's election. The High Court has deferred the hearing until after election.

The leaders of Indian National Congress and Indian left say that these facts highlighted are a clever mixture of truth, half-truths and exaggerations. They have also said that these issues have never been raised in the past while she was a deputy chairwoman of the Rajya Sabha, or during her tenure as a governor. They accused the BJP of launching a "malicious, unsubstantiated and deliberate" slanderous campaign just to damage her reputation. Prime Minister Manmohan Singh defended Pratibha Patil and dismissed the charges as "mud-slinging". On Monday 2 July 2007 breaking her long silence Pratibha Patil described the allegations leveled against her as "false, malicious and baseless".

Here's a copy of Mrs Pratibha Patil's CV, when she enrolled her candidature.

CV OF SMT. PRATIBHA DEVISINGH PATIL, GOVERNOR OF RAJASTHAN

Father's Name Shri Narayanrao

Date of Birth 19th December, 1934

Place of Birth Distt. Jalgaon (Maharashtra)

Marital Status Married on 7th July 1965

Spouse's Name Dr. Devisingh Ramsingh Shekhawat

Children-One son and one daughter

Educational Qualification M.A., L.L.B.

Educated at M.J.College, Jalgaon (Maharashtra) & Govt. Law College, Mumbai

Profession Social worker, practiced as Advocate at Jalgaon

Permanent Address -57, New Congress Nagar, Opp. Govt. Milk

Scheme, Amravati (Maharashtra)

1701, Vainganga, Worli Sagar Co-operative Housing Society, Pochkhanwala Road,Worli,Mumbai-400025. Tel.24950888

Position held – 1962-85 Member, Maharashtra Legislative Assembly

1967-72 Deputy Minister, Public Health, Prohibition, Tourism, Housing and Parliamentary Affairs, Govt. of Maharashtra

1972-74 Cabinet Minister, Social Welfare, Govt. Of Maharashtra

1974-75 Cabinet Minister, Public Health and Social Welfare, Maharashtra

1975-76 Cabinet Minister, Prohibition, Rehabilitation and Cultural Affairs, Govt. of Maharashtra

1977-78 Cabinet Minister, Education, Govt. Of Maharashtra

July 1979 to Feb.1980 Leader of Opposition, CLP(I), Govt. Of Maharashtra.

1982-85 Cabinet Minister, Urban Development and Housing, Govt. of Maharashtra

1983-85 Cabinet Minister, Civil Supplies and Social Welfare, Govt. of Maharashtra

June, 1985-90 Elected to Rajya Sabha

18 Nov. 1986 to 5 Nov. 1988

Deputy Chairperson, Rajya Sabha

1986-88 Chairperson, Committee on Privileges, Rajya Sabha Member, Business Advisory Committee, Rajya Sabha

1991 Elected to 10th Lok Sabha, Chairperson, House Committee, Lok Sabha

8 November, 2004 Governor of Rajasthan

Other positions held President – P.C.C. Maharashtra 1988-1990,

Director of National Federation of Urban

Cooperative Banks & Credit Societies, Member of Governing Council, National Cooperative Union of India.

Social & Cultural Activities

- Welfare of Women, established a Hostel for working women in Mumbai and Delhi
- Engineering College at Jalgaon for the benefit of rural youth
- Managing Trustee, Shram Sadhana Trust
- Chief Promoter and Chairperson of a Sugar Factory in Jalgaon, District Maharashtra
- Established Mahila Vikas Mahamandal, a Government owned cooperation
- Industrial Training School for Blind in Jalgaon and Managing a school for poor children of Vimukta Jamatis & Nomadic Tribes
- Establishment of Mahila Cooperative Bank at Jalgaon, Maharastra while a Minister in the Govt. of Maharashtra, established Govt. owned Corporation Mahila Vikas Mahamandal.

Special Interests Development of Rural Economy, Welfare of Women

Sports and clubs Champion in table tennis during college days and won shields in Inter-college tournaments

Countries visited and widely travelled –

Attended International Council of Social Welfare Conference, Nairobi and Puerto Rico

- Leader, Delegation to Austria on Status of Women
- Conference Member, A.I.C.C. (I)
- Delegation to Bulgaria, 1985
- Attended Common Wealth Presiding Officers Conference, London 1988
- Attended World Women Conference at Beijing –China.

India's Murkiest Presidential Campaign Ever

After a month of one of the dirtiest and most controversial Presidential campaign, UPA candidate, Pratibha Patil, was preparing for a five year reign at the Rashtrapati Bhavan. She has travelled across the country canvassing support and UPA Chairperson, Sonia Gandhi, left no stone unturned to make sure Patil was *numero uno* — even hosting an election dinner on her behalf. Numerically, Patil had a huge headstart and on the eve of the Presidential poll, the UPA camp sounded confident. The country will never forget NDA for maligning Pratibha Patil," said Union Railway Minister, Lalu Prasad. But for Bhairon Singh Shekhawat, whose electoral track record is enviable, that had turned out to be a career-ending defeat. Shekhawat's RSS past let him down in the end. Several NDA allies including Trinamool Congress and JD(S) were unwilling to vote for him and the Shiv Sena didn't want to upset the chances of a Marathi nominee. It was an election where the result was a foregone conclusion.

Open defiance, abstentions — both individually and as a group, cross-voting, last minute U-turns and sulking parties brought a dramatic element in the voting trends in one of the most bitterly fought Presidential elections. The elections also saw four jailed MPs — Shibu Soren, Mohd Shahabuddin, Babubhai Katara and Pappu Yadav — not missing out on exercising their franchise but not before Shahabuddin threw tantrums and refused to be taken to Patna from Siwan jail by a jail van. Shahabuddin was later provided a car. Various reasons were cited for abstentions by the smaller parties and individuals ranging from Centre not spelling out its stand on a separate Telengana state to UPA-Left nominee Pratibha Patil's controversial remarks on the 'pardah' system. One MLA cited inconsistency in his party's leadership. Despite being in government, ruling parties in one state abstained. Mizo National Front and its coalition partner Mizoram Congress Party stayed away nursing a grouse against the Centre and NDA-backed independent candidate and Vice President Bhairon Singh Shekawat. After the abstention announcement made by their leader Jayalalitha last Saturday on behalf of the eight-party UNPA, AIADMK legislators' volte face raised the political heat. Seeking to justify the voting by AIADMK MPs and MLAs, the party chief said this turn of events has occurred only because of the "extreme confusion" generated by Election Commission's "unwarranted and unnecessary" note on July 17 note and not due to any other reason.

About 88.5 per cent of Parliamentarians and 91 per cent of the State legislators cast their votes in the 13th Presidential election. Eight States registered 100 per cent polling. Elsewhere, the turn-out was generally high. The eleventh hour decision of the All-India Anna Dravida Munnetra Kazhagam to participate in the polling provided a surprise element in a contest that otherwise went along expected lines. According to Parliamentary Affairs Minister Priyaranjan Dasmunsi, some members of the Telugu Desam Party and the Samajwadi Party also voted. All three parties — constituents of the United National Progressive Alliance — had earlier decided to abstain. While the AIADMK went back on the decision early on Thursday, the TDP and SP legislators acted on their own without any party directive. Confident of a "massive" victory for the United Progressive Alliance-Left candidate Pratibha Patil, the Minister, who is also her election agent, said the AIADMK decision had not upset the ruling combine's calculations. However, he conceded that there were unexpected abstentions from the UPA-Left camp: A.F. Golam Osmani,

Congress MP from Assam and Asaduddin Owaisi of the All-India Majlis-e-Ittehadul Muslimmen (AIMIM), who represents Hyderabad in the Lok Sabha. Five MLAs of the AIMIM in Andhra Pradesh are also reported to have abstained.

Electoral officials open a sealed ballot box before counting votes in the Indian presidential elections in New Delhi, 21 July 2007. India's first female president, Pratibha Patil, savoured her election win as supporters hailed the victory as a significant step forward for women in the South Asian nation.

Lawmakers elected India's first female president, officials announced 21st June, in a vote seen as a step forward for hundreds of millions of Indian women and girls who face bitter discrimination in everyday life. The position is largely ceremonial. But observers said the selection of Pratibha Patil, 72, in a vote by the national Parliament and state politicians, will widen the role of women in the country's often male-dominated political scene. "This is a victory of the principles of which the Indian people uphold," said Patil, wearing her signature oversize glasses and a red and gold celebratory sari. As she waved a V-for-victory sign on television, marigolds and coloured powders used in Hindu celebrations (holi) were tossed at her feet. Patil had been expected to win because of support from the governing Congress party and her deep political ties and friendship with Sonia Gandhi, leader of the party and the powerful Gandhi dynasty. Patil is a steadfast loyalist of the Gandhi family, which has long maintained a strong hold over Indian politics. Patil took in nearly two-thirds of the votes, defeating Vice President Bhairon Singh Shekhawat, the candidate of the opposition Bharatiya Janata Party.

For evidence that there may, after all, be some virtue in dynastic succession, monarchists need look no further than the muddle India is making of choosing its president. The Indian job is largely titular but, like the British monarchy, carries clout when an election produces a hung parliament and the president chooses whom to invite to form a government. For that reason, governments try to ensure that a new incumbent is on their side, or at least is not an opponent.

Mr. Abdul Kalam with his eccentric floppy hair style, had managed to demystify the job and appeal to India's young people. From a poor Muslim background, he was a neat choice in 2002 for the government, then led by the Hindu-nationalist Bharatiya Janata Party (BJP). But the current Congress-led coalition did not want him for another term. The president is indirectly elected for a five-year term by members of parliament and of state assemblies. It is customary for the ruling party to make its choice, and then to try to achieve a consensus. But Sonia Gandhi, who heads the coalition, as usual failed to give a lead and half a dozen or so names were in the air. One was that of Pranab Mukherjee, the foreign minister, but he was too useful as a politically astute deputy to Manmohan Singh, the prime minister.

Pratibha Patil- the President

"I......Pratibha Patil......................... do swear in the name of God that I will

bear true faith and allegiance to the Constitution of India as by law established and that I will, as in duty bound honestly and faithfully serve in the Indian Air Force of the Union of India and go wherever ordered by Air, Land or Sea and that I will observe and obey all commands of the President of the Union of India and the commands of any officers set over me even to the peril of my life."

After Sixty years of Independence, a Woman leader is going to lead us for the next five years of our country, which, some say is a beginning of a Revolution.

Shrimati Pratibha Patil is a Taurean. Her stars suggest that she is very intelligent and she is supposed to take very daring decisions. Well, her stubborn demeanour could be grasped from the fact that after marriage she refused to keep the surname of her husband and kept her own, 'Patil' which could have zoomed as a very unorthodox- unsocial practise in that time.

Portrayed as a symbol of an empowered woman herself, the country's first woman President Pratibha Patil had wasted no time in giving women's empowerment and their role in nation-building the necessary impetus. Even before she made her debut at public ceremonies as President, she had already interacted with non-government organisations and women's groups in the precincts of the Rashtrapati Bhavan to draw up a blueprint for the subject.

Setting the pace for prioritising the issue of women's empowerment, Ms. Patil at her swearing-in ceremony on July 25, had equated women's empowerment with that of the nation. And though she was still to move into her residential quarters in the erstwhile Viceregal Lodge, she has held deliberations on the issues of empowerment of women and their role in nation-building. At a meeting with a confederation of non-government agencies that work in the rural areas, she made out a case for concerted efforts to ensure the welfare of women.

Promising her support and participation, Ms. Patil is said to have told the delegations that she will try to be present at the zonal meetings and remain available for advice.

Ms. Patil, who also met the chairperson of the National Commission for Women and the chairpersons of the State Commissions for Women, said efforts should be made to empower women who constitute 50 per cent of the country's population.

She met a delegation of the Muslim Vikas United Front from Maharashtra and about 300 members of Rajput Kshatriya Sangh. A delegation of the All-India Jamait Ul-Quresh apprised the President of the lot of the minority community and the hardships being faced by the underprivileged. They demanded early implementation of the Sachar Committee recommendations.

Ms. Patil, who has made a reference to the need for waging a relentless campaign against poverty, ignorance and disease, she had presided over a special function to mark 60 years of Indian Independence at the National Academy of Agriculture Sciences. This was her first public appearance as President.

For Smt. Pratibha Patil, it seems like a daunting task to follow her predesessor Mr. Abdul Kalam. Mr. Kalam possessed an air of enigmatic charm which was unstained and innocuous. He was a model of empathy and wisdom. The image of Mr. Kalam even before Mr. Kalam- the President we love and adore was of honour and decree. It almost seemed just that he lived up to his image of a rational man.

Mrs. Pratibha Patil's shaky credentials or may we say her rather stained reflection doesn't seem to suggest a cake walk for Mrs. Patil on the throne. She would have to stand up to the dauby challenge that lay in front of her. But there are instances where some mortals seem to raise their bar once they are confronted with affliction. It would be fair to give her time to prove herself and to prove that the trust of this great nation upon her is just and upright.

12
Here After

"I will be a political President"

First there was her nomination. Then there were allegation regarding her political history and also regarding her character. And then finally there were the elections. Pratibha Patil won by a landslide majority, a truth that was known by all, right from the very onset and a fact that even her adversaries were trying to elude from. Pratibha Patil finally assumed the office of the President of the Republic of India.

It was only in the interviews that she gave after her becoming the President of the country that people got to gauge the true character and personality of their Head of State. President Patil now displays her iron interior as she finally speaks to the media, giving them her side of the story. Plus another aspect that has to be borne in mind when any point is raised about Pratibha Patil, is that all the information that the nation was fed about her, came from myriad sources and therefore people should question the integrity and sincerity of these allegations and defences. One thing that was clearly evident in this particular Presidential election was that even the office of the Head of State was not kept outside the purview of politics. Just as the NDA kept targeting the character of Pratibha Patil, the UPA candidate, their opposition in the ruling alliance also started targeting Bhairon Singh Shekhawat, the NDA candidate. Therefore to arrive at conclusions depending on the reports claimed by various political entities is an extremely dangerous thing to do in the Indian environment.

Pratibha Patil, in one of her first interviews inside Rashtrapati Bhavan, one that she gave in perfect English, stated categorically that she was not going to relinquish her presidency to a mere rubber stamp. She immediately asks the media to check her previous track records and ascertain for themselves whether she has displayed in the past, any incident of political pressure or force. And that fact remains true. When she was the Governor of Rajasthan, she sent back the Anti-conversion Religious Bill two successive times refusing two implement it with the record of her signature. As a natter of fact, Pratibha Patil as the Governor of the state did not let the Congressmen of Rajasthan to pressurize her into submitting her report to the Centre is the wake of the Gujjar – Meena face off early in 2007. She rather asked the Chief Minister Vasundhara Raje to immediately look into the matter and take necessary actions to solve the problem.

Pratibha Patil even takes cognizance of the fact that out of the two presidents who preceded her, KR Narayanan was considered to be a political president and APJ Abdul Kalam was said to be a apolitical president. In that context, Patil clarifies that she would prefer to be remembered as a political president. She strongly believes that there is a lot of scope and potential within the activities of the government, where a president can play an active role – be it the budget or other such critical issues, after which it is left to the government's discretion as to whether they want to accept or reject the president's advice. Patil also goes on to mention that individually she is extremely interested in looking into issues pertaining to rural development, the rural economy, women's development, welfare of backward castes, scheduled castes, scheduled tribes, health and the like.

Her immediate predecessor, Abdul Kalam was reported within the media circles to be a "people's president." On being asked whether it was ever going to be difficult for her to follow the giant footsteps that he had already marked, she always provides a rather circumspect answer – she believes that accessibility should not be a problem as she comments that within the first two days, she had already entertained over a thousand people at Rashtrapati Bhavan, most of them people who had come all the way from Maharashtra just to get a glimpse of her or even to just click a photograph. People close to her report that she was extremely touched when people well below the poverty line also spent a portion of their measly income to make the long journey and come and meet her. As her sources report, the rush at Rashtrapati Bhavan was so huge that they had to open out the large Ashoke Hall, which is generally kept close to facilitate important events like the president's installation and also to host foreign ambassadors.

Pratibha Patil's first political encounter came after assuming the offices of the president, when a BJP delegation sought permission to meet her and discuss the political turmoil in Goa. Patil was kind enough to meet them immediately and entertained them, even though the group was half-an-hour late. It should be kept in mind herewith that if this were the era of her predecessor Kalam, the meeting would have been cancelled as he was extremely particular about punctuality. However, Patil offered them tea and also added her sympathy to the whole issue. She convinced them that the Governor of Goa must be well informed about the constitutional problem and consequently he would take the necessary steps to solve the fiasco. Even the BJP who had targeted this woman for a whole month during the run-up to the elections, acknowledged her political skills and decency to become the president of the country.

Pratibha Patil has a huge history in politics behind her. She spent sixteen years as a minister in Maharashtra and then again as a Governor. Just as there are controversies surrounding her, there are also many proofs regarding her unparalleled record as a politician which have been completely overlooked by a blatant oppositional campaign by the NDA. Pratibha Patil's role will become extremely sharp in the 2009 Lok Sabha elections, when the tide of events may see another alliance forming the government at the Centre. She is absolutely certain when she comments, *"The Constitution says it all – the roles of the various organs of state, the executive, judiciary and legislature are well-defined. I will just be guided by the Constitution. I don't really envisage any problems."*

13

Speeches made by President Patil on Various Occasions

Dr. A.P.J. Abdul Kalam

Avul Pakir Jainulabdeen Abdul Kalam was the twelfth President of India, serving from 2002 to 2007. A notable scientist and engineer, he is often referred to as the Missile Man of India for his work and is considered a progressive mentor, innovator and visionary in India. He is also popularly known as the People's President. His term as president ended on July 25, 2007.

During his presidential period he proved that the post can be platform for inspiration and progressive leadership. He endeared himself to the public like no one before him. Kalam entered the Rashtrapati Bhavan as a surprise consensus candidate, left it as a folk hero.

Personal Life

APJ Abdul Kalam was born in 1931 to Jainulabdeen and Ashiamma in a middle-class family in Rameshwaram, a town well-known for its Hindu shrines. His father, a devout Muslim, owned boats which he rented out to local fishermen and was a good friend of Hindu religious leaders and the school teachers at Rameshwaram. APJ Abdul Kalam mentions in his biography that to support his studies, he started his career as a newspaper vendor. This was also told in the book, A Boy and His Dream: Three Stories from the Childhood of Abdul Kalam by Vinita Krishna. The house Kalam was born in can still be found on the Mosque Street at Rameswaram, and his brother's curio shop abuts it. This has become a point-of-call for tourists who seek out the place. Kalam grew up in an intimate relationship with nature, and he says in Wings of Fire that he never could imagine that water could be so powerful a destroying force as that he witnessed when he was six. That was when the cyclonic storm swept away the Pamban Bridge and a trainload of passengers with it.

Kalam observes strict personal discipline, vegetarianism, teetotalism and celibacy. Kalam is a scholar of Thirukkural; in most of his speeches, he quotes at least one kural. Kalam has written several inspirational books, most notably his autobiography Wings of Fire, aimed at motivating Indian youth. Another of his books, Guiding Souls: Dialogues on the Purpose of Life reveals his spiritual side. He has written poems in Tamil as well. It has been reported that there is considerable demand in South Korea for translated versions of books authored by him.

On a lighter note, Kalam is unmarried, and a teetotaler and vegetarian. He also plays the Veena and has an appreciation for Tamil poetry. He often quotes the famous Tamil poets Bharatidasana and Subramania Bharatiyar ("who died in 1939 at the age of 35, killed by an elephant while giving it a coconut"). In one recent Parliamentary speech, I saw a quote from the great Bhatki/Sufi mystic Kabir: "Kaal Kare So Aaj Kar, Aaj Kare So Ab" ("What you want to do tomorrow do it today, and what you want to do today do it now").

Dr. Kalam, a bachelor is a connoisseur of classical Carnatic music. He plays veena in his leisure. He writes poetry in Tamil, his mother tongue. Seventeen of his poems were translated into English and published in 1994 as a book entitled

'My Journey'. He reads the Quran and the Bhagavad Gita with equal devotion. He is also the Author of the books 'India 2020 : A vision for the New Millennium'(1998 with YS Rajan), 'Wings of Fire : an Autobiography' and 'Ignited Minds – unleashing the power within India'. Totally dedicated to the nation, Dr. Abdul Kalam's vision is to transform India into a developed nation by the year 2020 through hard work and perseverance. He holds a first world dream for the third world nation.

Books authored

- India 2020: A Vision for the New Millennium by A.P.J. Abdul Kalam, Y.S. Rajan (Penguin Books India, 2003) ISBN 0-14-027833-8
- India-my-dream by A.P.J. Abdul Kalam (Excel Books, 2004) ISBN 81-7446-350-X
- Envisioning an Empowered Nation: Technology for Societal Transformation by A.P.J. Abdul Kalam (TATA McGraw-Hill Publishing Company Ltd., 2004) ISBN 0-07-053154-4
- Guiding Souls: Dialogues on the Purpose of Life by A.P.J. Abdul Kalam, Arun K Tiwari, (Ocean Books, 2005) ISBN 81-88322-73-3

Biographies and Autobiographies

- Wings of Fire: An Autobiography of APJ Abdul Kalam by A.P.J. Abdul Kalam, Arun Tiwari (Orient Longman, 1999) ISBN 81-7371-146-1
- Ignited Minds: Unleashing the Power Within India by A.P.J. Abdul Kalam (Penguin Books, 2003) ISBN 0-14-302982-7
- Scientist to President by Abdul A.P.J. Kalam (Gyan Publishing House, 2003) ISBN 81-212-0807-6
- Eternal Quest: Life and Times of Dr. Avul Pakir Jainulabdeen Abdul Kalam by S. Chandra (Pentagon Publishers, 2002) ISBN 81-86830-55-3

- President A.P.J. Abdul Kalam by R. K. Pruthi (Anmol Publications, 2002) ISBN 81-261-1344-8
- A. P. J. Abdul Kalam: The Visionary of India' by K. Bhushan, G. Katyal (A.P.H. Pub. Corp., 2002) ISBN 81-7648-380-X

Education and Awards

Abdul Kalam, a graduate from the St. Joseph's College, Tiruchirapalli, and Abdul Kalam later studied aeronautical engineering in the Madras Institute of Technology which was regarded as the crown jewel of technical education in Southern India in the fifties. After passing out as a graduate aeronautical engineer, Abdul Kalam joined the Directorate of Technical Development and Production of the Ministry of Defense.

He has been awarded Padma Bhushan in 1981, Padma Vibhushan in 1990 and Bharat Ratna in 1997.Dr. Kalam was conferred with the degree of Doctor of Science (D.Sc. Honoris-causa) by twenty eight universities. He is the recipient of several awards including the National Design Award. Dr. Biren Roy Space Award; Prof. Y Nayudamma Memorial Gold Medal (1996): GM Modi Award for Science (1996): R K Firodia Award for Excellence in S&T (1996): Veer Savarkar Award (1998): and Indira Gandhi Award for National integration (1997).

The Technocrat

From a humble beginning, Dr. Kalam had an unparalleled career as an Aerospace and Defence Scientist, leading the nation with a vision of "Developed India." Dr. Kalam as an eminent Aeronautical Engineer, contributed for the development of India's first Satellite launch vehicle SLV III, became the architect of Indian Guided Missile development programme, led to the successful Nuclear experiments and envisioned a road map for realising "Developed India" within 20 years.

He later joined the Indian Committee for Space Research (INCOSPAR) as a Rocket Engineer, which during the later half of 1962 had decided to set up the Equatorial Rocket Launching

Station at Thumba. He became a member of team led by Prof. Vikram Sarabai which aimed at organising an integrated national space programme for the manufacture of rockets and launch vehicles indigenously.

Dr. Abdul Kalam was chosen to lead a team for the design and development of Satellite Launch Vehicle, SLV III which was successfully launched on 18th July, 1980, and injecting Rohini satellite into low earth orbit. He later became Director of ISRO Launch Vehicles/Systems and contributed for the evolution of launch vehicle configurations.

Dr. Abdul Kalam was appointed Director of the Defence Research and Development Laboratory, Hyderabad in 1982. As Director, DRDL, he was the Chief of integrated Guided Missile Development Programme and led to successful completion of Prithvi and Agni missiles. He was appointed as the Scientific Advisor to the Defence Minister, Secretary to Department of Defence Research and Development and Director General of Defence Research and Development Organisation in 1992. Many new technology projects towards building self-reliance in defence and also spin-off to society emerged during this period. Later he became the Principal Scientific Advisior to the Government of India in the rank of Cabinet Minister and served in this capacity from November 1999 till November 2001. He was primarily responsible for evolving policies, strategies and missions for generation of innovations in technology development for multiple applications through Government departments, academic institutions and industries as partners. Dr. Kalam was also the Chairman, Ex-officio of the Scientific Advisory Committee to the Cabinet (SAC-C). Dr. Kalam believes that Technology can be used as a tool for national development. In December 2001 he moved over to Anna University as Professor of Technology and Societal Transformation.

Dr. Kalam took up academic pursuit as Professor, Technology and Societal Transformation at Anna University,

Chennai and involved in teaching and research tasks. Above all he is on his mission to ignite the young minds for national development by meeting high school students across the country.

He is a Fellow of many professional societies including Aeronautical Society of India: Astronautical Society; Indian National Academy of Engineering; Indian Academy of Sciences and Institution of Electronics and Telecommunication Engineers.

Political Views

Kalam's probable views on certain issues have been espoused by him in his book "India 2020" where he strongly advocates an action plan to develop India into a knowledge superpower and into a developed nation by the year 2020. Kalam is credited with the view that India ought to take a more assertive stance in international relations; he regards his work on India's nuclear weapons program as a way to assert India's place as a future superpower.

Kalam continues to take an active interest in other developments in the field of science and technology as well. He has proposed a research programme for developing bio-implants. He is a supporter of Open source software over proprietary solutions and believes that the use of open source software on a large scale will bring more people the benefits of information technology.

Kalam's belief in the power of science to resolve society's problems and his views of these problems as a result of inefficient distribution of resources is modernistic. He also sees science and technology as ideology-free areas and emphasizes the cultivation of scientific temper and entrepreneurial drive. In this, he finds a lot of support among India's new business leaders like the founders of Infosys and Wipro, (leading Indian IT corporations) who began their careers as technology professionals much in the same way Kalam did.

Presidential Election

After an unparalleled career as a defense scientist, the 71-year-old Bharat Ratna took over from President K R Narayanan on July 25 Eminent missile technologist A P J Abdul Kalam was on Thursday elected India's 11th President in a highly one-sided contest in which he trounced the Left-backed Colonel Lakshmi Sehgal bagging nearly 90 per cent vote value in a preferential system of election.

The 71-year-old Kalam, born in a boatman's family in Rameswaram in Tamil Nadu, got 4,152 votes with a vote value of 9,22,884, against Sehgal's 459 votes accounting for 1,07,366 votes value in a race in what was heavily loaded against her with the entire political spectrum supporting Kalam.

Immediately after the results were declared, Mahajan drove to Kalam's residence to hand over the declaration. Kalam told Mahajan he was delighted to get elected as President of India and immediately came out with a message that the country needs a 'second vision' to transform into a prosperous, poverty free, healthy and developed nation.

While Kalam secured 89.58 per cent of the value of votes, Sehgal got 10.42 per cent. Of the total value of votes secured by Kalam, the highest came from Uttar Pradesh with 386 members giving a total value of 80,288 votes followed by Maharashtra where 280 members voted for him giving a vote value of 46,200. While Tamil Nadu gave a vote share of 38192, Bihar contributed 37195 votes to Kalam's success graph. From Delhi, Kalam secured 65 votes, leaving two to Sehgal, while three votes were invalid.

Outgoing President K R Narayanan on the very day extended his greetings to A P J Abdul Kalam, who was sworn in as the 11th head of the Republic afterward. Wishing him success and fulfillment in this highest office, Narayanan said in his farewell address to the nation: "I applaud him as a distinguished scientist and technologist and as a scholar and a humanist."

Post Presidentiality

With the search for his successor over, the hunt for a suitable house for outgoing President A P J Abdul Kalam has begun.

According to government sources, Kalam has informally expressed his desire to urban development ministry for a duplex accommodation. Sources said that the President was keen on retaining the ground floor for public meetings while reserving the upper floor for his vast library.

The urban development ministry, according to sources, had earlier identified two sprawling type VIII bungalows — 31, Aurangzeb Road and 7, Tughlak Road — in Lutyens' Delhi and offered it to the President. But, Kalam's desire has got the ministry mandarins to hunt afresh. Keen to offer suitable house to the First Citizen, the ministry is caught in a dilemma as there are not many duplex type VIII bungalows on Rajaji Marg and Akbar Road and the few which are there are occupied.

However, the ministry is hoping to accommodate the eminent scientist with some skilful juggling. "If a type VIII bungalow is not available, the ministry may offer him two type VII bungalows by amending allotment manual," said a source.

With a month left of his five-year tenure to end, Kalam is likely to put the hustle and bustle of politics firmly behind him and concentrate on getting back to his academic career and scientific research with the Capital as his base. Kalam, whose tenure is till July 24, has on several occasions expressed his desire to get back to teaching.

According to sources close to him, Kalam is keen on combining his love for teaching with science. "He has said that he would like to teach in colleges or seats of higher learning in predominantly rural areas," a source said.

The President is likely to be a visiting faculty at Anna University (where he is professor emeritus) and the ambitious space training centre being planned by the Indian Space Research Organisation (Isro) at Thiruvananthapuram. The institute is planned along the lines of Mumbai's Bhabha Atomic Research Centre.

Sources said that Kalam might also unofficially advise ISRO on Chandrayan-I, the unmanned mission to the moon, that is slated for February 2008. The President, during his tenure at Raisina Hill, had evolved a plan to revive Nalanda University as a seat of higher learning and is likely to play an important advisory role there as well.

But much before that, Kalam will be embarking on his 161st and perhaps last domestic tour this week. He is expected to visit Hyderabad and Secunderabad on June 28-29 where he will attend functions at the Nizam Institute of Medical Sciences and address an international conference on 'high speed trans-atmospheric air and space transportation'. The conference is likely to be attended by speakers from Japan, Australia, South Africa, Russia and Israel.

The President has been on an unprecedented number of domestic tours and his advisers feel that this is likely to continue after the tenure. "The President is a very active person and is likely to be on lecture tours. He has expressed his keenness on interacting with the youth and has proved an inspiring speaker," a source said.

Meanwhile, officials in the President's office are in a tizzy over their own postings. Besides the 600-odd permanent staff, there are about 10-12 persons in the President's office who are appointed to aid and advise the leader. Their tenure is traditionally co-terminus with that of the President's.

Kalam leaved a legacy that no president before him has left. By combining modernity and idealism, he proved that the presidential post was also a platform for providing leadership and practical vision. He was also during those five years a personification of secularism. As former Karnataka chief minister Dharam Singh remarked, "President Kalam brought a whole new meaning of secularism. A man who could sing "Tyagaraja kritis" plays the veena and read the Bhagavad Gita and the Koran with equal favour; he symbolized the true Indian".'

Kalam believes that the President of India can play a much greater role in the affairs of the State. "If he thinks big, he can. The post does not restrict the person at all" he said. It certainly didn't in his case. As Gujarat chief minister Narendra Modi puts it, "he spoke from his heart and whenever he expressed his concern about a problem, he appeared genuine. A star has left Rashtrapati Bhavan." The final word came from the man who tried to get him re-elected, former Andhra Pradesh chief minister N. Chandrababu Naidu, "He represents a defining moment in Indian democracy".

Five years after the choosing of his successor, there were only two words that can sum up the nation's farewell message, "Thank you, Mr. President".

PRANCE OF PRATIBHA

Preamble

Pratibha Devisingh Patil, the 1st Maharashtrian lady swore on 25th of July 2007 as the 13th and current president of India. With her unique modus operandi dealing with diplomatic formality, precedence, and etiquette she made the political parties and disciple to have a premonition of her debut.

Patil, the only female state governor in India, a member of Indian National Council (INC) was nominated by the ruling alliance of political parties in India headed by Congress and the Indian left, defeated her rival, Vice-president Bhairon Singh Shekhawat by thumping margin of 3, 06,810 votes and succeeded Dr. A.P.J. Abdul Kalam.

Homely Pratibha

This septuagenarian was born in a Kunbi family to Shri Narayan Paglu Rao on 19th December, 1934 in Jalgaon, Maharashtra. She had her schooling in R.R. School at the same place and received her MA from Mooljee Jaitha College, Jalgaon (affiliated to North Maharashtra University). Later on, she went to Mumbai and completed LLB from the Government Law College and started practicing as a law year after wards till joining the political party.

Whether it was a judiciary conference call with her colleagues or concentrating to nitty-gritty of any officials she was as comfortable as she was in the tennis court during her college period. She accolade with several shields in the inter-college tournaments. Probably it was the time and work pressure made her abstinent from this practice. Usha Bhowmik, she likes to name her as one of the dearest acquaintances of her early life, to whom she used to share her laugh and sorrows. It also has been said that, Patil regards the former Union home minister S B Chavan as her mentor.

The food habit says this political skipper is pretty much calorie conscious. Pratibha is likely a vegetarian from her early age and loves utthapam and dal but avoids spinach and potatoes. Her restricted cuisine also indicates her devout. In her recent visit to Brahmakumari University at Mount Abu, she revealed, apparently, the spirit of Lekh Raj, the founder of the Brahmakumari sect, alias "Baba" entered the body of his current spiritual head, Hriday "Dadiji" Mohini informed Patil about the "greater responsibility" coming her way. However it's a matter of controversy.

M.J College, Jalgaon, designated Pratibha as the "College Queen" in 1962 and at the very same year she got a party ticket to the Assembly election from Edlabad constituency, near to Jalgaon, on the Indian National Congress and went on to win the election with a huge margin till 1985, when she got elected for the Rajya Sabha as a Congress candidate.

By this time, Patil tied her nuptial naught with educator Dr. Devisingh Ransingh Shekhawat on July 7, 1965. It's needless to say Pratibha got very supportive in-laws which helped her to ensue in her career. During that period of time, if her political work was important, so was her son Rajendra, and daughter Jyoti. Later on she became grandma of four grand daughters and four grand sons by them and in turn she made a successful household as well.

Benevolent Pratibha

Besides having been president of the Maharashtra congress, she established "Vidya Bharati Shikshan Prasarak Mandal" an educational institute in assistance with her husband. This epic endurance for the welfare of rural youth lately became one of the upcoming universities in India having a number of schools and colleges under its affiliation in Jalgaon and Mumbai. While she was a Minister in the Govt of Maharashtra, she established Govt owned Corporation Mahila Vikas Mahamandal and also Hostel, Shram Sadhana Trust, for working women in Mumbai, New Delhi and Pune.

She also founded a cooperative sugar factory known as "Sant Muktabai Sahakari Sakhar Karkhana" at Edlabad in Jalgaon, Sonia Gandhi inaugurated the factory on 23 January 1999 and Patil became the chairperson from 1988 to 1996. Primarily the object was to export the product for the foreign trade but later on in collusion with export agents, they diverted the sugar to the domestic market.

A cooperative bank named after Patil as "Pratibha Mahila Sahakari Bank" was also founded in 1973, with the object to guarantee the franchise of rural woman.

She was also involved in setting up an Industrial Training School for the blinds in Jalgaon and running a school for poor children of Vimukta Jatis and Nomadic tribes.

Politician Pratibha

Pratibha Patil began her political career in 1962 at the age of 27. Under the mentorship of senior Congress leader and ex-Chief Minister Yashwantrao Chavan, she became a deputy minister for education after re-election in 1967 (in the Vasantrao

Naik ministry). In her next terms (1972-78) she was a full cabinet minister for the state. In successive congress governments, she handled the portfolios of tourism, social welfare and housing under several chief ministers, Vasantdada Patil, Babasaheb Bhosle, S.B. Chavan and Sharad Pawar. She was continually re-elected to the assembly, either from Jalgaon or the nearby Edlabad constituencies, until 1985, when she was elected to the Rajya Sabha as a Congress candidate. She has never lost an election that she has contested.

Post-Emergency Indira loyalist

In 1977, the Congress party split up after Indira Gandhi's defeat following the Indian Emergency (1975–1977). Many senior leaders of state Congress(I), including Pratibha's mentor Chavan and his protege Sharad Pawar, as well as much of the rank and file joined the Congress (Urs) party floated by Devraj Urs. However, Pratibha preferred to remain with Indira Gandhi, though it verged on inviting political ridicule. In fact, few know that Pratibha managed Indira Gandhi's kitchen when Sanjay died. She protested the arrest of Indira Gandhi in December 1977 and spent 10 days in prison in 1978, when the Congress (Urs) came to power in Maharashtra, she became Leader of the Opposition in the state assembly.

In 1980, the Congress (I) swept back into power, and her name was considered a front-runner for the Chief Minister's post. However, the post went to Sanjay Gandhi's confidant A. R. Antulay, who was soon forced to resign on corruption charges. Subsequently, she became a minister again in the Vasantdada Patil ministry. Following differences between Patil and then Maharashtra Pradesh Congress Committee (MPCC) chief Prabha Rau, Rajiv Gandhi appointed her as MPCC chief (1988-90).

Occupancy at Centre

In 1985, she was elected to the Rajya Sabha, and served as its deputy chairwoman from November 1986 to November

1988. Her term expired in April 1990. The following year, in the elections when Rajiv Gandhi was assassinated she won election 10th Lok Sabha from at Amravati constituency, her husband's city, where he had once been mayor, thus first time entering in lower house of national parliament Lok Sabha.

She has also served as Director of National Federation of Urban Co-operative Banks and Credit Societies and the Member of Governing Council, National Co-operative, Union of India.

Governor of Rajasthan

In November 2004, eight years after she had completed her term in the 10th Lok Sabha, Pratibha Patil was recalled from political hibernation to become the first woman Governor of Rajasthan. She was the second politician from Maharashtra in this post, the first being Vasantdada Patil. With Pratibha Patil as Governor, Rajasthan had women in three significant positions of power in the state, including Chief Minister Vasundhara Raje and Assembly Speaker Sumitra Singh.

In April 2006, the Rajasthan Legislative Assembly passed the Rajasthan Freedom of Religion Bill 2006 (originally titled as "Rajasthan Dharma Swatantrya Bill, 2006"). The objective of the bill was to control "unlawful conversion from one religion to another by allurement or by fraudulent means or forcibly." However, some Christian organizations opposed the bill alleging that the bill was an outcome of the rightist policies of Sangh Parivar. Pratibha Patil returned the bill unsigned, stating certain clauses in the Bill infringed on "the fundamental rights such as freedom of speech and expression, freedom of conscience and freedom to profess, practice and propagate religion."

The Government of Rajasthan re-sent the bill to her in May 2006 noting that similar anti-conversion laws enacted by Congress governments in Madhya Pradesh and Orissa over 40 years ago were upheld by the Supreme Court of India and that the head of the Constituent Assembly, Dr B R Ambedkar, while drafting Article 25 of the Constitution had said that it would be best to leave it to the state legislatures to make laws to regulate conversions. After sitting on the bill for over a year she sent it to the President of India just a day before she resigned as governor of Rajasthan. A similar bill named Himachal Pradesh Freedom of Religion Act 2006 passed later was promptly signed by the state governor.

Pratibha Patil resigned as the Governor of Rajasthan on June 21, 2007, due to her presidential candidacy.

Presidency

On 14th June, United Progressive Alliance (UPA), the ruling alliance of political parties in India headed by Congress (I), and the Indian left nominated her as their candidate for the Presidential Election to be held on 19 July 2007. She emerged as a compromise candidate after the Left parties would not agree to the nomination of present Home Minister Shivraj Patil. At that point, Sonia Gandhi proposed Pratibha Patil's name. Her loyalty to Nehru-Gandhi family was widely perceived to be a major factor in her nomination as UPA-Left Presidential candidate.

As a result of the potential that she would become the first female President of India, UPA Chairwoman Sonia Gandhi described her nomination as a "historic occasion" in India's 60th year of independence. Before leaving Jaipur for New Delhi, she thanked Sonia Gandhi for choosing her and said that her first job as president would be to make National Rural Employment Guarantee Act (NREGA) started by UPA a success. In Delhi she asserted that she would not be a rubber stamp president. Accompanied by Prime Minister Dr. Manmohan Singh and Congress chief Sonia Gandhi she filed her nomination on 23 June which was found to be valid after scrutiny. She faced Bhairon Singh Shekhawat, an NDA supported candidate, in a straight contest, and visited state capitals to garner support. Her campaign got a major boost with decision of UNPA to abstain from voting.

The Leader of the Opposition L K Advani sought intervention of Election Commission of India to get Pratibha

Patil to declare her assets, but this was rejected by the Commission. Shiv Sena, an important ally of NDA, declared its support to Pratibha Patil on the grounds that she will be the first Maharashtrian to hold this prestigious post. This decision of Shiv Sena has created trouble in BJP-Sena alliance.

Ms. Patil defeated her lone opponent, Vice-President Bhairon Singh Shekhawat, by an impressive margin of 3, 06,810 in an electoral college with votes valued at 10.98 lakh, in what has been described as the most keenly and, hotly contested poll. As a candidate of the United Progressive Alliance and the Left parties, Ms. Patil secured 65.82 per cent of the total votes cast, while the NDA-supported Shekhawat polled 33.18 per cent.

Reflecting the UPA-Left's national spread, Ms. Patil made her presence felt in every State, whereas Mr. Shekhawat drew a blank in West Bengal, Kerala, Tripura and Mizoram. He secured healthy margins in Gujarat, Madhya Pradesh and Rajasthan. Prime Minister Manmohan Singh described Ms. Patil's victory as "a vote against divisive forces."

At the Parliament level, 16 "extra" votes came for Ms. Patil. Exceeding the Congress calculation that 426 MPs from the ruling arrangement and the Bahujan Samaj Party would vote for her, Ms. Patil got 442 votes from both Houses of Parliament.Counting for the States took much of the time because of the variation in the value of votes. While results from all States came in by 4.30 p.m., counting of votes polled by MPs was wrapped up within the next hour. At the end, Ms. Patil's tally stood at 6, 38,116 and Mr. Shekhawat's 3, 31,306. After counting of votes from the States was through, Ms. Patil established a lead of 1, 58,130, bagging votes valued at 3, 25,180.

At her first day in her debut she said "I am deeply committed to the cause of education and would like to see every person, man and woman, boy and girl, be touched by the light of modern education. Empowerment of women is particularly important to me as I believe this leads to the empowerment of the nation".

"It is a special moment for us women, and men of course, in our country because for the first time we have a woman being elected president of India," said Congress leader Sonia Gandhi, who hand-picked Patil and was one of the first to congratulate her.

Dancing and bursting of crackers marked the celebrations outside the AICC headquarters on Akbar Road. Immediately after the national anthem was played, Patil met the ministers and people.

The First Citizens of India Since Independence

Dr. Rajendra Prasad

Dr. Rajendra Prasad was born on December 3, 1884 and died on February 28, 1963.

Long before the Gandhian era had set in, he was born in an obscure village Zeradei, in the Siwan district of North Bihar near Patna. His life was to be an embodiment of the Gandhian principles. Prasad was an independence activist and, as a leader of the Congress Party, played a prominent role in the Indian Independence Movement. He served as President of the Constituent Assembly that drafted the constitution of the Republic from 1948 to 1950.

The Learner

Dr. Rajendra Prasad was born to a Persian and Sanskrit language scholar Mahadev Sahai and his devout wife Kamleshwari Devi. At the age of five, the young Rajendra Prasad was sent to a Maulavi for learning Persian. After that he had his primary schooling in Chhapra Zilla School. He was married at the age of 12 to Rajvanshi Devi and then went on to study at R.K. Ghosh's Academy in Patna to be with his elder brother Mahendra Prasad. Soon afterward, however, he rejoined the Chhapra Zilla School, and it was from there that he passed the entrance examination of Calcutta University, at the age of 18. He stood first in the first division of that examination. He joined the Presidency College in 1902. His intrepid determination towards the service of nation encouraged the students and some of them came under his tutelage. He passed in 1915 with a Gold medal in Masters in Law examination with honors and went on to complete his Doctorate in Law. After that he started his early career as a lawyer.

The Activist

During his college days, he joined the Dawn Society, run by Satish Chandra Mukherjee. There he had the opportunity to meet and exchange ideas with sister Nivedita, Surendra Nath Banerjee and many others. A new awareness was now dawning on him. The anti-partition agitation stirred him with its state and slogans. He gathered students from Bihar in Calcutta and founded the Bihari Students Conference in 1908, which nurtured and produced practically the entire political leadership of the twenties in Bihar. At the time he set himself up as a legal practitioner in Calcutta. In 1911 he also joined the Indian National Congress. He shifted to Patna in 1916 after the establishment of the High Court of Bihar and Orissa. It was his innate integrity and purity of character, his inability to stoop to any tactics to score a point that established his supremacy over the minds of the judges. Notwithstanding a brilliant career at the Patna High Court, he decided to become a modest political worker.

He was drawn into the Indian freedom struggle soon after the decision. During one of the fact-finding missions at Champaran, Mahatma Gandhi asked him to come with volunteers. Rajendra Prasad was greatly moved by the dedication, courage, and conviction of Mahatma Gandhi and he quit as a Senator of the University in 1921. He also responded to the call by the Mahatma to boycott Western education by asking his son Mrityunjaya Prasad, a brilliant student to drop out of the University and enroll himself in Bihar Vidyapeeth, an institution he had along with his colleagues founded on the traditional Indian model. He wrote articles for Searchlight and the Desh and collected funds for these papers. He toured a lot, explaining, lecturing and exhorting. He took active role in helping the affected people during the 1914 floods that raged in Bihar and Bengal. When the earthquake of Bihar occurred on January 15, 1934, Rajendra Prasad was in jail. During that period, he gave the entire responsibility on his behalf to his close colleague and eminent Gandhian Dr. Anugrah Narayan Sinha.. He was released two days later. He set himself for the task of raising funds. The Viceroy had also raised a fund. However, while Rajendra Prasad's fund collected over 38 Lakhs (Rs. 3,800,000), three times of what the Viceroy could manage. During the 1935 Quetta earthquake, when he was not allowed to leave the country, he set up relief committees in Sindh and Punjab.

He was elected as the President of Indian National Congress during the Bombay session in October 1934. He again became the President when Netaji Subhash Chandra Bose resigned in 1939.

After India became independent he was elected the President of India. As the first President, he was independent and unwilling to allow the Prime Minister or the party to usurp his constitutional prerogatives. However, following the tussle over the enactment of the Hindu Code Bill, he moderated his stance. He set several important precedents for later Presidents to follow.

The Presidency

His stewardship of the Constituent Assembly was exemplary. He guided, regulated, controlled, but did so with such infinite endurance, skill, grace and firmness that not only none had a sense of grievance but all felt that the discussions were always full, free and frank and left nothing to be desired. During the very first session of the Constituent Assembly, he had announced that though the Assembly was born under limitations it would outgrow those and function as a sovereign body, recognizing no outside authority. The proceedings of the last day of the Constituent Assembly read like pages from a book of tributes and, in a way, indicate how loved and respected he was by each section of the House.

His elevation to the Presidentship in 1950 came as a matter of course. There were some doubts in some quarters. Could a person who was temperamentally a peasant, who lived and dressed like one, impress in an office where ceremonialism and gilded trappings counted? But nothing else was possible. He was the only choice and there could not be another.

As President, he exercised his moderating influence and moulded policies or actions so silently and unobtrusively that many were led to think that, unlike any other Head of State, he neither reigned nor ruled.

He never worried about what people said about him. He never looked into the mirror of history. There were occasions when he differed from the Prime Minister. But that was nothing new. They had differred for almost three decades and yet worked together in the Congress. The differences never embittered their personal relations. Perhaps, both realized that they arose out of their differing backgrounds, beliefs, approaches and attitudes.

The Leaving

It was in 1960 that he announced his intention to retire, and though there were many regrets and many tried to persuade him to continue for a third term, his mind was made up. Jayaprakash Narayan, an Indian freedom fighter and political leader, welcomed the decision, suggesting that his direct guidance might be available after retirement to the Sarvodaya Movement, a self-governance movement in Sri Lanka, which provides comprehensive development and conflict resolution programs to villages. But the 1961 illness, severed and protracted, shattered Rajendra Prasad's health completely. Many therefore, worried at his decision to go back to the Sadaquat Ashram. It was a big questions that how could he guide any constructive movement with his infirmity.

Within months of his retirement, early in September 1962, passed away his wife Rajbanshi Devi, whose contribution to making him what he was, though indirect and silent gesture; was considerable. Frail and an invalid for a long time, she was the very embodiment of the spirit of renunciation, self-sacrifice, self-effacement and loyalty. No wonder, his last days were days of anguish. The Chinese aggression had traumatized him completely.

His sister Bhagwati Devi died on the night of 25 January 1950, a day before the Republic Day of India. She doted on her dearly-loved younger brother. It was only on return from the parade that he set about the task of cremation. In 1962, after 12 years as President, he announced his decision to retire

Because of the enormous public reverence, he was referred to as Desh Ratna or the Jewel of the country. He wrote a number of books including "Satyagrah at Champaran", "Bapu ke kadmon mein", "India divided" and "Atmakatha". Dalai Lama in his autobiographical book, "Freedom in Exile" described him as a "true Bodhisatva" and said that his humility made him snuffled.

Within months of his retirement, early in September 1962, his wife Rajvanshi Devi died. In a letter written a month before his death to one devoted to him, he said, "I have a feeling that the end is near, end of the energy to do, end of my very existence". He died on 28 February 1963 at Sadaqat ashram, Patna with 'Ram Ram Ram' on his lips.

Dr. Sarvepalli Radhakrishnan

Dr. Sarvepalli Radhakrishnan was born on September 5, 1888 and died on April 17, 1975.

Dr. Sarvepalli Radhakrishnan was the first Vice President (1952-1962), and the second President (1962-1967) of India. He was one of the most eminent ambassadors, scholar of comparative religious conviction and philosophy and teacher, apart from being the President of India. Throughout his life and extensive writing career, Radhakrishnan sought to define, defend, and promulgate his religion, a religion he variously identified as Hinduism, Vedanta, and the religion of the Spirit. He sought to demonstrate that his Hinduism was both philosophically coherent and ethically viable. He built a bridge between Eastern and Western thought showing each to be comprehensible within the terms of the other. He often appeared to feel at home in the Indian as well as the Western philosophical contexts, and drew from both Western and Indian sources throughout his writing. Because of this, Radhakrishnan has been held up in academic circles as a representative of Hinduism to the West. He introduced Western idealism into Indian philosophy and was the first researcher of importance to provide a comprehensive annotation of India's religious and philosophical literature to English speaking peoples. His academic appointments included the 'King George V Chair' of Mental and Moral Science at the University of Calcutta, in1921 and 'Spalding Professor Chair' a Chair funded by the Indian Government of Eastern Religions and Ethics at Oxford University (1936-1939).

As a tribute to this great teacher, his birthday is granted as Teacher's Day. As a matter of fact when his students and friends asked him for the consent to celebrate his birthday, he asked them to celebrate the day as Teacher's day.

Early being

Rather little detail is known of Radhakrishnan's earliest childhood and education. Radhakrishnan rarely spoke about his personal life, and what he does reveal comes to us after several decades of reflection.

Radhakrishnan was born in Tiruttani, a well-known temple town and popular religious and pilgrimage center, forty miles to the north-east of Madras State, Andhra Pradesh, into a Brahmin family, likely smarta in religious orientation. He was the second son of Veera Samayya, a Tehsildar, an Indian revenue administrative officer, in-charge of a Tehsil (in word a District Collector) in a zamindari. It was a middle-class, respectable Hindu Brahmin family. Indeed, the placo, the time and the family were most suitable, from every point of view, for the advent of a new philosopher-statesman, so directly needed in those turbulent days of the awakening of a very primeval and glorious nation, drowsy and sluggish in its own ignorance and indolence, for reasons well known to all.

Bright and brilliant, with a scholarly disposition and a serene and saintly demeanor, from the very beginning, Radhakrishnan spent the first eight years of his life happily and fruitfully in his home town with his parents. The peaceful and exhilarating atmosphere of that well-known and well-loved place, as well as the benign influence of his parents who, as was common in the South, were intensely religious in the traditional sense, went far in molding his character and sowing a lively seed of religiousness and ethics in him.

It was, indeed, an indubitably significant fact that Radhakrishnan's parents, though orthodox, thought it fit to send their beloved son to Christian Missionary schools and colleges. In 1896, Radhakrishnan was sent to school in the nearby pilgrimage center of Tirupati, a town with a distinctively cosmopolitan flavor. For four years, Radhakrishnan attended the 'Hermannsburg Evangelical Lutheran Missionary School'. It was there that the young Radhakrishnan first encountered non-Hindu missionaries and 19th century Christian theology with its inclination toward personal religious experience. The theology taught in the missionary school may have found resonance with the highly devotional activities connected with the nearby Tirumala temple, activities that Radhakrishnan undoubtedly would have witnessed taking place outside the school. The shared emphasis on personal religious experience may have suggested to Radhakrishnan a common link between the religion of the missionaries and the religion practiced at the nearby Tirumala temple.

Between 1900 and 1904, Radhakrishnan attended Elizabeth Rodman Voorhees College in Vellore, a school run by the American Arcot Mission of the Reformed Church in America. The mandate of the Mission was to advocate the gospel, to publish dialect tracts, and to educate the "heathen" masses. It was here, as Robert Minor points out, that Radhakrishnan was "introduced to the Dutch Reform Theology, which emphasized a righteous God, unconditional grace, and election, and which criticized Hinduism as intellectually incoherent and ethically unsound." At the same time, the Mission demonstrated an active concern for education, health care, and social uplift through its participation in famine relief, the establishment of hospitals, and education for all irrespective of social status. Such activities were not conflicting with the consent of the Mission as they often served as incentives for conversion. In was in this atmosphere that Radhakrishnan encountered what would have appeared to him as crippling assaults on his Hindu sensibilities. He also would have witnessed the positive contributions of the social programs undertaken by the Mission in the name of propagation of the Christian gospel.

Thus, Radhakrishnan inherited from his upbringing a implicit acceptance of Vedanta and an awareness of the centrality of devotional practices associated with the smarta tradition. His experiences at Tirupati brought him into contact with Lutheran Christian missionaries whose theological emphasis on personal religious experience may have suggested to him a common ground between Christianity and his own religious heritage. In Vellore, the presence of a systematic social gospel was intimately bound up with the religion of those who sought to censure Radhakrishnan's cultural norms and religious worldview.

As usual in those days, Radhakrishnan was married in 1906 while living in Vellore, at the tender age of 18 and while still a student, to Sivakamamma, and spent a happy conjugal life with her for half a century, having six children: five daughters and a son. She did on 1956.

It is in these historical and hermeneutic contexts and with these experiences informing his worldview that Radhakrishnan encountered a resurgent Hinduism. Specifically, Radhakrishnan encountered the writings of Swami Vivekananda and V.D. Savarkar's The First War of Indian Independence. The Theosophical Society was also active in the South Arcot area at this time. The Theosophists not only applauded the ancient wisdom they claimed to have found in India, but were persistent advocates of a philosophical, spiritual, and scientific meeting of East and West. Moreover, the Society's role in the Indian nationalist movement is evidenced by Annie Besant's involvement with the Indian National Congress. While Radhakrishnan does not speak of the Theosophists presence at this time, it is unlikely that he would have been unfamiliar with their views.

What Vivekananda, Savarkar, and Theosophy did bring to Radhakrishnan was a sense of cultural self-confidence and self-reliance. However, the affirmation Radhakrishnan received from this resurgence of Hinduism did not push Radhakrishnan to study philosophy nor to interpret his own religion. It was only after Radhakrishnan's experiences at Madras Christian College that he began to put down in writing his own understanding of Hinduism.

Academics

Radhakrishnan's choice of Philosophy as his main or Honours subject in his B.A. degree course was due to a very fortunate accident. At that time, he was really rather baffled as to what particular Honours subject to choose from amongst the possible five, viz., Mathematics, Physics, Biology, Philosophy and History. Then, purely accidentally, and out of a mere boyish curiosity, he read three well-known works on

Philosophy, passed on to him by one of his cousins who had that year obtained the B.A. degree with Philosophy Honours and that definitely decided his future course of studies.

He studied Sanskrit and Hindi also; and had a good deal of interest in the traditional languages of India. He read also the Vedas and the Upanishads with great care and reverence.

In fact, Radhakrishnan was, and is, still today, a reader and a digester in the true sense of the terms. For, what he read - and he read widely and lovingly all kinds of good books - did not remain an external acquisition, an ornamental decoration, with him; but blossomed forth in him in fullest glory and grandeur.

It is not always that in this strange world of ours inner worth is accompanied by outer success. But Radhakrishnan is a glorious exception in this regard. For, all throughout his brilliant career, honour after honour was showered on him.

In 1904, Radhakrishnan entered Madras Christian College. At this time Radhakrishnan's academic sensibilities lay with the physical sciences, and before beginning his MA degree in 1906 his interest appears to have been law.

Two key influences on Radhakrishnan at Madras Christian College left an indelible stamp on Radhakrishnan's sensibilities. First, it was here that Radhakrishnan was trained in European philosophy. Radhakrishnan was introduced to the philosophies of Berkeley, Leibniz, Locke, Spinoza, Kant, J.S. Mill, Herbert Spencer, Fichte, Hegel, Aristotle, and Plato among others. Radhakrishnan was also introduced to the philosophical methods and theological views of his MA supervisor and most influential non-Indian mentor, Professor A.G. Hogg. Hogg was a Scottish Presbyterian missionary who was educated in the theology of Albrecht Ritschl and studied under the philosopher Andrew Seth Pringle-Pattison. As a student of Arthur Titius, himself a student of Albrecht Ritschl, Hogg adopted the Ritschlian distinction between religious value judgments, with their emphasis on subjective perception, and theoretical knowledge, which seeks to discover the nature of ultimate reality. Religious value judgments give knowledge which is different from, though not necessarily opposed to, theoretical knowledge. For Ritschl, and subsequently for Titius and Hogg, this distinction led to the conclusion that doctrines and scriptures are records of personal insights and are therefore necessary for religious, and specifically Christian, faith. This distinction left its mark on Radhakrishnan's philosophical and religious thinking and resonates throughout his writing.

A second key factor shaping Radhakrishnan's sensibilities during this time is that it was at Madras Christian College that Radhakrishnan encountered intense religious polemic in an academic setting. Radhakrishnan later recalled: "The challenge of Christian critics impelled me to make a study of Hinduism and find out what is living and what is dead in it... I prepared a thesis on the Ethics of the Vedanta, which was intended to be a reply to the charge that the Vedanta system had no room for ethics".

Elucidation and Inspiration

Upon the completion of his MA degree in 1908, Radhakrishnan found himself at both a financial and professional crossroads. His obligations to his family precluded him from applying for a scholarship to study in Britain and he struggled without success to find work in Madras. The following year, with the assistance of William Skinner at Madras Christian College, Radhakrishnan was able to secure what was intended to be a temporary teaching position at Presidency College in Madras.

At Presidency College, Radhakrishnan lectured on a variety of topics in psychology as well as in European philosophy. As a junior Assistant Professor, logic, epistemology and ethical theory were his stock areas of instruction. At the College, Radhakrishnan also learned Sanskrit.

During these years, Radhakrishnan was anxious to have his work published, not only by Indian presses but also in

European journals. The Guardian Press in Madras published his MA thesis, and scarcely revised portions of this work appeared in Modern Review and The Madras Christian College Magazine. While Radhakrishnan's efforts met with success in other Indian journals, it was not until his article "The Ethics of the Bhagavad Gita and Kant" appeared in The International Journal of Ethics in 1911 that Radhakrishnan broke through to a substantial Western audience. As well, his edited lecture notes on psychology were published under the title Essentials of Psychology. Badminton.

Radhakrishnan accepted an Assistant Lectureship at the Madras Presidency College in1909. While at the College, he mastered the classics of Hindu philosophy, namely the Upanishads, Bhagvad Gita, Brahmasutra, and commentaries of Sankara, Ramunuja and Madhava. He also acquainted himself with Buddhist and Jain philosophy. At the same time he read philosophical commentaries of Plato, Plotinus, Kant, Bradley, and Bergson. Later on in his life, he studied Marxism and Existentialism.

In 1914, in a strange twist of fate, Radhakrishnan met Srinivasa Ramanujan, the mathematical genius. Srinivasa was leaving for Cambridge for studies and had come to seek Radhakrishnan's blessings because a goddess came in his dream and told him to do so before undertaking the trip. The two never met again.

In 1918, Radhakrishnan was selected as Professor of Philosophy by the University of Mysore. By the time, Radhakrishnan had written many articles for journals of repute like The Quest, Journal of Philosophy and the International Journal of Ethics. He completed his first book "The Philosophy of Rabindranath Tagore." He believed Tagore's philosophy to be the "genuine manifestation of the Indian spirit." Radhakrishnan's second book, "The Reign of Religion in Contemporary Philosophy" was published in 1920.

Radhakrishnan's books and articles drew the attention of Ashutosh Mookerjee, Vice Chancellor of Calcutta University.

He nominated Radhakrishnan to the prestigious George V Professor of Philosophy at the Calcutta University, 1921. In 1923, Dr. Radhakrishnan's "Indian Philosophy" was published. The book was in response to the request made by Prof. J. H. Muirhead, to write a book on Indian philosophy for the Library of Philosophy. Radhakrishnan accomplished this mammoth task by producing a systematic and readable account of Indian philosophy. The book was hailed as a "philosophical classic and a literary masterpiece."

Radhakrishnan was called to Oxford University, England, to deliver the prestigious "Upton Lectures" on "The Hindu View of Life." The lectures were followed by an invitation to head the Department of Comparative Religion at Oxford. A philanthropist, Spalding, created a professorship for Radhakrishnan to teach Religion and Ethics at Oxford.

Radhakrishnan used his lectures as a platform to further India's cause for freedom. He thundered, "India is not a subject to be administered but a nation seeking its soul." He would graphically describe the "shame of subjection and the lines of sorrow" apparent on every Indian's face.

In 1931, Radhakrishnan was elected Vice Chancellor of the Andhra University. The University was in a state of stagnation. Radhakrishnan restructured the Honors and Post-Graduate teaching in Humanities and Languages, and Science and Technology Departments from scratch. By the time he left in 1936, he had transformed the University into a robust and well-recognized institution.

In 1939, Radhakrishnan became the Vice Chancellor of the Benaras Hindu University, Uttar Pradesh, founded by Pt. Madan Mohan Malaviya. The University was under pressure from the Governor, Sir Maurice Hallet, to turn the campus into a war hospital in response to the Quit India Movement launched by Gandhiji and the Congress. Radhakrishnan rushed to Delhi and successfully persuaded the Viceroy, Lord Linlithgow, to halt the Governor's action. The Governor instead suspended financial support to the University. Radhakrishnan went on "a Begging Pilgrimage," to collect funds from sympathizers and philanthropists. When Malaviyaji retired from University work completely, the Benaras Hindu University requested Radhakrishnan's services for an indefinite period which Radhakrishnan acquiesced to.

After independence on August 15, 1947, Radhakrishnan was requested to Chair the University Education Commission in 1948. The Radhakrishnan Committee's suggestions helped mould the education system for India's needs. In 1949, Dr. Radhakrishnan was appointed ambassador to the Soviet Union. The appointment raised many eyebrows because people wondered what kind of an impression Radhakrishnan, a student of idealist philosophy, would make on Joseph Stalin, an ardent communist. In 1950, Radhakrishnan was called to the Kremlin to meet with the Premier. This was rather irregular. Radhakrishnan was accompanied by Indian Embassy Minister, Rajeshwar Dayal and Soviet Foreign Minister Andrei Vyshinsky and interpreter Pavlov. Radhakrishnan told Stalin, "We had an emperor in India who, after bloody victory, renounced war and became a monk. You have waded your way to power through force. Who knows that might happen to you also." Radhakrishnan was referring to Stalin's infamous "bloody" purges. Stalin smiled and replied, "Yes, miracles do happen sometimes. I was in a theological seminary for five years!"

On April 5, 1952, a few days before Radhakrishnan's departure for India, Stalin called on Radhakrishnan. Radhakrishnan records Stalin's face being bloated. Radhakrishnan patted him on the cheek and on the back. Stalin said, "You are the first person to treat me as a human being and not as a monster. You are leaving us and I am sad. I want you to live long. I have not long to live." Stalin died six months later. Radhakrishnan's legacy in Moscow was a firm and friendly understanding between India and the Soviet Union and a relationship which has flourished over the years and has become even stronger.

Radhakrishnan was elected Vice-President of India in 1952. The Vice-President presides over the Rajya Sabha (Upper House) sessions, much like the Speaker does in the Lok Sabha (Lower House). Often, during a heated debate, Radhakrishnan would intervene with *Slokas* from the Sanskrit classics or quotations from the Bible to calm the charged atmosphere. Nehru commented later, "By the way in which Radhakrishnan conducted the proceedings of the Rajya Sabha, he had made the meetings of the House look like family gatherings!"

The Philosopher

Radhakrishnan argued that Western philosophers, despite all claims to objectivity, were biased by theological influences of their own culture. He wrote books on Indian philosophy according to Western academic standards, and made Indian philosophy worthy of serious consideration in the West. In his book "Idealist View of Life" he has made a powerful case for the importance of intuitive thinking as opposed to purely intellectual forms of thought. He is well known for his commentaries on the Prasthana Trayi namely, the Bhagavadgita, the Upanishads and the Brahma Sutra.

He was elected as a Fellow of the British Academy in 1938. He was awarded the Bharat Ratna in 1954, and the 'Order of Merit' in 1963. Around the same time, an 883-page compilation titled "The Philosophy of Dr. Sarvepalli Radhakrishnan" was released in America. He received the Peace Prize of the German Book Trade in 1961, and the Templeton Prize in 1975, a few months before his death. The Oxford University instituted the Radhakrishnan Chevening Scholarships and the Radhakrishnan Memorial Award in his memory.

Thought and Existentialism

The philosophy of Radhakrishnan is an attempt to reinterpret and reconstruct the Advaita Vedanta of Sankara in the light of scientific knowledge and technique of modern time. The philosophy of Advaita follows the basic tenets of the Upanishadic philosophy. Radhakrishnan does not propound any system of philosophy. He is bound to tradition like his contemporaries. But, his philosophy is distinct from others by some of its peculiar features. It is based on his own experiences and reflections.

Existentialism is an attitude and outlook that emphasizes human existence. 'Existence precedes essence'-this is the maxim of existentialism. Existentialism deals with the problems the individual has to face in life, with the ways how he faces them, with his feelings and emotions and above all, with his outlook on life and experience. It recognises freedom and responsibility of the individual man.

Soren Kirkegaard is regarded as the father of 'Existentialism'. He starts discussion on it. It is further developed in the hands of subsequent thinkers like Karl Jaspers, Gabriel Marcel, Martin Heidegger and Jean Paul Sartre. It must be admitted that there are divergent interests and points of view within existentialism.

There are certain affinities between the viewpoints of Rahdakrishnan and the existentialist thinkers.

Indian thought, in general; investigates into the self. Radhakrishnan also maintains that "In India, 'Atmanam Viddhi,' know the self, sums up the law and the prophets." (1) We do hear in this 'Atmanam Viddhi' the voice of existentialism.

The two great propositions of the Upanishads are 'Tattvamasi' (Thou art that) and 'Aham Brahmasmi' (I am Brahman). These two propositions assert that man is neither a thing nor an object. Man is not the product of something. He is one with Brahman. Thus, the self is identified with Brahman, the one. For Radhakrishnan, man is essentially subject, not object. The ultimate reality is one with our deepest self. Brahman is Atman, the Universal Spirit. The existentialists assert that man is not an object to be known, but a subject.

Karl Jaspers, one of the existentialists maintains that "My true self is not the individual soul, but the supreme self, the one, and therefore. I reach my authentic being in identifying myself with the one."

According to Radhakrishnan, man is more than matter, life or mind or all these taken together. Man has grown out of physical, vital and animal life into the power of manhood. Kierkegaard speaks of the 'individual existence' in a sense in which a man is not simply a biological, psychological or social animal, but in which a man is a 'human being.'

In Radhakrishnan, we often find that "Man is always more than he is able to comprehend of himself." Radhakrishnan is quite akin to Jaspers as Jaspers also holds the view that man is always more than himself.

Both Radhakrishnan and the existentialists emphasize on the immense potentialities of man. Radhakrishnan maintains that man must be transformed and transmuted to a higher level of existence in course of evolution. Man's greatness is not in what, he is but in what he can be. Jean Paul Sartre asserts about man that- "it-is-what-it-is-not and that it is not what-it-is." Man exists and makes himself develop into what he wants to be.

Radhakrishnan realises deeply the present-day condition of man. The present period is a period of uncertainty. Man has lost his happiness and peace. The life becomes artificial and mechanical. Radhakrishnan writes, "We live in a period of agonizing strain, of grave anxiety, of manifold disillusionment. The world is in a condition of trance."

Existentialism is also deeply concerned with the condition of man in the modern age. In the present time man has lost his freedom, individuality, humanity. Man is reduced to a machine. Different disciplines treat man not as an individual, but as an object. Existentialism points out that a type of thought which dominates the treatment of objects is inadequate to the existing individual.

Radhakrishnan, in spite of the crisis of present time maintains an optimistic attitude. According to him, man's unrest is not a mere negative force. He is not only oppressed by new doubts but is inspired by new horizons, new perspective and a thirst for new relations with fellowmen. We are in the beginning of a new age. Jaspers also believes that present discontents and unrest indicate the birth of a future. He expresses, "we live, so to speak, in a seething cauldron of possibilities, continually threatened by confusion, but always ready in spite of everything to rise up again."

Radhakrishnan acknowledges the reality of suffering and misery of worldly existence. This empirical world is the source of all kinds of sorrows and suffering. Man is the victim of suffering so long as he confines himself to this world. Like other Advaita thinkers, Radhakrishnan affirms the inevitability of death and transitoriness of human existence. But he also affirms that the suffering of life can be transcended. Man is intended for something greater than confinement in this world. He can rise above it. Radhakrishnan makes suffering and misery of worldly existence an aspect of the process of spiritual growth. Again, death is not a denial of life. It is only a condition. Death is only a change from one life to another Death terminates the present life of man in order to substitute a new life for it. It is not possible for man to exhaust all the potentialities of life in a single life. Hence, we must accept some possible forms of life after death.

The existentialists depict a gloomy picture of life. There are antinomies, contradictions and distress at the root of existence. The feeling of anxiety or anguish or dread (angst, agonizes) is a peculiar feature which characterizes the outlook of the existentialist thinkers. We have to face all these; otherwise we evade the truth of our own being. Existentialists think that an important fact of life is death. Death is man's inevitable end. Heidegger has carried out the detailed study of the existential meaning of death. It pulls man up into authentic existence out of his inauthentic existence. Jaspers refers to death, chance, guilt, suffering struggle as boundary situations. These boundary situations reveal to us our 'Existence'-the authentic self.

Radhakrishnan, like the existentialists distinguishes between the inauthentic and the authentic existence as between bondage and liberation. Bondage is the self-alienation of man from his real being. Liberation results from the realisation of the real nature of man. Inauthentic existence is the life of worldliness. It signifies the ignorance of man of his real nature. The authentic existence is the way of man who wants liberation. It signifies the attempt of man to liberate himself from egocentric limitations and the realisation of the real-self.

Like other thinkers, Radhakrishnan is primarily concerned with liberation. Liberation is a state of freedom. It means the realisation of the self in its pure nature. Freedom is the central concept around which the existential enquiry revolves. Freedom constitutes man's basic nature. Freedom is inherent to human existence. The practice of freedom is man's authentic existence. It is to be lived through responsible decision and action.

According to Radhakrishnan-moksa, nirvana, eternal life is not an escape from life, but the realisation of life's fullest possibilities, the perfection of personality. Each one's life is a road to him, to self-realization.

In the existentialists we find that man seeks to liberate himself from his state of 'fallenness' and direct it towards the realisation of his highest potentialities. Herein lies man's freedom.

In his later writings, Radhakrishnan often refers to existentialism. He maintains that existentialism is one of the basic types of thought. It appears in the history of philosophy whenever we stress the difference between the individual being of man and the being of objects in nature. Though Radhakrishnan has much more in common with existentialism, he regards it as a transitional phase of individual development. He states, "Existentialism is a stage in man's pilgrimage through life. It has to transcend itself: for an analysis of the human predicament reveals the fact of God as being and God as perfection."

The confrontation

By 1914, Radhakrishnan's reputation as a scholar was beginning to grow. However, the security of a permanent academic post in Madras eluded him. For three months in 1916 he was posted to Anantapur, Andhra Pradesh, and in 1917 he was transferred yet again, this time to Rajahmundry. Only after spending a year in Rajahmundry did Radhakrishnan find some degree of professional security upon his acceptance of a position in philosophy at Mysore University. This hiatus in his occupational angst would be short lived. His most prestigious Indian academic appointment to the George V Chair in Philosophy at Calcutta University in February of 1921 would take him out of South India for the first time only two and a half years later.

Between 1914 and 1920, Radhakrishnan continued to publish. He authored eighteen articles, ten of which were published in prominent Western journals such as The International Journal of Ethics, The Monist, and Mind. Throughout these articles, Radhakrishnan took it upon himself to refine and expand upon his interpretation of Hinduism.

There is a strong polemical tenor to many of these articles. Radhakrishnan was no longer content simply to define and defend Vedanta. Instead, he sought to confront directly not only Vedanta's Western competitors, but what he saw as the Western philosophical enterprise and the Western ethos in general.

Radhakrishnan's polemical sensibilities during these years were heightened in no small part by the political turmoil both on the Indian as well as on the world stage. Radhakrishnan's articles and books during this period reflect his desire to offer a sustainable philosophical response to the unfolding discontent he encountered. World War One and its aftermath, and in particular the events in Amritsar in the spring of 1919, further exacerbated Radhakrishnan's patience with what he saw as an irrational, dogmatic, and despotic West. Radhakrishnan's 1920 The Reign of Religion in Contemporary Philosophy is indicative of his heightened polemical sensibilities during this period.

A more positive factor in Radhakrishnan's life during these years was his reading of Rabindranath Tagore, the Bengali poet. Radhakrishnan joined the rest of the English-speaking world in 1912 in reading Tagore's translated works. Though the two had never met at this time, Tagore would become perhaps Radhakrishnan's most influential Indian mentor. Tagore's poetry and prose resonated with Radhakrishnan. He appreciated Tagore's emphasis on aesthetics as well as his appeal to intuition. From 1914 on, both of these notions — aesthetics and intuition — begin to find their place in Radhakrishnan's own interpretations of experience, the epistemological category for his philosophical and religious proclivities. Over the next five decades, Radhakrishnan would repeatedly appeal to Tagore's writing to support his own philosophical ideals.

The, War, Tagore and Mysore (1914-1920)

By 1914, Radhakrishnan's reputation as a scholar was beginning to grow. However, the security of a permanent academic post in Madras eluded him. For three months in 1916 he was posted to Anantapur, Andhra Pradesh, and in 1917 he was transferred yet again, this time to Rajahmundry. Only after spending a year in Rajahmundry did Radhakrishnan find some degree of professional security upon his acceptance of a position in philosophy at Mysore University. This hiatus in his occupational angst would be short lived. His most prestigious Indian academic appointment to the George V Chair in

Philosophy at Calcutta University in February of 1921 would take him out of South India for the first time only two and a half years later.

Between 1914 and 1920, Radhakrishnan continued to publish. He authored eighteen articles, ten of which were published in prominent Western journals such as *The International Journal of Ethics*, *The Monist,* and *Mind.* Throughout these articles, Radhakrishnan took it upon himself to refine and expand upon his interpretation of Hinduism.

There is a strong polemical tenor to many of these articles. Radhakrishnan was no longer content simply to define and defend Vedanta. Instead, he sought to confront directly not only Vedanta's Western competitors, but what he saw as the Western philosophical enterprise and the Western ethos in general.

Radhakrishnan's polemical sensibilities during these years were heightened in no small part by the political turmoil both on the Indian as well as on the world stage. Radhakrishnan's articles and books during this period reflect his desire to offer a sustainable philosophical response to the unfolding discontent he encountered. World War One and its aftermath, and in particular the events in Amritsar in the spring of 1919, further exacerbated Radhakrishnan's patience with what he saw as an irrational, dogmatic, and despotic West. Radhakrishnan's 1920 *The Reign of Religion in Contemporary Philosophy* is indicative of his heightened polemical sensibilities during this period.

A more positive factor in Radhakrishnan's life during these years was his reading of Rabindranath Tagore, the Bengali poet. Radhakrishnan joined the rest of the English-speaking world in 1912 in reading Tagore's translated works. Though the two had never met at this time, Tagore would become perhaps Radhakrishnan's most influential Indian mentor. Tagore's poetry and prose resonated with Radhakrishnan. He appreciated Tagore's emphasis on aesthetics as well as his appeal to intuition. From 1914 on, both of these notions — aesthetics and intuition — begin to find their place in Radhakrishnan's own interpretations of experience, the epistemological category for his philosophical and religious proclivities. Over the next five decades, Radhakrishnan would repeatedly appeal to Tagore's writing to support his own philosophical ideals.

The Presidency

The years following Indian independence mark Radhakrishnan's increasing involvement in Indian political as well as in international affairs. The closing years of the 1940s were busy ones. Radhakrishnan had been actively involved in the newly incorporated UNESCO (United Nations Educational, Scientific, and Cultural Organization), serving on its Executive Board as well as leading the Indian delegation from 1946-1951. Radhakrishnan also served for the two years immediately following India's independence as a member of the Indian Constituent Assembly. Radhakrishnan's time and energy to UNESCO and the Constituent Assembly had also to be shared by the demands of the University Commission and his continuing obligations as Spalding Professor at Oxford.

With the Report of the Universities Commission complete in 1949, Radhakrishnan was appointed by then Prime Minister Jawaharlal Nehru as Indian Ambassador to Moscow, a post he held until 1952. The opportunity for Radhakrishnan to put into practice his own philosophical-political ideals came with his election to the Rajya Sabha, in which he served as India's Vice-President (1952-1962) and later as President (1962-1967).

Radhakrishnan saw during his terms in office an increasing need for world unity and universal fellowship. The urgency of this need was pressed home to Radhakrishnan by what he saw as the unfolding crises throughout the world. At the time of his taking up the office of Vice-President, the Korean War was already in full swing. Political tensions with China in the early 1960s followed by the hostilities between India and

Pakistan dominated Radhakrishnan's presidency. Moreover, the Cold War divided East and West leaving each side suspicious of the other and on the defensive.

Radhakrishnan challenged what he saw as the divisive potential and dominating character of self-professed international organizations such as the League of Nations. Instead, he called for the promotion of a creative internationalism based on the spiritual foundations of integral experience. Only then could understanding and tolerance between peoples and between nations be promoted.

Radhakrishnan retired from public life in 1967. He spent the last eight years of his life at the home he built in Mylapore, Madras. Radhakrishnan died on April 17, 1975.

Dr. Radhakrishnan is, indeed, a versatile genius - a great scholar, a great philosopher, a great seer, a great writer, a great orator, a great statesman, a great administrator, all combined.

And above all, he is a Man - a full real Man, who has always lived men, served men, worshipped men, not as a superior being, not as a superman; but only as a Man, as their fellow being, as their friends, as their nearest and dearest one.

Jawaharlal Nehru, who was one of his closest friends throughout, said about Radhakrishnan: "I join you in paying my tribute to our President, Dr. Radhakrishnan. He has served his country in many capacities. But above all, he is a great Teacher from whom all of us have learnt much and will continue to learn. It is India's peculiar privilege to have a great philosopher, a great educationist and a great humanist as her President. That in itself shows the kind of men we honor and respect".

Dr. Zakir Hussain

Dr. Zakir Hussain was born on February 8, 1897 and suddenly demised on 3 May, 1969.

Dr. Zakir Hussain was the highest Indian national award, the 'Bharat Ratna' winner third President of India from May 13, 1967 until his death on 3 May 1969.

Early Life

DR. ZAKIR HUSSAIN was born at Hyderabad on February 8, 1897; he came of a Pathan family of the upper middle-class, settled at Qaunganj in the District of Farrukhabad, Uttar Pradesh. His Pashtun father, Fida Hussain Khan, went to Hyderabad, studied Law and had a most successful career. Unfortunately, he died when Dr. Zakir Hussain was only ten years old.

Dr. Zakir Hussain was sent first for his education to the Islamia High School in Etawah (U.P.) which specialized in puritanical strictures. After finishing school, he joined the M.A.O. College at Aligarh and studied up to the M.A. When the Indian National Congress and the All India Khilafat Committee joined hands in launching the Non-Cooperation Movement, Mahatma Gandhi toured the country to induce teachers and students to leave Government administered schools and colleges. The young Zakir Hussain, who was then half-student and half-teacher, very prominent among the students and very popular with a large section of the staff, persuaded Hakim Ajmal Khan and other leaders to establish a national institution at Aligarh, and the Jamia Millia Islamia came into being on 29 October, 1920. But Zakir Hussain did not wish to leave his studies incomplete and he went to the University of Berlin in Germany for higher studies in 1923, returning with a doctorate in Economics three years later. He rejoined the Jamia Millia in February-March, 1926 and became the Shaikhu Jamia (Vice-Chancellor). It was at the Jamia Millia that Dr. Zakir Hussain developed his gifts as an educationist. It was his experience here as well as his deep study of the philosophy of education which enabled him to take charge of the scheme of Basic National Education when it was launched in 1938. He was the President of Hindustani Talimi Sangh, Sevagram from 1938 to 1948.

Career

In November 1948, Dr. Zakir Hussain was appointed Vice-Chancellor of the Aligarh Muslim University. He was also nominated a member of the Indian Universities Commission. The World University Service made him the Chairman of the Indian National Committee and in 1954 he was elected the World President of the organization. He was also nominated to the Rajya Sabha and made the Indian representative on the Executive Board of the UNESCO from 1956 to 1958. He remained the Chairman, Central Board of Secondary Education, till 1957, a member of the University Grants Commission till 1957, a member of the University Education Commission in 1948-1949 and of the Educational Reorganisation Committee of Bihar, Uttar Pradesh and Madhya Pradesh. In 1957 he was appointed the Governor of Bihar and in 1962 he was declared elected as the Head of the State and was formally sworn in as the Third President of the Indian Republic four days later. He held the highest office of the country with exemplary grace and dignity till his sudden death..

Dr. Zakir Hussain was awarded Padma Vibhushan in 1954 and Bharat Ratna in 1963. He was awarded D.Litt. (Honoris Causa) by the Universities of Delhi, Calcutta, Aligarh, Allahabad and Cairo.

Many demands were made on Dr. Zakir Hussain's time and he was not able to undertake many scholarly projects which he had in mind. His interest in literary and academic work was so keen that he translated Plato's 'Republic' and Cannon's 'Elementary Political Economy'into Urdu soon after joining the Jamia Millia in 1920. While in Germany, he got an edition of the 'Diwan-I-Ghalib' printed - doing much of the compositing himself, because the press did not have enough staff - and also brought out a book in German on Mahatma Gandhi (Die Botschaft des Mahatma Gandhi') . He delivered a series of lectures on economics under the auspices of the Hindustani Academy and another series in English, on Capitalism: Essays in Understanding, under the auspices of the Delhi University in 1945. He also translated Friedrich List's 'Nationalockonomie'. His Convocation Addresses have been collected and published under the title "The Dynamic University". But he excelled in writing for children and his stories are masterpieces of style.

Tall, well-built, fair in complexion, with broad forehead, a sensitive aristocratic nose, and a well-trimmed beard and always neatly and tastefully dressed in sherwani and pyjama, Dr. Zakir Hussain was an imposing embodiment of culture and refinement. He was sensitive to beauty in all its forms and had an intense passion for excellence. His varied tastes and hobbies, his love of roses, his collection of cacti, fossils, paintings and specimens of calligraphy, objects the art, and curios and above all, his rich library are evidence of his versatile personality.

He was steeped in the spiritual and aesthetic culture and the ethical principles of the Muslim Sufis and poets. He had the Sufi's indifference towards the externals of religion and, though a deeply religious man, his religiosity was never obvious. It was the inspiration for secularism by which he endeared himself to men of different religious communities.

Dr. Zakir Hussein's nationalism was, like Gandhiji's, a reflection of his allegiance to the highest moral values and to the ideals of a culture which had become the whole of his own self. It was a nationalism which demanded for the individual that freedom which is the essence of democracy, that self-discipline which is the foundation of democratic citizenship and that identification with the good of the society which gives substance and meaning to the life of the individual.

Dr. Hussein died suddenly on 3 May, 1969 at the age of 72 working at an optimum pace till his last day.

Sri Varahagiri Venkata Giri

Shri Varahagiri Venkata Giri was born on August 10, 1894 and died on June 23, 1980.

The Flipside

Varahagiri Venkata Giri, the second son of V.V. Jogiah Pantulu and Venkata Subbamma, was born on August, 10,1894 at Berhampur in the district of Ganjam in Orissa which was part of the then Madras Presidency. Even while in his teens, Giri interested himself actively in public service. He was hardly 12 years old when, along with the youth of his place and under the inspiring guidance of his uncle, D. Viswanatha Rao, who greatly moulded his outlook on life, Giri pioneered the Young Men's Library Association as also the library movement in the country. After passing the Senior Cambridge examination, Giri went to the U.K. in 1913 to study law.

The Dynamic Life

He joined the Institute of Court and the National University in Ireland. In Dublin, Giri organized the Indian Students Association' of which he was the Secretary throughout his stay there. The members of this Association took active interest in the political events in India and also followed the course of events in South Africa where Gandhiji was engaged in peaceful 'Satyagraha' to secure for Indian settlers their basic rights as of events in South Africa where Gandhiji was engaged in peaceful 'Satyagraha' to secure for Indian settlers their basic rights as citizens. Giri prepared a pamphlet entitled, 'South African Horrors' which narrated graphically the humiliation to which the Indians were subjected.

Giri and some of his colleagues actively participated in the Irish nationalist movement and identified themselves totally with the sentiments and aspirations of the Irish people in their struggle for freedom. When the Easter Rebellion broke out in 1916, Ireland was placed under Martial Law and the military authorities decided to extern Giri for his involvement in the nationalist movement. He was given notice to quit the U.K. by July 1, 1916. This prevented Giri from taking his degree, though by then, he had been called to the Irish Bar. Giri returned to India in September, 1916 and was soon enrolled as an Advocate of the Madras High Court as a junior to the eminent lawyer, T. Prakasam. In the same year, Giri joined the Congress and the Home Rule Movement of Mrs. Annie Besant. In 1921, in response to Gandhiji's call, he threw away his flourishing practice at the bar and joined the freedom movement.

Giri always wanted to organize the workers as part of the national struggle. He became the President of the B.N. Railway Indian Labour Union in 1922. The Bengal Nagpur Railway, a British managed company, was one of the biggest in the country, employing nearly a lakh of workers and its lines running through nearly 3,000 miles or so over four provinces. Along with organizing the B.N. Railway Union, Giri undertook the strengthening of trade unions in other railways also, notably the East India Railway, the M. S. M. Railway, the Nizam State Railway and the Mysore State Railway and became their President. Simultaneously, Giri, N. M. Joshi and other wanted to form a federation of all the railway unions to focus attention on the views and demands of all the workers together. The All India Railway men's Federation came into being in 1924 with its headquarters at Berhampur.

Soon all the unions in different railways were affiliated to the AIRF and the Federation became the sole and powerful spokesman of all railway workers. It was organized on sound trade union principles and became, within a few years of its existence, the main pillar of the Indian Trade Union Movement. It drew its strength and sustenance from the inspiring guidance and personal attention of Giri who placed it on a sound footing and organized scientifically the entire working class in the railways. The Federation believed in the basic tenets of truth and non-violence which Gandhiji had enunciated in his political struggle.

In 1926, Giri was elected President of the All India Trade Union Congress at its Madras session. In his presidential address he stressed the need of organizing the agricultural workers in India, a field comparatively neglected till then. In 1926-27, the B. N. Railway Indian Union waged a historic struggle against the management for reprisal of the workers grievances. This strike by more than 35,000 workers and their solidarity was epoch-making in the history of trade union movement in India and abroad. What was initially a strike turned out to be a lockout. It was called off when the management and the Government of India conceded to pay the full lock-out wages for three months to the workers. The unity and the sense of dedication and sacrifice of nearly 40,000 workers evoked support and sympathy throughout the world. National leaders, notably Gandhiji, hailed the victory of the working class as a triumph of moral force.

In 1927, Giri went to Geneva to represent the workers of India at the International Labour Conference. Speaking at the conference, he referred to the unemployment situation prevailing in the country and suggested the setting up of Employment Exchanges and also making provision for unemployment benefits to the working classes. He also pleaded for retrenchment benefits for the workers so that the unreasonable attitude of the employers in dismissing the workers on 'trivial' faults or on their 'first offense' could be eliminated. Giri entered the Central Legislature in 1935 and was the Congress spokesman on matters relating to labour. He was elected as a Congress candidate in the polls conducted for provisional assemblies under the Government of India Act, 1935 and became a Minister under Rajaji in the Madras Province. He held the important portfolios of Labour, Industry, Cooperation and Harijan Uplift.

Contribution to the Labour Welfare

Giri was a pioneer in many respects. For the first time in the history of Labour-Management relations in our country, in April 1938 he convened a tripartite conference of the representatives of Employers, Workers and Government, the underlying idea being that discussion of differences and issues between labour and management across the table would reduce the area of conflict and widen the field for cooperation.

That Giri was one of the originators of planning in India is a fact relatively not well known. He was one of those few leaders who considered planning vital to the country's progress. He took active steps to establish an all-India planning machinery and for this he secured the whole-hearted support of the then President of the Indian National Congress, Subhash Chandra Bose, and the engineer-statesman. Sir M. Visweswarayya. Later in October 1938, at a conference of Industrial Ministers of Congress provinces, held in Delhi, Giri stressed the necessity of co-operation not only to Congress Governments but also of the non-Congress and Princely State Governments in the matter of planning and development of industries. The Conference authorized Giri to take necessary steps to bring into existence the All India Planning Commission and also to convene the first meeting of the preliminary committee.

By the beginning of 1939, the National Planning Committee was established with Jawaharlal Nehru as Chairman and Giri as Convener. In the meantime, the Congress Governments refused to co-operate with the British in the war effort and the ministries in different provinces resigned in October, 1939. Giri was arrested in January 1940 and was sentenced to 15 months' imprisonment. He was released by March 1941 but was again arrested on August 17 during the 'Quit India' Movement.

In 1946, Giri once again, became a Minister in Madras but resigned when the Prakasam Ministry fell. Giri was appointed the first Indian High Commissioner in Ceylon in 1947. The noteworthy event during his tenure in Colombo was the first meeting of the Prime Ministers of the India and Ceylon. Giri relinquished office in 1951 paying a tribute to his work there. Prime Minister Pundit Nehru wrote that Giri had kept 'a balance of firmness and flexibility'.

In the 1952 General Elections, Giri was elected to Parliament as a congress candidate. He became the Minister of Labour at the Centre, the first trade union leader to occupy that high office. As Labour Minister, Giri reiterated his faith in collective bargaining rather than compulsory adjudication. Popularly known as the "Giri-approach", he spelt it out in his opening address at the Twelfth Session of the Indian Labour Conference in October, 1952:

Compulsory adjudications had cut at the very root of Trade Union Organization. If workers find their interests are best promoted only by cooperation/ no greater urge is needed to forge a band of strength and unity among them. But compulsory arbitration sees to it that such a bond is not forged. It stands there as a policeman looking out for signs of discontent and at the slightest provocation takes the parties to the Court for a dose of costly and not wholly satisfactory justice. The moment the back of the policeman is turned, the parties grow red in face with redoubled determination and the whole cycle of litigation starts over again. Let the Trade Unions become strong and self reliant and learn to get on without assistance of policeman.

To safeguard the workers against indiscriminate and involuntary pay off and retrenchment, Giri brought into force legislation for the payment of compensation to workers under the Industrial Disputes (Amendment) Act, 1953. The Act lies down that 'no worker who has rendered a year's continuous service or more may be retrenched without being given a month's notice (or a month's wages in lieu) as well as compensation for losing his job.

Giri's dedication to the cause of Labour came under severe test when he had to choose between the dictates of his conscience and the high office of Labour Minister. He left the Central Cabinet when the Government decided to upset by executive action, the Award of the Tribunal, on Bank Dispute. His resignation on August 30, 1954 from the Central Cabinet will ever adorn the pages of Labour History in India. While some of his colleagues felt that the acceptance of the Award of Justice Rajadhyaksha would unfavorably affect the banking system and would have consequences so grave as to upset the economy and stability of the country, Giri differed. He felt that the Appellate Tribunal's award should be accepted and enforced.

Giri's resignation created such a strong opinion in the country that the Government was forced to appoint another Commission under Justice Gajendragadkar to go into the whole issue. This Award was accepted by the Government. It was not only a moral victory for Giri personally but the stand of the entire working class was vindicated.

Giri was actively associated with academicians and public men engaged in promoting the interests of labour and industrial relations and were largely responsible for the founding of the Indian Society of Labour Economics in 1957. He was the first President of the Indian Society of Labour Economics (ISLE) and remained as the kingpin of the organization during its formative years.

ISEL

This was founded in 1957 by a distinguished group of academicians and public men engaged in promoting the study of labour and industrial relations, The group headed by Shri V.V. Giri consisted of Professors Gyan Chand, Baljit Singh, V.B. Singh, S.D. Punekar, Radha Kamal Mukherjee, C.N. Vakil, P.S. Lokanathan, G.P. Sinha and others. The Society, among others, owes its birth and growth largely to the nurturing care of Shri V.V. Giri, who later became the President of India. Among those who able assisted Shri Giri in his endeavour was Professor V.B. Singh, who not only edited ISLE's journal – The Indian Journal of Labour Economics – but remained the kingpin of the organization till he breathed his last in 1978.

Today the Indian Society of Labour Economics (ISLE) is a broad based organization, which promotes comprehensive scientific studies of labour and related matters, provides a forum for free and frank exchange of views on various aspects of labour and related issues among all the people concerned, and disseminates information and knowledge for a wider debate.

The Presidency

After 1957, Giri held successively gubernatorial assignments for about a decade: Uttar Pradesh (1957-60), Kerala (1960-65) and Mysore (1965-67). After the Fourth General Election in 1967, Giri was elected Vice-President of India.

On the sudden demise of President Zakir Hussain on May 3, 1969, Vice-President Giri was sworn in as the acting President of India. He resigned his office on 20th July, 1969 and contested the Presidential election as an Independent candidate. He was elected President on 20th August and was sworn in as the fourth President of India on 24th August 1969.

Serving as the President of India during 1969-1974, Giri provided positive thinking and constructive action in promoting unity, goodwill, tolerance and mutual understanding. He always stood for the upliftment of the economically and socially deprived sections of the society and urged all concerned to work together for bringing about social and economic equality. He continued to be an active participant in the working class Movement and addressed the special sitting of the 54th session of the International Labour Conference in 1970.

His tenure as the President of India ended on 24th August 1974, and the nation honoured his service as a freedom fighter, trade unionist, diplomat, minister, governors, the Vice-President and the President by conferring on him the highest honour of the country, Bharat Ratna, in 1975.

The absolute completion of his work and assignments came to an end in the year of 1980, 3rd June and he passed away left the world behind.

Shri Fakhruddin Ali Ahmed

Shri Fakhruddin Ali Ahmed was born on May 13, 1905 and died on February 11, 1977.

Early Days

Shri Fakhruddin Ali Ahmed born on May 13, 1905 at Hauz Qazi area of Old Delhi with a silver spoon in his mouth, Fakhruddin Ali Ahmed was one of those few Muslims who by virtue of his service to the country under the leadership of Mahatma Gandhi reached the pinnacle of honour as the President of the Indian Republic, the fifth in the roll.

Shri Fakhruddin's grandfather, Shri Khaliluddin Ali Ahmed, of Kacharighat near Golaghat town in the Sibsagar district, Assam, married in one of the families who were the relics of Emperor Aurangzeb's bid to conquer Assam. Ali Ahmed's father Col. Zalnur Ali, of the Indian Medical Service, had to leave Assam while he was a bachelor doctor following an incident in Shillong. Col. Ali and one of his Assamese contemporaries, Col. Sibram Bora, were allotted seats at a function in the Shillong Club away from the European guests. The two Assamese Colonels boycotted the function in protest against the segregation meted out to them. This naturally enraged the European bosses who transferred Col. Zalnur Ali to distant North-West Province. This provided him with an opportunity to come in contact with the Nawab of Lohari in Delhi whose daughter he married. Here was born Fakhruddin Ali Ahmed.

Education

Educated first in the Bonda Government High School in U.P., Fakhruddin matriculated from the Delhi Government High School then under the Punjab University. He was sent to England for higher education in 1923 in order to groom him for the I.C.S., though his mother was opposed to his son being sent abroad. He joined the Catherine College of Cambridge University and was called to the Bar from Inner Temple of

London. He could not compete for the I.C.S. examination due to illness. On return to India he started legal practice in the Lahore High Court in 1928. In October that year, Col. Zalnur Ali, accompanied by his Barrister son, Fakhruddin paid a visit to Gauhati ostensibly to look after his paternal property which included a few hundred acres of land in and around Gauhati. Obviously, the Ahmed family's link, snapped on the Colonel's posting in N.W.P. was thus re-established after several years. Two years later Fakhruddin Ali Ahmed revisited Gauhati and came in contact with the leaders of the Congress in Assam and in 1931 enrolled himself as its primary member. This was a turning event in the life of Ahmed.

Political Vocation

During his stay in England he met Jawaharlal Nehru in 1925 whose progressive ideas impressed him very much; in fact, Nehru became his mentor and friend from the thirties onwards(Lord Bulter, one of the luminaries of the Tories was a classmate of Fakhruddin Ali Ahmed). Once Ahmed joined the Indian National Congress he steadfastly adhered to it though his co-religionists in the Muslim League tried to persuade him to join the latter. As a Congressman, Ahmed Saheb actively participated in the freedom movement. To begin with, he offered individual satyagraha on 14 December, 1940 for which he was imprisoned for a year under Section 5 of the DIR. Again, in the 'Quit India Movement' he was arrested on 9 August, 1942 while he was returning after attending the historic session of the AICC meeting held at Bombay and detained as a security prisoner for three and a half years till April 1945. In the Congress organization he occupied several positions of responsibilities. He remained a member of the Assam Pradesh Congress Committee since 1936 except for a small break. He retained the membership of the AICC from 1947 till 1974. He was elected to the Assam Assembly for the first time in 1935 and became the Minister of Finance, Revenue and Labour in the Congress Coalition Ministry formed by the late Gopinath Bardoloi on 19 September, 1938. In the first spell of his Ministerial office Ali Ahmed demonstrated his acumen and ability in administrative sphere. His initiative in introducing the Assam Agricultural Income Tax Bill, the first of its kind in India, that levied taxes on tea garden lands in the Province and his pro-labour policy in the labour strike in the British-owned Assam Oil Company Ltd. At Digboi irked the European planters and their henchmen who considered that the measures of the Congress Coalition Government were revolutionary and, therefore, constituted a danger signal to the interests of the British commercial community. But Ali Ahmed did not heed to such opposition and went ahead with the measures which brought him and the Bardoloi Ministry a good deal of popular applause. However, the Bardoloi Ministry had to resign on 16 November, 1939 on the war efforts issue, but that Fakhruddin Ali Ahmed was an able administrator was established.

After Independence he was elected on Congress ticket to the Assam Assembly on two terms (1957-1962) and (1962-1967). Earlier, he was elected to the Rajya Sabha (1952-1953) and thereafter became Advocate-General of the Government of Assam. Though Ali Ahmed occupied a senior position in the Chaliha Ministry from 1957 he was asked by Jawaharlal Nehru to join his Cabinet at the Centre in January 1966. He was elected to the Lok Sabha from the Barpeta constituency in 1971. In the Central Cabinet he was given important portfolios relating to Food and Agriculture, Cooperation, Education, Industrial Development and Company Laws. His induction to the Central Cabinet was perhaps because of his close link with, and loyalty to the Nehru family and also for his acumen in administration.

In the Congress hierarchy Ali Ahmed enjoyed an enviable position being a member of the Congress Working Committee for several years. In the Great Split of the Congress (1969), Ali Ahmed remained with Indira Gandhi, may be his deep-rooted association with the Nehru family made him adhere to Indira Gandhi's leadership till his death. He was elected to the highest post of the land - the Presidentship of the Indian Republic on 29 August, 1974, but his tenure in the office was cut short (1977) by his sudden death due to a heart attack which he suffered on his return from a tour of the South-East Asian countries only a day before. In the wake of the Emergency Ali Ahmed became the target of criticism of his detractors. It was alleged that he put his signature as President to the order on promulgation of Emergency on 25 June, 1975 at the behest of the Prime Minister, though he assured at the time of his election to Presidentship that he would not be a yes-man of the Cabinet. Notwithstanding this criticism, Ali Ahmed's personality, integrity and ability in administration were never questioned.

Suave and sober, Ali Ahmed seldom allowed anger and prejudices to get better of him, at the same time; he did not compromise with unprincipled issues. These traits of his character were apparently the key to his success in the public life and enabled him to acquire a respectable position in the society. Towards the end of his political career, he was, however, accused of being communal by certain quarters, but this accusation was hardly warranted. Mention of an incident in this connection would perhaps be relevant. In 1935, when Mohammad Ali Jinnah, Liaquat Ali Khan, Nazimuddin and a few starwarts of the Muslim League came to Assam to campaign against Fakhruddin Ali Ahmed who was pitted by the Congress against a Muslim League candidate in the Assembly poll, a common friend at the instance of Sir Mohammad Saadullah suggested that Fakhruddin Saheb should pay a courtesy call to the Muslim League leaders at Gauhati. Liaquat Ali, however, reacted to the suggestion somewhat tersely saying that he would not shake hands with a Kafir meaning Ali Ahmed. Thus, the suggestion was scotched. It is apparently difficult to believe that he could be communal with a long record of service to the country under the banner of the Congress. It is, nonetheless, a fact that he tried to bring to the Congress fold a number of Aligarh Muslim University educated youths of his community whose communal outlook was a public knowledge. If this had created an impression in certain quarters that Fakhruddin Ali Ahmed was communal, that was entirely a different matter. But his love for the country and faith in secularism were profound and therefore, were not in doubt in the least.

Individuality

Though politics was Ali Ahmed's forte, his deep interest in sports and other extra-mural activities were well-known. Himself a tennis player and golfer, he was elected President of the Assam Football Association and the Assam Cricket Association for several terms; he was also the Vice-President of the Assam Sports Council. In April, 1967 he was elected President of the All India Cricket Association besides being a member of the Delhi Golf Club and the Delhi Gymkhana Club since 1961. His love for music and finer arts was no less; he was deeply interested in poetical works of Ghalib. His travels in the USSR, the USA, the UK, Japan, Malaysia and many Arab countries as a Minister and afterwards as the President of India widened his urbane outlook that endeared him to all sections of the people, irrespective of caste, creed and avocation. Elegantly dressed he was always courteous but firm in what he considered to be just and fair and presented himself as a Moghul, as it were, which quality he perhaps inherited from his maternal side.

At forty Ali Ahmed married Abida (21) of a respectable family of U.P. educated in Aligarh Muslim University. When negotiations for the wedding were under way Ahmed was undergoing a jail term in Jorhat as security prisoner. At a certain stage of the negotiations Abida's family wanted to know what the prospective bride groom was doing. The answer came from one of the relatives of the would-be bridegroom: "Fil hal to jail men Hai" (At present he is in jail). But Destiny so ordained that Fakhruddin Ali Ahmed and Abida were happily married on 9 November, 1945. Begum Abida Saheba was elected to the Lok Sabha in 1981 from a U.P. constituency in a by-election.

Ali Ahmed passed away on 11 February, 1977 in the Rashtrapati Bhavan leaving behind his wife, two sons and a daughter.

Shri Neelam Sanjiva Reddy

Shri Neelam Sanjiva Reddy was born on May 18, 1913 and died on June 1, 1996.

Shri Neelam Sanjiva Reddy, the sixth President of India, was a veteran statesman and bureaucrat. He held many eminent positions in public life both before and after independence. It is often said that Presiding Officers should strive not only to be fair and impartial but should also appear to be so. This difficult task is further complicated since they are usually elected to the House on a political party's ticket. Some are of the view that Speakers should not remain party members once they are elected to office. Others feel that in our party system, it may be unfair to ask the Speaker to dissociate fully from the political party on whose ticket he had won the election. In our parliamentary history, Dr. Neelam Sanjiva Reddy is the only Speaker since Independence who after assuming the office of Speaker formally resigned from his political party. He also had the distinction of being the only Speaker who was later unanimously elected as the President of the Republic. His distinguished public life was marked by high standards of performance in several capacities in which he served the country with deep commitment to parliamentary democracy and its essential norms.

Back Ground

Neelam Sanjiva Reddy born in a peasant family in the Illur village of district Anantapur in the State of Andhra Pradesh, Reddy belonged to an enlightened middle class family.

He had his primary education at the reputed Theosophical High School, Adayar at Madras. The spiritual atmosphere of the school left a deep impact on the mind of young Reddy. Later, he joined the Government Arts College at Anantapur for his higher studies. However, destiny had something else in store for him. He did not continued his studies there after as because the despondent status of India.

Mahatma Gandhi's visit to Anantapur in July 1929 was the turning point in Reddy's life. Like many other young people of his generation, Reddy too came under the profound influence of Gandhiji's thoughts, words and actions. He discarded his foreign clothes and took to Khadi as his dress. In 1931, the young Sanjiva Reddy gave up his studies to take part in the freedom movement, and threw himself into the struggle. He never regretted the decision of leaving his college. He first came into limelight when he participated in a student satyagraha.

The Legislature

Reddy actively participated in various Youth Congress activities and in 1937, at a young age, he became the Secretary of the Andhra Provincial Congress Committee (APCC). True to his character, Reddy managed the affairs of the APCC meticulously and methodically. It was a testimony to his qualities of leadership and his organizing ability that he remained in that post continuously for a long span of ten years. During 1940-45, he underwent imprisonment several times for participating in the freedom movement.

Reddy's legislative career began in 1946 when he was elected to the Madras Legislative Assembly and became the Secretary of the Madras Congress Legislature Party. The following year, he was elected a member of the Constituent Assembly of India and actively participated in the proceedings of the Constituent Assembly which was shaping the destiny of the nation for the generations to come. In 1949, he was back in the State politics and from April 1949 till April 1951, he served as the Minister for Prohibition, Housing and Forests in the then Madras State.

In 1951, Reddy was elected the President of the APCC where he served for a year before returning to the Centre as a member of the Rajya Sabha in 1952. However, he remained a member of the Upper House only for a short while. In 1952, in recognition of his political sagacity, drive and dynamism, he was appointed the Deputy Chief Minister of the new-born State of Andhra and Played a very important role in the formation of the Andhra State. Subsequently, following the reorganization of the States in October 1956, the State of Andhra Pradesh was constituted and the choice for the Chief Minister of the newly formed State fell on Reddy.

As Chief Minister, Reddy realised that democracy could function effectively only when the people at the grass-root level were politically educated, trained and equipped. He had a vision of an era of decentralised power and he always strove to strengthen democracy at the grass-root level. His creative leadership and progressive outlook, coupled with his pragmatic approach to the multifarious problems of the newly set up State, were widely appreciated.

Soon, Reddy began to emerge as a political leader of national stature. In 1959, he resigned as the Chief Minister of Andhra Pradesh to take up the post of the President of the Congress Party. To Reddy, power was never an end in itself but only a means to an end, that being the welfare of the people.

After serving for two terms as the President of the Congress Party, Reddy went back to Andhra Pradesh for a second term as the Chief Minister. In February 1964, when the Supreme Court made certain observations in the Bus Routes Nationalisation case against the Government of Andhra Pradesh for not filing an affidavit, he voluntarily tendered his resignation from the office of the Chief Minister, thus setting an example of high standards in public life.

On 9 June 1964, Reddy joined Lal Bahadur Shastri's Government as the Minister of Steel and Mines. In the same year, he was elected to the Rajya Sabha. He also served for a very brief period as the Minister of Transport, Aviation, Shipping and Tourism in Indira Gandhi's Government in 1967.

Reddy was elected to the Fourth Lok Sabha from the Hindupur constituency in Andhra Pradesh. On 17 March 1967, Reddy was elected the Speaker of the Fourth Lok Sabha, amidst widespread acclaim and admiration. Sanjeeva was speaker of the Lok Sabha from 1967 to 1969. He then contested for the office of the President as the official Congress candidate as against V. V. Giri who was then the Vice-President. The Presidential contest proved to be of momentous significance in the history of the Congress, resulting in the split of the Congress with an overwhelming section siding with Mrs. Indira Gandhi, who had rebelled against the old guard, headed by Mr. Nijalingappa, which came to be known as the Congress (O). Thus the Congress came to be divided into the Congress (O) and Congress (R) parties. The President election went in favour of Mr. V. V. Giri.

The, split in the Congress gradually widened. In the 1971 mid-term election, the Congress (R) had a landslide victory and the Congress (O) was reduced to a party of little significance. After the defeat of the Congress (R) in the Lok Sabha elections of 1977, Sanjeeva Reddy was elected at the instance of the Janata Party as the President of the Republic.

He was very particular about maintaining the independence and impartiality of the august office as he considered them to be indispensable for the successful working of parliamentary democracy. Immediately after his election as the Speaker, he resigned from his 34-year-old membership of the Congress Party, thus becoming the first Speaker since Independence to have formally severed his party affiliation. He believed that the Speaker belongs to the whole House, he represents the totality of members and as such he should belong to no party or rather he should belong to all parties.

Though Reddy remained the Speaker only for a little over two years, he lent dignity and distinction to the office by the exemplary manner in which he presided over the deliberations of the House. He possessed a large measure of personal authority, a willingness to appreciate the others' point of view and a deep understanding of the sense of the House which enabled him to conduct the parliamentary business in an orderly and effective manner. With his vast experience of men and matters, Reddy tactfully handled delicate situations within the House by his commendable patience and common sense. He conducted the proceedings of the House with such dexterity that there was not even a single occasion when the Opposition resorted to staging a walkout from the House. Also, no member was named when Reddy was in the Chair.

During Reddy's Speakership, many significant rulings were given and conventions laid down which have enriched the parliamentary traditions and practices. Reddy, for the first time, allowed a No-Confidence Motion to be taken up for discussion on the same day when the President addressed both the Houses, He believed that urgent matters should not be delayed by taking recourse to traditions and precedents.

Reddy was always conscious of affording equal opportunity to each and every member of the House to express his or her views. He defended, with utmost concern, the rights and privileges of the members both inside and outside the House. It was during his tenure as Speaker that for the first time in the history of the Lok Sabha, the House sentenced a person to imprisonment for committing contempt of the House by shouting slogans and throwing pamphlets on the floor of the House from the Visitors' Gallery.

The setting up of the Committee on the Welfare of the Scheduled Castes and Scheduled Tribes was another significant innovation during Reddy's Speakership. Inaugurating the first sitting of the Committee on 18 December 1968, he hoped that the Committee would ensure that the measures taken by the Union Government for the advancement of the Scheduled Castes and Scheduled Tribes were effectively implemented.

Annulment

On 19 July 1969, Reddy resigned the Speakership of the Sabha to contest the Presidential election which he lost by a narrow margin. After a period of voluntary exile from politics, Reddy was back in the Sixth Lok Sabha. On 26 March 1977, he was unanimously elected the Speaker of the Sixth Lok Sabha. However, this time too, he could not complete his full term as the speaker and after serving for four months, he again resigned from the high office to file nomination papers for the Presidentship of India.

Reddy achieved the pinnacle of glory when he was elected the President of India on 25 July 1977. During his tenure as President, he took various historic decisions on crucial issues.

By his long years in public life and by virtue of his close association with leaders of all sections of opinion in the country, President Reddy could steer the destiny of the nation at a critical stage in its history. His sagacious leadership, affability and accessibility endeared him to people belonging to all walks of life. He also lent a rare distinction to the highest office in the land by his pragmatism, idealism and patriotism. As a world statesman, Reddy articulated the nation's views with utmost finesse in the international fora. Following the completion of his term, Reddy retired to private in his home town, Anantapur.

Dr Neelam Sanjiva Reddy passed away at his native place, Anantapur, Andhra Pradesh in 1996 at the age of 83.

Address by the President of India Smt. Pratibha Devisingh Patil to commemorate the 60th anniversary of India's independence in the Central Hall of Parliament.

New Delhi, 15th August 2007

Hon'ble Vice President,
Hon'ble Prime Minister,
Chief Justice of India,
Speaker of Lok Sabha,
Members of the Union Council of Ministers,

Deputy Chairman of Rajya Sabha,
Deputy Speaker of Lok Sabha,
Members of Parliament,
Excellencies, Ladies and Gentlemen,

Today, we celebrate an important event in the history of India. On this day, 60 years ago, there was jubilation as the long struggle against foreign rule had culminated in the freedom of India. This year we also celebrate another historic event in India's path to freedom as we mark the 150th anniversary of the War of Independence of 1857. We bow our heads in reverence to pay tribute to the brave men and women of that era. I can quote a few names like Mangal Pandey, Tatia Tope, Rani Lakshmibai, Begum Hazrat Mahal and Kitturu Rani Chennamma, but there remain many more whose supreme sacrifices had shown us the road to freedom.

This unique moment in history provides us an opportunity to look at the past with pride and to the future with hope and confidence. Pandit Jawaharlal Nehru, at the dawn of India's freedom, while addressing the nation said, and I quote, " It is fitting that at this solemn moment, we take the pledge of dedication to the service of India and her people and to the still larger cause of humanity." Unquote. Let us reaffirm our commitment to work with determination and dedication for a glorious future of India.

On this day, let us remember the devotion and sacrifice of our freedom fighters and pay homage to them. We shall forever remain indebted for their selfless service. Mahatma Gandhi, Pandit Jawaharlal Nehru, Netaji Subhas Chandra Bose, Sardar Vallabhbhai Patel, Subramaniam Bharathi, C. Rajagopalachari, Dr. Rajendra Prasad, Maulana Abul Kalam Azad and many others have immortalised themselves in the pages of our country's history. We must not forget the brave women of this nation who participated in the freedom struggle, who were not secondary to the men, but equals in their zeal and commitment to the cause of freedom. Prominent among them were Kasturba Gandhi, Dr. Sarojini Naidu, Aruna Asaf Ali, along with many others.

India's freedom came not by the efforts of a few, but with the united support of multitudes - those millions of unknown and unsung champions of our freedom. We gratefully pay our homage to them and ensure that they inspire us today to dedicate ourselves to the cause of upholding those timeless values of freedom, tolerance, justice, equality and harmony and pledge to build a strong and modern India of the 21st Century.

Dr. Ambedkar said, and I quote, "Democracy is not merely a form of Government. It is primarily a mode of associated living, of conjoint communicated experience. It is essentially an attitude of respect and reverence towards fellowmen." The multi-lingual, multi-cultural, multi-religious and multi-ethnic character of India continues to be our greatest strength and the harmonious coexistence of such diversity remains an exemplary role model for the world at large.

Today, India stands at the threshold of a new era of progress. We are witnessing historically unprecedented rates of economic growth. It should be our combined endeavor to sustain this growth and ensure that it is socially inclusive, particularly for the disadvantaged and the marginalised. We must ensure that every region of the country participates in and benefits from the process of economic growth that is destined to transform India.

In agriculture and allied sectors, modern technology and improved farm practices can further sustain the gains in these areas and ensure food security for our future generations.

In modern India, development in all sectors of industry have shown remarkable achievements. We should continue to march ahead to scale new heights in the face of stiff global competition.

To realise the full potential of our people, we must invest in their capabilities and empower them with modern education and comprehensive health care. We must continue our campaign against poverty, ignorance and disease and seek a better future for the coming generations.

Education should be one of our primary focus areas. Every citizen of this country - man or woman, boy or girl - must be given the opportunity to be educated. Universal education is the key to a prosperous and successful India. Demographically India has one of the world's youngest populations, and the active participation of the youth and empowering them with education is necessary to eliminate the social evils that spring from ignorance.

We have a glorious history in art and culture. We are duty bound to pass on this proud legacy to our younger generation. We should expose them to the treasure of great Indian art and culture and help them inherit our traditional and moral values and basic tenets of humanism.

As we move into the 7th decade of our independence, let us ensure that the pride in our nations' democratic traditions does not give way to complacency. Parliament is the edifice of democracy and freedom, representing the will of the people. It therefore becomes important that our Parliamentarians efficiently meet the aspirations of our people. For our efforts to yield results, we need to improve implementation mechanisms of our programmes. Corruption today poses a grave challenge to our system and it is time that the nation begins to determinedly combat this menace.

As we surge ahead on the path of growth and development, the world today is compelled to take notice of this awakening power that is India. India has a crucial role to play in the world order. As a nation we have always believed in "वसुधैव कुटुम्बकम्", the world is one and humanity is a single family. The world, in this hour of uncertainty and darkness, plagued by wars and terrorism, can take inspiration from India and our commitment to values such as non-violence and tolerance. India is committed in its resolve to foster friendly ties with the nations of the world and together with the international community work towards a united and prosperous world.

Thus, on this sixtieth anniversary of our Independence, let us pledge to dedicate ourselves to the welfare and happiness of the people of India, and humanity at large.

JAI HIND !

Address to the Nation on the eve of the 60th Anniversary of India's Independence by Smt. Pratibha Devisingh Patil, the President of India.

My Dear Fellow Citizens,

On the eve of the momentous occasion of the 60th anniversary of our Independence Day, I extend my warmest greetings to my fellow-citizens in India and the world over. This is also the 150th year of our historic War of Independence in 1857.

The saga of our Independence involved the sacrificial struggle of many freedom fighters – some whose names are etched in history as stalwarts and the countless, relatively less-known souls - whose silent contribution conjointly helped to realize the dream of an Independent India under the charmisitic leadership of the Father of our Nation, Mahatma Gandhi. Let us solemnly remember them with gratitude and reverence and pay homage to their sacrifice for the liberation of our motherland from the colonial yoke.

I am happy that the two events are being celebrated in a befitting manner to inspire our younger generation, remind them about glorious past and inculcate in them a spirit of sacrifice, dedication and patriotism.

Having traversed sixty long years since independence, it is time for us to introspect on the progress achieved so far and ponder over the future course of action. We have excelled in many areas; and in many others we still have immense scope for improvement.

Democracy in India has taken deep roots. But it cannot be appreciated in its fullest glory if we construe it merely as a political arrangement. The real test lies in internalizing the spirit of democracy and making it a habit of our minds. We have ably demonstrated to the world, how India – a developing nation of more than a billion people – can give its people a better quality of life within the framework of a secular democracy. It is the greatness of the people of India that amidst all trials and tribulations, they have kept the sacred flame of democracy burn ever-bright illuminating India's journey in the new millennium. As members of the largest thriving democracy in the world, it continues to be the bounden duty of every citizen to ensure that the system of parliamentary democracy which we have worked successfully grows from strength to strength.

What is of still greater significance is that the framework of democratic governance and the reach of representative institutions have percolated down to the common man. The wisdom of the Founding Fathers of our constitution has been vindicated in that the process of democratic decentralization has acquired healthy roots intimately encompassing village panchayats and urban local bodies. Our endeavour should be to stamp out the imperfections and entrench democratic decentralization to ensure participative decision-making of the people in the planning process at the grass-root level to build a more vibrant India. Along with such decentralization it is equally important to provide a morally superior and clean administration. This would empower every citizen, especially the poor, the disadvantaged and the marginalized to enjoy the real fruits of democracy.

The father of the nation, Mahatma Gandhi once said, "Salvation of India lies in the elevation of her women." It is indeed encouraging that assured representation has been provided to nearly one million women in our local bodies. History bears sufficient proof that our womenfolk have excelled themselves not only as able home-makers but in devoting themselves to the noble task of nation building. Let us resolve that they are not left marginalized in our society. Let us also resolve to expand opportunities for their wholesome participation in every field of activity and make them harbingers of sustainable development.

Fostering equilibrium in diversity is the hallmark of democracy. What sets our nation apart is that in spite of criss-crossing of a plethora of culture, languages, religions, customs, faith and traditions, our people are bound together in unison by a deep-rooted secular Indian identity. Evolution through synthesis and inherent respect for pluralism has been the golden thread which has run through our millennia old civilization. Non-violence, tolerance, acceptance of all religions and different ways of life, search for truth and fearlessness are cherished values that have become the cornerstone of our heritage. We must recapture the spirit of unity that marked our freedom struggle, linking the people of all parts of our country in a common endeavour of ultimate loyalty to the nation.

We have to weld the entire nation into a strong, unassailable unity in which there is no room for distrust between man and man. For any nation and its people to become great, there is a need to pursue the path of collective vision. The more developed amongst us should inspire and enthuse the less developed to race ahead on the road to development. We must strive to maximize our collective performance so as to build a nation of equal opportunities. Today, we are, where we are, entirely due to the collective participation of our people and our endeavour should be towards fostering an environment of cooperative federalism and collective pursuit of national goals.

Working within the canons of parliamentary democracy and through the mechanism of planned economic development, we have made commendable economic progress. India's stature as an economic entity has gone up manifold. We are fortunate to live in the times of a buoyant and upswing economy. Steady industrial growth, growing exports and sound foreign exchange reserves are all signs of growing economic strength and resilience. A surplus current account and sizeable capital inflows are other indicators of the strong fundamentals of our country's economy. World over, there is a growing realization that India's business environment is changing. We are being watched with singular interest and both developed and developing countries have shown great eagerness to forge economic partnerships with us. If we draw up a balance sheet, listing our strengths and weaknesses, we would perhaps find more pluses than minuses. Nevertheless, we have to take special care to bring in egalitarian reforms to ensure that the full benefit of economic liberalization reaches people at all levels.

Growth, when unevenly spread, dwarfs overall prosperity. Only through socially inclusive growth can there be sustained consistency in our growth rates. We have to ensure equitable growth for all. The fruits of economic development must necessarily touch, especially, the living and working conditions of our toiling masses and people below the poverty line. It should be remembered that our freedom fighters toiled not only for political freedom but dreamt of transforming political freedom into a vehicle for attaining the goal of equality and prosperity for all. As Pandit Jawaharlal Nehru said "Democracy means equality, and democracy can only flourish in an equal society." Empowerment of our economically deprived section of the society still remains unaccomplished. Progress must relate to the lives of the people and we have to conscientiously discharge our responsibilities towards uplifting the socially and economically disadvantaged and weaker sections of the society. For this let us resolve to rededicate ourselves to rid the country of poverty and build a strong and resurgent India.

Agriculture has a critical role to play for balanced development and especially a better life for our farmers. Apart from overall contribution to the national income and helping in the attainment of the goal of food security for all, a strong and robust growth in agriculture can help reduce rural poverty. A vibrant agriculture sector will create a dynamic rural economy which will further drive our economic growth. The success of the First green Revolution has been significant and helped us to feed a population, which has crossed the one billion mark and I express our nation's gratitude to our farmers, labourers and congratulate our scientists who are responsible for this glorious accomplishment. However we cannot remain complacent, we need to sustain the momentum of the first revolution and must analyze the challenges that we face in the present agricultural scenario. Recently I had the occasion to interact with the top agricultural scientists in a seminar that discussed the issues related to eradication of hunger and poverty vis-a-vis agricultural development. I am confident that the synergized endeavour of our policy makers, the farming community, farmers organizations, voluntary agencies and agricultural scientists and agri-business enterprises can help us meet the challenges that beset the agricultural front and tackle distressful situation faced by farmers in some pockets of the country. In the coming years we need to ensure that agriculture becomes more rewarding with formulation of appropriate policies, measures and technologies.

This year as in previous years we have seen floods in some parts of the country resulting in loss of lives and damage to property. My heartfelt sympathies to the people in the flood ravaged areas of the country. The seriousness of the matter makes it imperative to take necessary steps to prevent this recurring phenomenon.

There is a new climate of growth and competitiveness in our industrial economy. A youthful India is taking its place on the world-stage surely and steadily. The world is on the threshold of a new wave, where the ability to create knowledge and innovate has become the key competitive differentiator between nations. The strength of our knowledge capital is now recognized worldwide and we need to ensure a supportive environment for it. We are fast emerging as a major economic power of the world and our entrepreneurs are surging ahead with fresh self-confidence. The achievements in knowledge economy, IT and IT enabled services, pharmaceuticals and other sunrise industries have been spectacular. Our corporate have made bold and successful forays into the global market and corporate acquisitions. My good wishes go for our entrepreneurs, big and small, in their continuing enterprise. The contribution of the working classes has been considerable and the nation owes a deep debt of gratitude to them.

A significant feature of our changing society is the transformation taking place in the country's demographic profile. As a people, we are growing younger. Youth in India constitute a sizeable, vibrant and resourceful segment of our society who are fired with the desire to scale greater heights. Children and youth are our hope for tomorrow. There can be no greater cause, no better investment, no greater priority for development consensus than bringing the needs, rights and expectations of the youth to the centre-stage of development concern. It is our duty to kindle the imagination of our youth so that the nation surges ahead with added strength and vigour.

This casts a greater responsibility on our educational institutions at all levels to harmonize the cognitive faculties of our youth in the direction of the continued well-being of our nation. While the prime concern of our educational institutions is and should be studies, it should not stagnate into a medium which merely facilitates mechanical acquisition of information. Knowledge imparted should have an organic and living relationship with the societal needs and help in mediating the strands of overwhelming challenges of a rapidly changing modern-day world. While we foster an atmosphere conducive to promoting higher standards of academic excellence, we should not overlook the need to nurture a system of holistic education that teaches positive values and makes good citizens.

It is also vital that we recognize the importance of health while planning our social infrastructure. Poor health shackles human capital. There is an imperative need to widen the coverage and qualitatively empower both the primary and secondary health care systems. Affordable health care has to reach the rural and urban poor and be supplemented by other inter-sectoral interventions like provision of safe drinking water, better sanitation facilities, coordinated slums management, nutritional programmes and family welfare measures.

Fellow-citizens, we cannot forget that we live in a world and in a neighbourhood. We stand for friendship with all nations and will continue to work for international peace and security. We should also continue to intensify cooperation to fight the global challenges of terrorism, poverty, ignorance, disease and climate change.

This is the occasion to express our gratitude to the brave personnel of our Armed Forces whose eternal vigil and protection of our borders, seas and skies under challenging circumstances have ushered in a climate of peace enabling us to plan the path of future progress and development of the nation.

As we watch the tri-colour unfurl tomorrow morning, let us all hold our heads high with pride and confidence and look ahead with optimism towards a better and brighter future for our great nation.

Dear citizens, rarely there comes a moment in time such as this when we as a nation stand firm on the solid foundations painstakingly established by our ancestors, and with nationalistic pride in our hearts, look ahead to the glorious path of infinite possibilities that await India with open arms. Today India is poised to take flight into this open sky of success and perfection, and as loyal citizens of this country, it is our duty, as individuals, and as a nation to ensure that we do not let this unprecedented moment in time go unutilized for the dream of a strong, robust and prosperous India. It is a vision, a dream, a goal; as success must be the anthem of every nation's awakening. For our nation to rise and claim its glorious destiny, we must realize that it is us, and our billion hands that can shape it, and in the immortal clarion call of Swami Vivekanada, I ask my fellow-citizens to "Arise, Awake and Stop not till the goal is reached."

JAI HIND !

Address by the President of India Smt. Pratibha Devisingh Patil on the occasion of special lecture on "Agriculture cannot wait"

New Delhi, 06th August 2007

I am very happy to be amidst you all today and it is immensely satisfying to note that to commemorate the 60th Anniversary of our Independence, the National Academy of Agricultural Sciences has organized a Special Lecture: '*Agriculture Cannot Wait*'. It is fascinating to note that Pt. Nehru, the visionary thinker, had echoed the same thoughts more than half a century ago when he remarked, "*Everything can wait, but not agriculture*'. The theme of today's lecture is of special relevance globally, as we are poised at a critical juncture grappling with the formidable task of eradicating hunger and poverty from our planet.

A nation is its people and our motherland is the abode of nearly one-sixth of all humanity. Securing a better life for our citizens where each one of us, can lead lives of dignity and fulfillment therefore merits undivided attention in our development strategy. A natural corollary to this is the attainment of the goal of food security for all. The need to catalyze agricultural growth through a result-oriented agricultural development strategy with the synergized endeavours of our policymakers, the farming community, farmers organisations, farming labour, agricultural scientists and agri-business enterprises is indeed the call of the moment.

During the 60 years after Independence, we have made spectacular strides in the field of agriculture. The chronic spectre of famine, which was commonplace during colonial rule, has long been obliterated from our memories. It is no mean achievement to be able to feed a population, which has crossed the one billion mark. I salute our farmers and congratulate our scientists who are responsible for this magnificent accomplishment and must add with all emphasis that the entire nation is proud of their dedicated work. We have amidst us, Dr. M.S. Swaminathan, a distinguished scientist who played a stellar role in ushering in the First Green Revolution. What is noteworthy of admiration is that he continues to be fired with the same zeal and spirit to pave the onward march of agriculture in our country. My special greetings also go to Dr. Jacques Diouf, Director General, Food and Agriculture Organization of the United Nations.

The success story of the First Green Revolution has run its course. We cannot afford to rest on our laurels. The fruits of the Green Revolution and the momentum generated by it, needs to be sustained. Towards this endeavour, we must analyse the challenges that beset the agricultural scenario. The Economic Survey 2006-07 has enlisted some of the structural weaknesses of the agriculture sector which include low levels of public investment, exhaustion of the yield potential of new high yielding varieties of wheat and rice, unbalanced fertilizer use, low seeds replacement rate and low yield per unit area across almost all crops. Agricultural growth has become lackluster, as rain-fed areas still constitute about 65 percent of the total net sown area. The diminishing size of land holdings; degradation in land quality and soil health due to improper nutrient application; the looming threats of global warming and climate change; emergence of new pests and diseases; production losses due to biotic and abiotic causes; weak linkages between research and extension; limited credit access at reasonable rates of interest; non-remunerative prices; inadequate market access; poor rural infrastructure and insufficient post-harvest infrastructure such as warehousing, cold chains, and agro-processing facilities are other features plaguing our agricultural production environment.

Notwithstanding these difficulties and constraints, we are endowed with certain inherent strengths, which can help us meet these challenges. Though 80 percent of our farming population comprises of small and marginal farmers, they are hard working "farming farmers". We have varied climatic and soil resources, abundant sunshine throughout the year, sizeable water resources, a long coastline and endowed with rich bio-diversity. To cap it all, we have a time tested scientific infrastructure with a proven record of technological achievements for enhancing agricultural productivity in a sustainable and substantial manner. For India, farming is a living heritage, which we should protect and preserve. Agriculture has to remain centre-stage in our nation's economic thinking, making it attractive and rewarding.

The per capita availability of land has also been shrinking due to population increase. This has been compounded by increase of wasteland. There is also spread of urbanisation and the growing demand for more land. We are left with a situation where we have to produce more from the limited land available to ensure food security. But in doing so, we must always keep in mind that any food production and consumption policy must safeguard that the integrity of natural eco-systems is not compromised. Mahatma Gandhi had warned that, *"trading in soil fertility for the sake of quick returns could prove to be a disastrous, short-sighted policy. It would result in virtual depletion of the soil"*.

New policy initiatives are a must. Some of the measures requiring attention would include improving the management of water resources, timely supply of quality inputs, easy and efficient access to credit at low interest rates, better post-harvest management, besides, enhancing knowledge and skills of farmers, traders and other stake-holders involved in agri business. The other priority for agricultural revival includes bridging the substantial yield gaps existing in all States. This requires localised, State-specific strategies based on local agroclimatic conditions and constraints. Precision farming should be developed as a special thrust area wherein a farmer adjusts farm practices to match the variation of soil and terrain of his plot rather than follow the one size, fits all approach. Agri-clinics to provide services such as soil health care, water conservation, integrated nutrient management, dissemination of information on value adding processes and marketing services at the farm gate can be a source of tremendous confidence to vulnerable farmers. Every Gram Panchayat should have a Knowledge Centre for our farmers. They can make use of radio, television and IT medium to know the latest techniques to improve farm productivity and to propagate these in farmers.

Efforts towards sustainable agriculture can be greatly augmented with the help of space technology and biotechnology advances.

There is a need for a climate literacy programme and for the training of local level climate managers to guide farmers on the methods of maximising the benefits of a good monsoon and minimising the hazards of a poor monsoon. We should encourage the application of computer simulation techniques, better forecasting techniques and remote sensing technology in our efforts for sustainable development in the agricultural sector.

There is also a need to learn to respect and encourage the traditional wisdom of our farmers and their traditional farming practices particularly in water conservation measures. We must continue to enable village communities to conserve their bio-diversities in the field of gene banks and to preserve water, seeds and grains in village water, seed and grain banks.

Information is power. We must try and ensure that the actual cultivator who tills the soil is himself encouraged to collect and maintain key information relating to his own arable land. We should enlist the support of Panchayati Raj institutions and some of our agricultural Universities in this task. It is essential to actively involve farmers in the development of new technologies for it is only with their active participation that we can achieve our goal of sustainable development.

Another important issue for consideration is crops diversification, both for production and consumption. We should not limit ourselves to a narrow crop basket. Widening and diversifying the current narrow food security basket to include local cereals, millets, sorghum, legumes, tuber crops, vegetables and fruits could be an effective strategy to combat hunger. A well-planned diversification strategy with crops, horticulture, livestock, poultry, fishery and other on-farm and off-farm enterprises need to be pursued.

It would be equally important to bear in mind that our agricultural strategies should not only be pro-poor and pro-nature but also pro-women. The pioneering role played by women in movements undertaken by them for preservation of forests and topsoil is well recognised. The big leap in our country's milk production can be credited to the toil and labour put in by nearly 75 million women who are involved in the care of the cow and the buffalo. We must therefore endeavour to mainstream gender considerations in all areas of agricultural research, education and extension. Women farm labour about 60 per cent is also playing an important role in our agriculture operations.

With these words and thoughts, I congratulate the organisers for holding this seminar and I sincerely wish that today's deliberations will add to the resource-base of knowledge on how to strike a balance between natural resources and population as also between the needs of man and environment so as to make India a strong and agriculturally prosperous country where the people can lead a fuller and better life.

JAI HIND!

Speech by Smt. Pratibha Devisingh Patil on her assumption of office as President of India

Central Hall of Parliament, New Delhi
25th July 2007

Respected Dr. Abdul Kalamji, Mr. Prime Minister, Chief Justice of India, Speaker of Lok Sabha, Members of the Union Council of Ministers, Governors, Chief Ministers, Deputy Chairman of Rajya Sabha, Deputy Speaker of Lok Sabha, Members of Parliament, Excellencies, Ladies and Gentlemen.

My greetings to you all. I thank the Members of Parliament and State Legislatures for electing me to this high office. I am overwhelmed by the affection and regard shown to me by so many people across the length and breadth of the country during the past few weeks. I stand here today as the Republic's first servant, humbled by this experience.

It will be my sincere endeavour to live up to the high expectations of all those who have chosen to elect me, and to serve the best interests of the people of India. I am fully aware of the great responsibility that has been placed on my humble shoulders.

This year we celebrate the 150th anniversary of the First War of Indian Independence. As I stand before you, I draw inspiration from the courage and sacrifice of all those who led our nation to freedom. One of the unique features of our national movement, of our freedom struggle, was the equal participation of men and women. Among the many who led that battle against foreign rule were brave women like Rani Lakshmibai, Begum Hazrat Mahal and Kitturu Rani Chennamma.

In a few days time we will be celebrating the 60th anniversary of our independence. I would like to remember with gratitude the great contribution to our freedom struggle made by leaders like Pandit Jawaharlal Nehru, Sardar Patel, Maulana Azad and Sarojini Naidu, who fought under the unique and path-breaking leadership of the father of our nation, Mahatma Gandhi. Therefore, I share the sense of pride of every Indian that the United Nations General Assembly has declared Gandhi Jayanti, the 2nd of October, as the International Day of Non-violence. We express our gratitude to the world community for this unique honour.

Ours is an ancient civilization but a young nation. We look back with pride to the tremendous achievements made during the 60 years of our independence in all spheres of life. More than anything else we have demonstrated to the world that a developing country of over a billion people, each aspiring for a better quality of life, can live harmoniously and move forward within the framework of a secular democracy.

As President I assure the people of India that in upholding the Constitution I will always be inspired by the stirring message of Dr. Babasaheb Ambedkar who, in his closing speech to the Constituent Assembly, emphasized the need to hold fast to the constitutional methods of achieving our social and economic objectives. Sixty years ago, speaking in these very premises, Pandit Jawaharlal Nehru had said, and I quote, "Freedom and power bring responsibility." He reminded us that this great responsibility, I quote "rests upon this Assembly, a sovereign body representing the sovereign people of India." Indira Gandhi as India's first and only woman Prime Minister, showed us that the upliftment of the underprivileged and alleviation of poverty must remain the foremost and sacred duty of those who hold public office.

Today India stands at the threshold of a new era of progress. The nation is moving at historically unprecedented rates of growth. It should be our combined endeavour to sustain this growth and ensure that it is socially inclusive. We must ensure that every section of our society – particularly the weak and the disadvantaged - are equal partners in, and beneficiaries of, the development process. We must also ensure that every region of the country participates in and benefits from the process of economic growth.

I am reminded of the words of the great seventeenth century, Marathi poet-saint, Sant Tukaram, who said:

"One who befriends the poor and the oppressed, Recognise him to be a Saint, for God is with him"

Today, I commit myself to work for the well-being of all our citizens.

To realize the full potential of our people, we must invest in their capabilities and empower them with modern education and comprehensive health care. We must banish malnutrition, social evils infant mortality and female foeticide. I wish to express my full commitment to the protection of child rights. We must wage a relentless campaign against poverty, ignorance and disease to seek a better future for our children. We must show wisdom and foresight in protecting our planet and our environment, for the good of all living species and future generations.

I am deeply committed to the cause of education and would like to see every person, man and woman, boy and girl, be touched by the light of modern education. Empowerment of women is particularly important to me as I believe this leads to the empowerment of the nation.

We must ensure that science and technology serve our needs better, and help us develop a scientific temper that will unleash the full potential of our people, of our farmers, our workers, our professionals and our entrepreneurs.

The people of our country desire better governance, faster development and a life of peace and security. We must all stand united in the fight against such divisive and destructive tendencies as communalism, casteism, extremism and terrorism.

The world has come to regard the success of social and economic development in India within the framework of a democracy as a symbol of hope for all humanity. As I think of the future of our great nation, and our duties and responsibilities in taking it forward, I am reminded of Gurudev Rabindranath Tagore's invocation about India awakening into that heaven of freedom where the mind is without fear and the head is held high. Let us all rededicate ourselves once again to our Constitutional ideals and work unitedly to build such an India.

Jai Hind!

What We Read

Many articles have been published on the nature and character of UPA Presidential nominee Pratibha Patil. It is indeed needless to say that most of the features appearing in dailies and other media based magazines, directing their efforts towards public approval or disapproval as the case may be, have necessarily been defamatory. These so called articles have gone on to target any loopholes that may have emerged in any of her social contracts. Prominent BJP member and earlier Cabinet Minister, Arun Shourie, in one of his articles began by listing the 'cooperative' bank begun with the aim of empowering women liquidated by the Reserve Bank of India, the bankrupt sugar mill and then went on to club them as one of the many objections that were being raised by her candidature.

He also questions the matter revealed by the documents. The money that was set up from the Medical Aid Account with the sole purpose of going on to help doctors, also went on to the pockets of her brother GN Patil. The employees of the college were marked as working at the residence of mostly all board members and that even went on to include Pratibha Patil herself. The college fund even went on to establish a guest house that was deemed fit for usage by all the members of the faculty of the college, but the truth emerged when it was found out that its services were being employed by the members of Patil's family. To make matters even worse, papers report that the money collected from students went on to be deposited at the soon-to-be-bankrupt sugar mill. This was negotiated as a pattern.

Priyaranjan Dasmunshi seemed visibly upset with defending all these allegations all the time. He believed that there was an immediate need to slap some morality on media activities. He blamed the NDA for trying the malign the character of Pratibha Patil. He said that the way they were drawing these reports on Patil's character, there have also been several other political leaders, whose relatives too were defaulters like Patil and therefore even they needed to be brought under the scanner.

This obviously means that there should be some sort of need to bring all these defaulters to book. There remains only one answer to this question according to Shourie and that is the need to publish each and every defaulters name and, as Shourie points out with a hint of irony, not make anyone the President of the country at random.

As earlier reported here, Shourie makes a list of each and every instance of the entire Vishram Patil murder and speaks at length about the man who is the chief accused by Vishram Patil's wife, Rajni Patil – Pratibha Patil's brother, GN Patil.

GN Patil has been seen in political circles as a close aid of Pratibha Patil's endeavors to empower women and also uplift the conditions of the rural youth. It is believed that GN Patil was a frustrated rival of Vishram Patil, mainly due to the fact that the latter had defeated him to the Presidency of the District Congress Committee. And moreover there were also reports that GN Patil had also used the Congress workers to collect funds for tsunami victims. However, where that money went is a case that should be pursued even till now, because these funds were never deposited in the Chief Minister's Relief Fund.

Congress workers were later used again to collect funds on the event of Pratibha Patil becoming the Governor of Rajasthan. However, even those funds got lost into obscurity.

The Congress workers filed an enquiry with the Maharashtra Pradesh Congress Committee Chief, Prabha Rau regarding these funds. However, the enquiry either never reached their destination, or there was no answer from the Chief.

It was then, on the 15th of August. 2005, that nine of these office-bearers of the DCC provided a press release reporting the case. They mentioned the name of GN Patil at the center of the fiasco and this caused Vishram Patil to immediately set-up and enquiry into the whole matter, something that was perhaps expected from Prabha Rau. Vishram Patil, along with the enquiry into the misappropriation of funds in this case, also set-up an enquiry into the financial dealings of Ulhas Patil and other NGOs that are run by him. This obviously made him push his concerns at the Congress headquarters.

What happened next was pretty theatrical, albeit frightening. Vishram Patil was the recipient of three anonymous mails which were written by hand, stating that he would be killed in three days. Ironically, the letters advised him that he should be careful. Vishram Patil remained true to his commitments and therefore persisted with the enquiry.

Vishram Patil died. Everyone could draw the obvious assumptions that the murder was the result of a political rivalry within the District Congress Committee. The local police acted fast on the fact that he was a famous local personality and within sometime, they arrested a few criminals. They claim that 90% of the investigation was through and within some more time, they would nab the villains.

However, suddenly everything went off trail. Police fed the media with the information that the murder happened over some monetary dispute between Vishram Patil and the chief suspect Raju Mali, a local goon. Rajni Patil refused to accept this logic. Local papers refused to buy this story either.

On September 26th, the widow of Vishram Patil, Rajni Patil writes to Sonia Gandhi asking for her help in the matter as she feels the obvious principle that the people responsible for the murder were trying to put the investigation out of context. She writes in her letter, "The brain behind the crime is pressurizing the investigation process."

Later, on the 27th, Rajiv Patil, the *parabhari adhyaksha* of the Congress claims to the local paper *Deshdhoot* that Raju Mali, the person arrested by the police in regard to the murder was actually an accomplice of GN Patil. The paper also reports that there have been great discussions in the entire town of

Jalgaon as to who the killers are and what were the finances involved in the murder. That very same day, nearly thirteen office bearers of the District Congress Committee write to the local Superintendent of Police, claiming that GN Patil and Ulhas Patil were responsible for the murder and that the investigation process should be accelerated.

September 28th saw another development in the entire incident. Papers like the *Deshdoot* and the *Deshonnati* print photographs of the day of the District Congress Committee elections. It shows that the group of people who are standing next to Vishram Patil, also include Raju Mali, the man who was eventually going to kill Patil.

The obvious question that comes out in such situation is that without actually being a member of the party, under whose permission and orders did Raju Mali enter the office? These make the picture more complete.

That day also saw Manikrao Gavit, Minister of State in the Home Ministry at the Center, write to the Chief Minister of Maharashtra, wherein he attached the letter of Rajiv Patil which named Ulhas Patil and GN Patil as the main perpetrators of the crime. He appended that the fact remained that there was a state of complete panic in the local Congress, hence he urged the Chief Minister to look into the matters at the earliest.

The local papers although kept up their efforts to bring the culprits to the books. They preach the names of Ulhas Patil and GN Patil all over the town thereby making it extremely evident that the culprits are still at large. Rajni Patil writes to the local Police Chief, stating that it seemed that the murder was committed majorly due to political rivalry and therefore the matter needed be looked at from that particular angle. This would obviously result in a more comprehensive probe into the matter and should therefore give the police force further impetus and direction. She believed that someone influencal was trying to mislead the police and thus she brought the matter under consideration.

Later then, on the 5th of October, Rajiv Patil writes to the Chief Minister, the Director General of Police and to the head of the Pune Branch of the CID and informs them that the investigations into the murder have arrived at a standstill, with no in-roads being made on any front. He mentioned the names of some Jalgaon based police officers who had been dealing with the case right from the beginning and therefore he concluded that they should be involved in the investigations, so as to save precious time in order to start the investigations right from scratch.

Ten days later he made another attempt to bring this matter to the attention of the concerned people enquiring into the case. He also informed them once again that the people who had been arrested by the police till then were actually Congress activists and had been appointed by the prime accused, GN Patil and Ulhas Patil only during the District Congress Committee elections.

From then to December, the investigations headed straight into unknown territory and at one point it seemed that there seemed no connection between what was assumed to be the murder and the actual inquisition. Rajni Patil wrote incessantly to RR Patil, the deputy Chief Minister and also the Home Minster of the state. She expressed her frustration at the pseudo-investigation that was being carried out by the criminal agencies. She reminded him that the police had assured her that nearly 90 per cent of the investigation and yet they could not catch the real culprits, as "the real conspirators have high-level connections ... when only 10 per cent of the investigation was left, the case was taken out of their hands and given to the state CID."

By the 8th of December, Rajni Patil again corresponds with the Chief Minister and clears her stand on the police's verdict that the murder was on the charge of financial misappropriation between her husband and the killers. She even makes matters simple for them by exclaiming that the police should question the people that they have in their custody. However, this solicited no response from the Chief Minister.

Finally, frustrated at the progress made by local authorities, Rajni Patil moves towards Delhi and speaks of her concerns to Sonia Gandhi herself. She puts her case forward even to other congress stalwarts like Ahmed Patel, Sushil Kumar and Margaret Alva to name a few.

Even the Congress top bracket remained tight lipped on the entire matter. On the local front, the FIR that had been launched again the 'financers' of the murder had also been dropped. In a remarkable twist of achievements, the case was now being taken over from the state CID and was being handed over to the CBI.

The next three months were a patient perusal of the CBI's attempts to arrive at some break-through in the case. Finally the CBI responds that as the case has no inter-state or international ramifications, they will not be the required criminal agency to investigate into the matter. Any fool would know that this was an obvious attempt to kill the probe and thereby free the real conspirators behind the murder. Now having no other alternative left, the widow moved the Aurangabad Bench of the High Court. Then she added an "Affidavit in Rejoinder" where she quoted from the CID's report saying,

"However during the course of the investigation I found no evidence or material to suggest that the political opponents of deceased Vishram Patil were in any manner involved in the conspiracy to murder."

The widow believed that none of the suspects were called by the investigating agency and therefore their case rests. Herein comes another piece of information that the Investigation Office has completely kept quiet about. The fact remains that both Raju Mali and Raju Sonawane had mentioned to the authorities that they were getting letters which threatened them with the cost of their lives. They wrote,

"We are being harassed. GN Patil and the former MP are pressurizing us to own up to the charge entirely and confess to the crime. Otherwise they have threatened us 'we'll finish you as we finished VG Patil..."'

This case remained like this till February 23rd, 2007, where the court issued orders against the CBI dismissing their problems regarding the case and asked them to take it on further. The court reminded the investigating agency that they are well aware of the exceptional cases that the agency handles and it is only after these considerations that they have been expected to take on the case. The Court mentioned,

"We have scrutinized the record with the help of the counsel of both sides. We have considered the chequered history of the present case, the developments which have taken place after filing of the charge-sheet, issues involved, and the reference to alleged conspiracy by influential political leaders of the region. Having regard to the importance of the issues involved and the alleged complicity of the influential political leaders...in our considered opinion, this is a fit case where the investigation should be conducted by the CBI."

In this process of transferring the case from the police to the CID to the CBI – only to have the CBI turn down the case – the people who had initiated this whole mess had achieved the delay of this entire process by nearly one and a half years.

By March, Rajni Patil once again writes to the Congress Chief Sonia Gandhi. She complained to her, that as they were both women who had lost their husbands, they would be able to understand and comprehend the pain of the other. She restated the letters that her husband had received warning him of a *supari* given in his name by GN Patil and Ulhas Patil. She stated.

"I fear that my whole family is likely to get liquidated by these brutal murderers if they continue to get politically patronized by the party..."

She submitted these to the then President APJ Abdul Kalam and she mentioned to him that she received no reply from any of the top channels that she had mentioned the incident to.

The CBI finally arrived in Jalgaon on the 4th of April 2007 and began their enquiry by first questioning the widow herself. Mysteriously though, on that very same day, Raju Mali died in prison.

The most important thing that has to be kept in mind in this entire process is that Rajni Patil is seen as always pleading before the State and Congress authorities. The aspect that is starkly prominent here is that Patil is just not the only one who is pleading; even all the functionaries of the local Congress also are trying to dispatch memorandums and letters whereby they are all pointing towards Ulhas Patil and GN Patil. All these letters are visible on the letterheads of the Congress party itself.

Finally, Rajni Patil arrived in Delhi on the 21st of June, 2006 with her son and a local Congress activist, and submits a petition to the President, APJ Abdul Kalam. She says in her memorandum –

"Justice has eluded me so far, even though I have moved from pillar to post hoping, in vain, that those in power in Mumbai and Delhi would listen to the cry of a helpless woman and discharge their lawful duty."

She finally remarks that since all this while there has been no mention of the main perpetrators, as named in so many letters and media releases, and the fact that they do not even have FIRs registered in their names, she demands for their immediate arrest.

It is here that she directly names the UPA's Presidential candidate, Pratibha Patil. She says,

"I am convinced – and it is my charge – that right from Day One of this case, Smt. Pratibha Patil has been trying to influence the investigation on order to protect her brother Dr

GN Patil. Towards this end, she has been misusing her authority and her high-level contacts in the governments in Mumbai and Delhi."

The Congress response according the Mr. Shourie has been extremely stereo-typical and from the point of view of politics, regular. They promptly ran it down as propaganda by the opposition to malign the character of their candidate. They claimed,

"It is all a BJP ploy. It shows their desperation at not being able to find a candidate of the stature of Pratibha Patil."

What Mr. Shourie points out correctly, is that even if this were to be a BJP ploy, what response can the UPA, viz. the Congress provide for the facts – the facts that have already been listed in this article, the facts that were reported by the media?

"But why now? The timing of these allegations itself shows that they have been manufactured only to tarnish the image of Pratibha Patil as she is standing for the Presidentship of the country. After all, why are they bringing up these right now?"

This is their only alternative response - the response used, when there is no other valid comment to make, nothing of any importance, based on the truth.

Mr. Shourie comments that these allegations that have been marked against Pratibha Patil have all taken place way before she was chosen upon to contest these elections. Till the time she was chosen as the Presidential candidate, these matters were considered to be frauds committed by some district politicians. This particular murder was only left as the concerns of the people of Jalgaon, who went on to question the way that they lived their lives. It is justifiably now that she has been chosen to be the next President of the country that people nationally have decided to scrutinize her and her actions. Mr. Shourie believes that there is absolutely no mismatch in the timings and her actions. He believes that if the frauds and murders are not exhumed today, then and only then would there be a real conspiracy behind these facts.

Once he is through with stating all the facts, Mr. Shourie tries to unravel the politics behind these facts. He tries to reason as to whether the primary Congress members, like Ms. Gandhi even knew about these allegations and these facts, because he realizes that Pratibha Patil's name had been selected right at the end, that too without any discriminative schedules. However, this looks like a complete fallacy as there are reports made by Rajni Patil wherein she states that she had met Sonia Gandhi and told her about the entire conspiracy. Looking at all these facts, it does look rather foolish to believe that the Congress High Command was completely oblivious of these facts. Most importantly, Mr. Shourie says that the murder accounted for the life of one of their own members, who had one the same post three times within the party. Such murders are not common at all and therefore the matter does not seem to be all that trivial. In which case, the conspiracy looks to include the Congress High Command into its wraps.

Finally, Mr. Shourie concludes that with a submissive Prime Minister at the helm of affairs, the Congress has gone on to create another rubber stamp for them. The Prime Minister at the end of the day is not vulnerable as he had a clean financial record, he is honest, but in this case, the matters may be different.

Index

M

N

Z